ARSNICK

ARSNICK

The Student Nonviolent
Coordinating Committee
in Arkansas

*Edited by Jennifer Jensen Wallach
and John A. Kirk*

THE UNIVERSITY OF ARKANSAS PRESS
FAYETTEVILLE • 2011

15 14 13 12 11   5 4 3 2 1

ISBN-10 (cloth): 1-55728-968-9
ISBN-10 (paper): 1-55728-966-2

ISBN-13 (cloth): 978-1-55728-968-1
ISBN-13 (paper): 978-1-55728-966-7

Text design by Ellen Beeler

⊗ The paper used in this publication meets the minimum requirements of the
American National Standard for Permanence of Paper for Printed Library
Materials Z39.48-1984.

Library of Congress Cataloging-in-Publication Data

Arsnick : the Student Nonviolent Coordinating Committee in Arkansas / edited
by Jennifer Jensen Wallach and John A. Kirk.
        p. cm.
    Includes bibliographical references and index.
    ISBN 978-1-55728-968-1 (cloth : alk. paper) — ISBN 978-1-55728-966-7
    (pbk. : alk. paper)
    1. Student Nonviolent Coordinating Committee (U.S.) 2. Civil rights
    movements—Arkansas—History—20th century. 3. African Americans—
    Civil rights—Arkansas—History—20th century. 4. African Americans—
    Segregation—Arkansas—History—20th century. 5. Arkansas—Race relations.
    6. Student Nonviolent Coordinating Committee (U.S.)—Sources. 7. Civil
    rights movements—Arkansas—History—20th century—Sources. 8. African
    Americans—Civil rights—Arkansas—History—20th century—Sources.
    9. African Americans—Segregation—Arkansas—History—20th century—
    Sources. 10. Arkansas—Race relations—Sources. I. Wallach, Jennifer Jensen,
    1974– II. Kirk, John A., 1970–
    E185.615.A788 2011
    323.1196'0730761—dc23
                                                                        2011019137

Note on the Title

The Student Nonviolent Coordinating Committee was often referred to in the media as SNCC or sometimes as "Snick." In 1960, a group of Arkansas student activists began humorously referring to themselves as "Arsnick," as both a tribute to the national organization and as an indication of the poisonous "arsenic" impact they hoped to have upon the system of white supremacy in the state. After SNCC officially began operating in Arkansas in 1962, field director Bill Hansen occasionally used this same play on words to describe the Arkansas project.

Contents

PART III: HISTORICAL DOCUMENTS

Acknowledgments

This book could not have been completed without the assistance of a number of people and institutions. Arkansas SNCC supporters and staff members Sanderia Smith, Nancy (Shaw) Stoller, Tim Janke, Millard "Tex" Lowe, Laura Foner, Gertrude Jackson, and Arlene (Wilgoren) Dunn not only allowed us to print their SNCC memories here, but they also patiently answered a stream of questions on the telephone, via e-mail, or in face-to-face interviews. Former SNCC Arkansas director Bill Hansen and former staff member Michael Simmons were particularly generous with their time over the past several years and contributed to this project in innumerable ways. Tim Janke deserves a special thank you for allowing us to publish many of the beautiful photographs he took while working in Arkansas, and Laura Foner also opened up her personal SNCC archives to us. Vincent J. O'Connor granted us permission to publish many of the wonderful photographs he took in Arkansas in 1965 and overwhelmed us with his enthusiastic interest in the project. SNCC volunteers Brian Rybolt, Howard Himmelbaum, and Dwight Williams also offered us valuable information. Mitchell Zimmerman was kind enough to allow us to publish excerpts from the journal that he kept while working as a SNCC volunteer in 1965.

We are indebted to archivists at the Martin Luther King, Jr. Center for Nonviolent Change, Inc., the University of Arkansas Special Collections, the Moorland-Spingarn Research Center, the Wisconsin Historical Society, and the Roosevelt Study Center, Middleburg, The Netherlands, for not only providing us with vital research support but also in some instances for granting us their permission to publish items housed in their collections. We would also like to thank Patrick Williams of the *Arkansas Historical Quarterly,* Frank Fellone of the *Arkansas Democrat Gazette,* and Hannah Kirsch of the Brandeis University student newspaper, *The Justice,* for allowing us to reprint items that originally appeared in their publications. (The notes after each chapter or document contain information concerning where the original is deposited or where previously published items originally appeared.)

Rita Reynolds, a fellow historian and good friend, donated her skills as a photographer during the SNCC Fiftieth Anniversary Conference in Raleigh, North Carolina, in April 2010. We thank her for allowing us to use her photographs in this book. Georgia College & State University graduate student Michelle Flirt offered research assistance at an early stage of the project. The University of North Texas, the Georgia College & State University Foundation, and the Roosevelt Study Center offered valuable travel funding. Charles Bittner gave miscellaneous assistance and much-needed advice on numerous occasions. Clayborne Carson generously allowed us to examine materials from his SNCC archives and gave us some important research tips.

Finally, we would like to express our gratitude to Larry Malley, the director of the University of Arkansas Press, for giving us this opportunity to publish these exciting materials. We are also grateful to our copy editor, Debbie Upton, whose assistance was invaluable. Our wonderful editor Julie Watkins has been unfailingly helpful at every stage of this project. We are mindful of all that she has done to bring this book to fruition.

Preface

The historiography of the Student Nonviolent Coordinating Committee (SNCC) over the past fifty years has traveled in two very different directions. On the one hand, signal works across the decades by Howard Zinn, Clayborne Carson, Cheryl Greenberg, and Wesley Hogan have by and large returned to the same events, figures, and turning points which have formed the core institutional memory of the organization.[1] Many of the key episodes in SNCC's history have received individual attention and have incorporated the history of the organization within their broader purview —including among them the 1960 sit-in movement; the 1961 Freedom Rides; the 1961–1962 Albany, Georgia, campaign; the 1963 March on Washington for Jobs and Freedom; the 1964 Mississippi Freedom Summer and the creation of the Mississippi Freedom Democratic Party; the 1965 Selma, Alabama, campaign and the Voting Rights Act; and the 1966 Meredith March, the Atlanta Project, and the emergence of Black Power.[2] On the other hand, a burgeoning number of grassroots studies of local-, county-, and state-level activism have incorporated SNCC's far-flung activism that interweaved with other civil rights efforts across the South in the 1960s. Rather than being signposted by landmark events, this literature represents the sprawling, fragmented, and sporadic nature of SNCC's activities out in the field.[3]

The bifurcated nature of SNCC scholarship provides a sense both of the enduring central concerns and aims of the organization and the multifaceted and eclectic ways in which they were pursued. But it also leaves gaps in the history of SNCC, especially in terms of activities that fall somewhere between the two national and local perspectives. Most notable by their relative absence in the literature are two dedicated long-term SNCC projects in southwest Georgia and in Arkansas that ran from roughly 1962 to 1967, paralleling, but very much overshadowed by SNCC's involvement in Mississippi.[4] The aim of this book is to correct the historical record by asserting the importance of the activities of SNCC in Arkansas which have previously been all but ignored. In so doing, the book puts down a marker to suggest new and fruitful approaches to understanding the history of one of America's most important, if most short-lived, civil rights organizations. As SNCC passes its fiftieth anniversary, now is an apposite time to take stock of the research that has already been done and to think about what remains to be covered to provide a more complete picture of SNCC activism.

This book is by no means intended to be the final word on SNCC in Arkansas. On the contrary, it consciously seeks to bring a research focus to the subject to act as a steppingstone for future more-expansive studies. It does this by bringing together for the first time all of the existing secondary scholarship on the subject; by providing firsthand testimonies of SNCC volunteers in the state, which are published here for the first time; by showcasing photographs taken in the state by SNCC workers; and by drawing together a wide variety of primary documents that speak to the many different types of activities and agendas that SNCC pursued in the state.

Part I includes all of the secondary literature written to date on SNCC in Arkansas. Collectively, the essays provide a useful overview of the organization's activities in the state. My own previously unpublished essay documents the early fledgling efforts of students from African American Philander Smith College in the state capital of Little Rock to organize sit-ins under the self-proclaimed banner of "Arsnick." Their efforts were largely unsuccessful at achieving their immediate goal of desegregation, although they did produce a lawsuit in *Lupper v. Arkansas* that eventually led to the dismissal of all arrests of sit-in demonstrators across the United States in December 1964. Brent Riffel contributes a profile of William (Bill) Hansen, a white SNCC volunteer who arrived in Little Rock in October 1962 to revive flagging attempts to mobilize a sit-in movement and who subsequently played a central role in SNCC's efforts throughout the state. Hansen came to Little Rock at the request of the Arkansas Council on Human Relations, a state affiliate of the Atlanta-based Southern Regional Council, and his efforts coupled with those of Philander Smith students eventually led to the successful desegregation of downtown facilities in 1963. Holly Y. McGee focuses on SNCC activism in Pine Bluff, Arkansas. After participating in successful demonstrations in Little Rock, SNCC volunteers began to focus their efforts on Pine Bluff, an important hub of African American history, politics, and culture in Arkansas, and a gateway to the surrounding Arkansas Delta areas where the vast majority of the state's African American population lived. Efforts in Pine Bluff, McGee notes, met with a mixed reception and with mixed results. Randy Finley's essay outlines the broad contours of SNCC activism in the Arkansas Delta between 1963 and 1967. Using Pine Bluff as a base, SNCC set up satellite projects in Helena, Gould, and Forrest City, in each place seeking to mobilize the local African American population to press for desegregation and voting rights. In turn, these projects were used to penetrate further into rural areas. Finally, Jennifer Jensen Wallach's essay charts the final years of SNCC in Arkansas, which, as developments within the organization elsewhere, were dominated by the question of Black Power and its meaning and intent. These discussions brought divisions within Arkansas SNCC ranks that contributed to the dissolution of activities under the SNCC banner by 1967.

Part II spotlights firsthand accounts of SNCC volunteers in Arkansas. Some are specially commissioned reflections written for this collection. Others are the result of personal interviews. One is an extract from a fictionalized account of an activist's experience. Visual firsthand testimony is provided via the photographs of three SNCC volunteers. The coeditors are immensely grateful to all of those who contributed. The material from Bill Hansen, Jim Jones, Michael Simmons, Sanderia Smith, Bob Cableton, Nancy (Shaw) Stoller, Tim Janke, Millard "Tex" Lowe, Laura Foner, Gertrude Jackson, Arlene Dunn (nee Wilgoren), and Vincent O'Connor encompasses SNCC volunteers, both men and women, African American and white, indigenous Arkansans and those who came from outside of the state, those who worked in urban and rural areas within Arkansas, and those who worked in Arkansas most of the time SNCC was there and those who worked there for only a short while. Together they reflect the diversity of experiences of SNCC in the state. If there is a common thread to be drawn from the testimonies it is that for those who participated as SNCC workers in Arkansas, as is surely true of SNCC workers elsewhere, their activism was part of an ongoing commitment to freedom, justice, and human rights, which both predated and outlasted their time in the state. The past experiences of SNCC volunteers shaped why they came to and what they did in the state and many were in turn transformed, or at least significantly affected by, what happened to them there. Their stories therefore not only chart the story of SNCC volunteers in Arkansas but equally provide a snapshot in microcosm of the impact that belonging to SNCC had on many people's lives.

Due to space constraints, all of the materials included in this section were shortened, but every effort was made to maintain the meaning and the style of the original documents. When making difficult editing decisions, material that dealt directly with SNCC in Arkansas was favored over information that dealt with other periods of the civil rights activists' lives. Furthermore, references to topics that were deemed repetitive were sometimes omitted. For example, nearly every SNCC Arkansas volunteer mentioned the impact that the events at Central High School in Little Rock in 1957 had on their growing consciousness and eventual decision to work for the movement in Arkansas, but for the sake of space this detail was occasionally excluded from the accounts that follow.

Part III draws on a variety of primary sources selected from a number of different places. It includes material from memoirs, personal letters, formal letters, incident reports, field reports, annual reports, press releases, press statements, letters to newspapers, newspaper articles, position statements, court cases, application forms, orientation schedules, poems, and minutes of meetings. The primary documents help to amplify some of the material in the secondary articles and firsthand accounts while also covering some of the key events and episodes that are not covered elsewhere.

Again, due to space limitations, several of the documents in this section were also shortened. Ellipses are used to indicate omitted material. While making these editorial decisions, every effort was made to avoid altering the intended meaning or tone of the texts. While transcribing these documents, obvious typographical errors were corrected. However, no effort was made to change syntax or spelling. In order to maintain the unique, historical character of these documents, we elected not to use the intrusive word *sic* to indicate unorthodox spellings or word usage. Occasionally, we have inserted notes to provide some additional historical context.

Taken together, this collection constitutes the best and most comprehensive introduction to SNCC's activities in Arkansas, an important though previously neglected episode in SNCC's history and, more broadly, in the history of the civil rights movement.

John A. Kirk

I.

Historical Assessments

1.

The Origins of SNCC in Arkansas

Little Rock, *Lupper,* and the Law

JOHN A. KIRK

On February 1, 1960, four African American students from North Carolina Agricultural and Technical College in Greensboro—Ezell A. Blair, Franklin McCain, David Richmond, and Joseph McNeil—shopped for school supplies at their local F. W. Woolworth's store. After making their purchases, McCain and McNeil went over to the lunch counter, took seats there, and asked for coffee and doughnuts. They were refused service on the grounds that the lunch counter was for whites only. Richmond and Blair joined them and engaged in a discussion with the waitress about the store's policy of racial exclusion. The store manager tried to persuade them to leave. Eventually, when the store was about to close, they left.[1]

Over the following days and weeks, more students held "sit-ins" in Greensboro at an ever-expanding number of local establishments as the protests began to snowball. The sit-ins quickly began to spread to other towns and cities, first in North Carolina and then to other states. Within a year, over one hundred cities had experienced sit-ins with over fifty thousand participants and over three thousand arrests. Under pressure from the direct-action demonstrations and the African American community's economic boycotts of businesses that often accompanied them, a number of businesses in Upper South states took the decision to voluntarily desegregate facilities rather than face continued disruption.[2]

More than fifty years later, the sit-ins have become part of American folklore as one of the most iconic forms of mass protest in the twentieth century. In particular, sit-in centers such as Greensboro, the scene of the first 1960 sit-ins; Nashville, Tennessee, which produced a cohort of influential student leaders; and Atlanta, Georgia, which made headlines because of Martin Luther King Jr.'s involvement and arrest, have received extensive coverage.[3] But as the historian Cynthia Griggs Fleming once noted, "each community's response to the sit-ins was different [and] shaped by the particular conditions that existed in that community." She concludes that "historians will never have a truly clear understanding of the sit-in movement of 1960 until each community has the chance to tell its own story."[4] A number of local studies have since appeared, providing insights into how the sit-ins impacted on a variety of different communities.[5] Meanwhile, sociologists and legal scholars have examined the sit-ins from different disciplinary perspectives.[6] While the historical literature has been strong on the local detail and historical context of the sit-ins, sociologists and legal scholars have tended to produce a much more comprehensive analysis of the overall trends of the sit-ins at regional and national levels. This essay seeks to combine the various insights of historical, sociological, and legal scholarship to demonstrate how these different perspectives can usefully complement one another.

In doing so, this essay uncovers an important though neglected episode in the region-wide sit-in movement of 1960. The sit-in movement in Little Rock has been sidelined largely because of the earlier dramatic national civil rights headlines that were made in the city over school desegregation. After the United States Supreme Court's *Brown v. Board of Education* (1954) school desegregation ruling, Little Rock, viewed as a relatively moderate Upper South city, was among the first to announce plans for compliance. However, in September 1957, as the school desegregation plan was about to be implemented, Arkansas governor Orval E. Faubus called out National Guard troops to prevent the entry of nine African American students into the city's Central High School. Faubus's actions eventually led to President Dwight D. Eisenhower sending federal troops to the city to ensure the safe passage of the nine African American students into the school. The Little Rock school crisis made international news headlines.[7]

One of the most recent and detailed accounts of the school crisis dismisses the subsequent sit-in movement in Little Rock in a two-sentence summary relegated to the book's epilogue: "In March of 1960 a sit-in movement developed in downtown Little Rock, led by students at Philander Smith College. In response, a 'secret committee' of businessmen entered into negotiations with black leaders and quietly desegregated many of the city's downtown business establishments."[8] In actuality, the story is far more complex and involved. When students from Little Rock's Methodist-supported African American Philander Smith College, with a student body of around seven hundred, held sit-ins in March and April 1960, they met with harsh fines and stiff prison sentences. Coupled with limited support from the wider African American community, the protests came to a premature and unsuccessful halt. Attempts to resurrect the sit-ins in November 1960 likewise met with failure. Not until fully two years later did local African American students, with outside help from SNCC, successfully mobilize to place enough pressure on downtown merchants to desegregate. The story did not end there. The cases of Frank James Lupper and Thomas B. Robinson, two students arrested in the April 1960 sit-ins, were not resolved until as late as December 1964. Their cases, consolidated with another case from South Carolina, turned out to be the very last sit-in cases heard by the U.S. Supreme Court and ultimately led to the dismissal of all such outstanding cases against more than three thousand other sit-in participants across the nation. The sit-in movement in Little Rock therefore not only formed the backdrop to the origins of SNCC in Arkansas but it also illuminates the larger legal context for direct action and desegregation, and how local, regional, and national levels of protest could often intersect in mutually beneficial ways.

The first sit-ins in Little Rock took place at 11:00 A.M. on March 10, 1960, when around fifty Philander Smith College students marched from campus to the F. W. Woolworth store on Fourth and Main Streets and asked for service at its segregated lunch counter. The students had been aware of the sit-ins taking place across the South and after discussions on campus they finally decided to act. The manager refused to serve the students and immediately alerted Little Rock chief of police Eugene G. Smith. The assistant store manager called Woolworth's home office in St. Louis for instructions and then closed the lunch counter to the public. When police chief Smith arrived he asked the students to leave. All but five did so. Those remaining—Charles Parker, twenty-two; Frank James, twenty-one; Vernon Mott, nineteen; Eldridge Davis, nineteen; and Chester Briggs, eighteen—were arrested for loitering. Shortly after arriving at the police station, the five arrested students made bail of $100 each posted by the Little Rock NAACP branch. The students had called state NAACP president and co-owner of Little Rock's leading African American newspaper, the *Arkansas State Press,* Daisy Bates, to inform her of the intended protest. Daisy's husband, L. C. Bates, arranged a bondsman, mobilized attorneys, and traveled to the jail himself to ensure the release of the students. Reporters on the scene asked L. C. Bates why the students had staged a sit-in. "Well, put it this way," Bates told them, "You can go anywhere in any store and buy anything but when you try to buy food you are trespassing and the kids can't understand it and neither can I."[9]

After the students left jail, police chief Smith consulted with the Little Rock city prosecuting attorney and the Arkansas state attorney general, resulting in two additional charges being brought against each student under Arkansas's Act 17 of 1958 and Act 226 of 1959.[10] The two acts had been passed amid a flurry of pro-segregation legislation in the Arkansas General Assembly of 1958 and the special session of the Arkansas General Assembly of 1959, with both legislative sessions taking place against the backdrop of the ongoing school desegregation struggle in Little Rock. Act 17 prohibited "any person from creating a disturbance or breach of the peace on any public school property, school cafeteria, or any public place of business." The act carried a maximum fine of $500 and a maximum six-month prison sentence.[11] Act 226 prohibited "any person from creating a disturbance or breach of the peace in any public place of business." The act carried a maximum fine of $500 and a maximum six-month prison sentence.[12]

The president of Philander Smith, Dr. M. Lafayette Harris, released a statement denying any foreknowledge of the students' actions, saying, "The college does not and has never subscribed to mass action in dealing with difficult problems. A full scale investigation is already under way to determine the facts relevant to the incident."[13] Like many other presidents of African American colleges, Harris trod a fine line between supporting his students, maintaining good relations with the city's white community, and placating the college's board trustees, who held varying opinions on the sit-ins.[14] Nevertheless, none of the students subsequently faced any further action by the college.[15]

Support from others in the African American community outside of the NAACP was in short supply. The events of the 1957 Little Rock crisis had disrupted existing lines of contact between African American leaders and the white community and had left a vacuum in African American community leadership that the Bateses temporarily moved to fill. The regional National Urban League representative C. D. Coleman reported in 1959 that "the one great problem facing Little Rock [is] the lack of unity, confidence and cooperation between Negro leaders and the lack of regular and orderly lines of communication between Negro organizations. . . . Disunity among Negro leaders [is of] greater concern than the school crisis."[16] John Walker, the African American associate director of the Arkansas Council on Human Relations (ACHR), the state affiliate of the Atlanta-based Southern Regional Council, observed in 1960 that "Negro leadership is virtually nil." Walker expressed the belief that "the 'masses' of Negroes are anxious for more progressive leadership from new people."[17] The sit-ins promised to do just that. Meanwhile, an impromptu poll of white community leaders by the *Arkansas Democrat,* a white newspaper, revealed that most rejected the sit-ins as an acceptable form of protest.[18]

On March 17, the five students arrested in the sit-in appeared for trial at Little Rock's Municipal Court. Other Philander Smith students packed the courtroom in a show of solidarity with their friends. Judge Quinn Glover found the students guilty under Act 266, but dismissed the charges against them under state loitering statutes and Act 17, insisting that Act 226 sufficiently covered the offenses with which the students were charged. Glover handed each student a $250 fine and a thirty-day jail sentence. The students' lawyers, Little Rock attorney Harold B. Anderson and Pine Bluff, Arkansas, attorney George Howard Jr., indicated that the students' fines and sentences would be appealed.[19]

In a show of defiance, and to place further pressure on downtown merchants, around forty to fifty Philander Smith students immediately left the courtroom and headed downtown to stage further sit-ins. This time they targeted not only Woolworth's but also other major downtown stores. All of the stores closed their lunch counters to customers when sit-ins took place. The students later convened at the state capitol where they sang "God Bless America" and "The Star Spangled Banner" before dispersing.[20]

When the Little Rock NAACP sought talks with the Little Rock Chamber of Commerce about desegregating lunch counters to halt the sit-ins they received a noncommittal response. The reluctance of whites in Little Rock to enter into a dialogue with African Americans mirrored the initial reactions to sit-ins in many other communities across the South. Public announcements by national chain stores such as F. W. Woolworth, S. S. Kressage, S. H. Kress, and W. T. Grant declared that the policy of segregation would continue. In light of this, the NAACP's national office called for a boycott of stores to support the aims of the sit-in demonstrators. On March 31, the Little Rock NAACP adopted what it called a "Racial Self-Defense Policy" against discrimination by urging people not to patronize stores that practiced segregation. Local NAACP branch president J. C. Crenchaw sent a memorandum to merchants at all downtown stores with segregated lunch counters to announce this policy. Crenchaw also pleaded with "all religious institutions, fraternal organizations, fraternities, sororities, civic and political groups" in the African American community to withdraw patronage from targeted stores. The memorandum called for a rallying of the community to help support the students. "HE NEEDS OUR HELP," it appealed, "we have the family purse and we have the ballot, and the NAACP is asking 'DO YOU HAVE THE WILL?'" The answer was seemingly no. Within just a week the boycott faded.[21]

As the NAACP mobilized economic boycotts to support the sit-ins, the NAACP Legal Defense Fund (LDF) discussed its legal strategy. On March 18, 1960, Thurgood Marshall called a conference of sixty-two LDF lawyers at Howard University in Washington, D.C., to discuss the cases. They considered a number of options. First, sit-in participants could claim a violation of the Fourteenth Amendment's guarantee of due process if they were charged with a breach of the peace without any actual evidence of a disturbance having taken place. Second, they could claim that segregation laws violated the Fourteenth Amendment's equal protection clause since whites were served at lunch counters when African Americans were not. Third, if sit-in participants were convicted of trespass in a place where segregation laws existed, this, too, would be a violation of the equal protection clause since the trespass laws were not being equally applied to whites. Fourth, for any sit-in participants convicted on state-owned property, the Fourteenth Amendment's equal protection clause prohibited states from enforcing segregation statutes.[22]

However, in the *Civil Rights Cases* (1883) the U.S. Supreme Court made explicitly clear that the equal protection clause did not cover private individuals, organizations, or establishments, which were free to choose their own clientele even if that meant discriminating on the grounds of race.[23] What, then, would happen in a case where there was no connection between state action and the conviction of sit-in participants? Did owners of private establishments still have the right to discriminate as the *Civil Rights Cases* suggested? The LDF lawyers looked to the more recent case of *Shelley v. Kraemer* (1948) as a precedent for extending the Fourteenth Amendment's equal protection clause to private discrimination.[24] *Shelley* involved the use of restrictive covenants in property contracts to prevent the sale of homes to African Americans. The U.S. Supreme Court ruled against the use of such covenants on the grounds that state action was required to enforce these private contracts. This allowed a very wide interpretation of what state action meant.[25] As LDF lawyer Jack Greenberg put it, "Since private decisions cannot be enforced without an ultimate, although sometimes only implicit, state sanction, is everything we do 'state action'? Do all personal decisions present constitutional questions? Where should the courts draw the line?"[26]

On April 11, 1960, the five Little Rock sit-in students arrested on March 10 appeared before Judge William J. Kirby in the city's circuit court to appeal their fines and sentences. In support of the NAACP's nonpatronage campaign, all wore badges reading, "I am wearing 1959 clothes with

1960 dignity. I refuse to patronize segregated stores." Kirby set the trial date for April 27.[27] The following day, April 12, ten students entered McLellan's at 10:15 A.M. and asked for service at the lunch counter. The manager promptly closed the counter. The same thing happened at Woolworth's, Blass's, and Pfeifers's.[28]

The next day, April 13, a group of six students—Eugene D. Smith, twenty-one; Melvin T. Jackson, twenty; McLoyd Buchanan, nineteen; William Rogers Jr., nineteen; Sammy J. Baker, eighteen; and Winston Jones, eighteen—held a sit-in at Pfeifers's department store. When the store manager asked the students to leave, all but one, Melvin T. Jackson, agreed to go. As with the first group of students arrested on March 10, the police charged the six students under Act 226.

In a separate incident, two students—Thomas B. Robinson, twenty, and Frank James Lupper, nineteen—requested service at Blass's lunch counter. The store manager told them that he was not prepared to serve them and he asked them to leave. They refused. The assistant manager then called the police, who escorted the two students from the building. In addition to being charged under Act 226, Lupper and Robinson were also charged under Act 14 for their refusal to leave the store at the request of the manager. Act 14, passed by the 1959 special session of the Arkansas General Assembly, made it "unlawful for any person to refuse to leave the business premises of any person when so requested by the manager or owner thereof." The maximum fine and jail sentence allowed under the act was $500 and thirty days.[29]

On April 15, students from local colleges and high schools, with the support of the local NAACP, sought to keep up pressure on downtown stores by picketing them. Around twenty students marched outside Blass's, Pfeifers's, and McLellan's holding placards that read "We are not buying where we can't eat," "Jailing our youth will not solve the problem," and "Help us make democracy work. NAACP Youth Council." L. C. and Daisy Bates joined them at various points. Daisy told reporters that "the picketing will continue indefinitely until the conscience of the community is made to realize that Negroes are being refused service in these places." She added, "The Negro is just not going to be satisfied with a situation where he can buy $1,000 worth of merchandise in one department of a store but he is considered trespassing and arrested if he attempts to spend one dime at the lunch counter." According to press reports, there were few incidents as a result of the picketing. Most shoppers ignored the protest, some gathered in groups to watch, and at one point a group of white teenagers sought to impede the pickets by standing in their way and blowing cigarette smoke in their faces. No arrests were made.[30]

On April 21, the trials of the second and third group of sit-in cases demonstrated the growing annoyance and irritation of the white community with the latest turn in events. In Little Rock's municipal court judge Quinn Glover imposed tougher penalties than in the first sit-in case. Glover handed the group of six students charged under Act 226 a $250 fine and a sixty-day jail sentence each. He handed the two students charged under Act 226 and Act 14 a $400 fine and a ninety-day jail sentence each.[31]

On April 27, at the appeal of the five students arrested for the first Little Rock sit-in, circuit court judge William J. Kirby handed each student a $500 fine and sixty days in jail, doubling the sentences imposed by Glover in the Little Rock Municipal Court.[32] On May 31, Kirby heard the second batch of sit-in appeals of the six students charged under Act 226. He again doubled the penalties for five of the six students, awarding them each the maximum fine of $500 and sixty-day jail sentences. In the case of Melvin T. Jackson, who had refused to leave the lunch counter at the request of store officials, as well as a $500 fine Kirby handed him a prison sentence of six months, the maximum allowed under the act.[33]

On June 17, Kirby presided at the appeal of Frank James Lupper and Thomas B. Robinson. On the advice of attorney Harold Anderson and Pine Bluff attorney Wiley Branton, who was chair of the Arkansas NAACP's Legal Redress Committee, the two students opted for a jury trial. The all-white jury took just fifteen minutes to find the students guilty. Kirby handed each of the students a $1,000 fine and a seven-month prison sentence. This was composed of the maximum fines and sentences allowed under Act 226, with the addition of another $500 fine and another thirty-day jail sentence allowed under Act 14.[34] In all of the cases heard by Kirby in the circuit court, the students' lawyers indicated that they would appeal their cases to the Arkansas Supreme Court.[35]

The summer recess at Philander Smith ended the sit-ins since many students left Little Rock to return to their homes in other towns and cities in Arkansas and in other states.[36] At the beginning of the fall semester, students attempted to revive sit-in protests. This time they went under the banner of the Arkansas Student Nonviolent Coordinating Committee or "Arsnick."[37] On November 8, election day, thirty students marched on the courthouse waving banners of protest at continuing segregation in the city.[38] On November 29, 1960, thirteen students demanded service at Woolworth's. When the new Little Rock police chief R. E. Glasscock asked the students to leave, they complied with his request. No arrests were made.[39]

The next day, seven students demanded service at the same lunch counter. This time, they refused to leave. All seven were arrested: Charles

Parker, twenty-two (who had participated in the first sit-in in March 1960 and whose conviction for this was already on appeal with the Arkansas Supreme Court); Lonnie McIntosh, twenty; Ted Hines, eighteen; Billy Bowles, eighteen; Edward Green, eighteen; Henry Daniels, eighteen; and Myrabel Callaway, eighteen, the only woman in the group. The students were charged under Act 226.[40] On December 1, Little Rock municipal court judge Quinn Glover deferred six of the seven new cases until after the Arkansas Supreme Court had had an opportunity to hear the earlier sit-in cases.[41]

On January 16, 1961, the Arkansas Supreme Court heard its first sit-in cases. Attorneys Wiley Branton and Harold Anderson represented the students. Branton raised several points along the lines that LDF lawyers had previously discussed. First, he argued that the students' Fourteenth Amendment right to equal protection was being violated. Branton conceded that businesses had the right to choose their own clientele, but he said that using criminal laws against African Americans who asked for service amounted to "state support [for] private prejudice" since whites asking for similar service were not treated in the same way. Second, Branton insisted that Act 226 and Act 17 should both be declared unconstitutional since they handed far too vague and sweeping powers to the state. He pointed out that Arkansas already had a statute that prohibited disturbing the peace, which referred to someone committing a "willful and malicious act." No such provision was made in the new acts. Third, even if the court found the state acts constitutional, Branton claimed that there was too little evidence upon which to find the students guilty. Fourth, Branton charged that the fines and the sentences handed down by the lower courts "were unusually harsh because the students had espoused an unpopular cause." Branton believed that the sentences were specifically aimed at halting protests and were intended to "break the spirit of other Negroes working for racial equality" rather than to ensure justice. He contended that if the court did uphold the students' sentences, at the very least the fines and jail terms should be reduced.[42]

Russell G. Morton, an administrative aide to Arkansas attorney general J. Frank Holt, argued the state's case. Morton said that the students had not been arrested for requesting service but for refusing to leave the premises when asked to do so and because their refusal to leave meant that there was a threat of disruption and violence. The charges against them, Morton insisted, had nothing to do with their color. Moreover, he pointed out, the students' fines and sentences did not exceed what was provided for under the law.[43]

The Arkansas Supreme Court took the cases under submission but waited almost two and a half years to hand down a ruling. The delay had a knock-on impact in the lower courts as Judge Quinn Glover refused to rule on the November 1960 sit-in cases, until, he said, the Arkansas Supreme Court decided the constitutional issues raised by the March and April 1960 sit-ins. Glover rescheduled the trials of the six students in the November 1960 sit-ins on no fewer than ten separate occasions. All of the students arrested in the sit-ins therefore found themselves in legal limbo.[44]

The Arkansas Supreme Court excused its own inaction by pointing to a lack of direction from the U.S. Supreme Court, which was reluctant to tackle the central constitutional question in the sit-in cases. In the trickle of such cases that arrived before the U.S. Supreme Court in its 1960 and 1961 terms, the Court consistently reversed sit-in convictions. At the same time, the justices refused to extend the Fourteenth Amendment's equal protection clause to instances of private discrimination as NAACP lawyers wanted. Doing so, the Court believed, would be tantamount to ordering private businesses to desegregate. Given the outcry that followed the Court's earlier *Brown* school desegregation ruling, it was understandably reluctant to go down this route. After *Brown*, 101 southern congressmen signed the so-called Southern Manifesto, condemning the Court's ruling in the case as "a clear abuse of judicial power" and accusing it of "undertaking to legislate."[45] Organized "massive resistance" to *Brown* had developed in the South and school desegregation slowed to a snail's pace.[46]

In the early sit-in cases the Court majority sought to sidestep the equal protection clause issue and devised other ways to reverse sit-in convictions. In the case of *Boynton v. Virginia* (1960), for example, the Court used the Interstate Commerce Act to reverse the conviction of Bruce Boynton. Boynton was an African American Howard University law student arrested for refusing to leave the white section of a bus terminal restaurant in Richmond, Virginia, in December 1958, while on an interstate coach trip from Washington, D.C., to Alabama. In the case of *Garner v. Louisiana,* the convictions of sit-in protestors in Baton Rouge were reversed on the grounds that there was insufficient evidence that their actions had caused a breach of the peace under state trespass laws.[47]

As well as the legal difficulties encountered by Little Rock's sit-in participants, another major obstacle was the ongoing difficulty in winning local support from the African American community that had already hampered efforts to extend the sit-ins to a boycott of stores. The ACHR lamented the lack of "coordinated support from the adult community which is showing its usual fragmentation and divisiveness." With the initial momentum for demonstrations lost and wary of the position of their friends who were still involved in protracted courtroom battles and facing large fines and jail sentences, protests were intermittent and eventually, again, ground to a halt.[48]

The situation in Little Rock progressed little the following year when another major new protest initiative, the Freedom Rides, hit the city. The Freedom Rides arose out of the first sit-in case heard by the U.S. Supreme Court in *Boynton v. Virginia*. In the earlier case of *Morgan v. Virginia* (1946), the Court had ruled against segregated seating on interstate travel. In 1947, the Congress of Racial Equality (CORE) tested this ruling by successfully holding an integrated "Journey of Reconciliation" through a number of Upper South states on interstate buses. When *Boynton* extended the *Morgan* ruling to interstate bus terminals, CORE reprised what it now called Freedom Rides to test facilities. On May 4, 1961, a group of thirteen African American and white Freedom Riders set off from Washington, D.C. The first leg of their journey, through Virginia, North Carolina, South Carolina, and Georgia, was largely incident free. However, on May 13, a white mob in Anniston, Alabama, attacked the first group of riders and firebombed their bus. The next day, whites attacked the second group as they pulled into the downtown Birmingham bus terminal.

The bus companies refused to transport any more Freedom Riders and CORE halted the campaign. However, SNCC declared that it would continue the rides. President John F. Kennedy responded to SNCC's decision by sending federal representatives to try to ensure the riders' safety. Nevertheless, when they reached Montgomery, Alabama, the riders were again attacked. Kennedy sent federal marshals and arranged a National Guard escort to ensure their safe passage to Jackson, Mississippi. Upon arrival in Jackson, by prearrangement police arrested the riders. The national publicity generated by the Freedom Rides led the Kennedy administration, through the Interstate Commerce Commission, to order the integration of all interstate buses and bus terminals. A Freedom Ride Coordinating Committee was set up to keep pressure on the federal government as well as encouraging African American communities to confront segregation in their own localities.[49]

The Freedom Rides arrived in Little Rock on July 10, 1961, when five members of the St. Louis branch of CORE rode into the city to test bus terminal facilities. The riders were arrested upon arrival. To avoid publicity, the city tried to dispatch the riders as quickly as possible. Judge Quinn Glover handed each of them the maximum sentence of a $500 fine and a six-month prison term, but he agreed to suspend their sentences if they left Arkansas immediately. The riders agreed to those terms. However, when they discovered that Glover actually meant for them to return to their homes in St. Louis and to abandon their plans to travel on and test facilities in Louisiana, they submitted themselves to re-arrest. The leader of the group, Rev. Benjamin Cox, told reporters that he would "much rather be dead and in my grave" than be "a slave to segregation" and threatened to go on hunger strike while incarcerated.[50]

For the first time since the school crisis, the Freedom Ride fiasco brought action from the city's white businessmen. The small but influential business elite in Little Rock had played a crucial role in ending the standoff over school desegregation in the city when they mobilized to oust pro-segregation members of the Little Rock School Board. However, since the token desegregation of the city's schools in August 1959, white businessmen had procrastinated over further calls for racial change. Thirteen business leaders met at the downtown First National Bank to discuss the situation with the Freedom Rides, and they formed an *ad hoc* Civic Progress Association to handle the matter. In a statement to the press, the business leaders diplomatically backed the city police in their actions. At the same time, they suggested they could learn from the incident in dealing with similar matters in the future. The following morning Judge Glover relented and allowed the Freedom Riders to continue their journey to Louisiana.[51]

Although the Freedom Ride failed to make the desired impact of forcing concessions for change, it did act as an important catalyst for a significant new African American community initiative. The failure of the sit-ins and the city's treatment of the Freedom Riders led to growing consternation among Little Rock's African American population. "I'm ashamed of the record Arkansas is making," lamented L. C. Bates in August 1961.[52] The "final straw" came in September 1961 when the African American composer and performer Duke Ellington was due to perform at Little Rock's Robinson Auditorium. L. C. Bates sent a telegram to Ellington's management company expressing disappointment "over your appearance . . . at Robinson Memorial Auditorium before a segregated audience." African Americans in Little Rock were still limited to segregated balcony seats at the auditorium, noted Bates, while neighboring cities such as Memphis, Tulsa, Oklahoma City, and Dallas had already desegregated their music venues. As a result, Ellington canceled the performance.[53]

In response to these developments, four young African American medical professionals, optometrist Dr. William H. Townsend, general practitioner Dr. Maurice A. Jackson, and husband and wife dentist team Dr. Garman P. Freeman and Dr. Evangeline Upshur, decided to act. They formed a Council on Community Affairs (COCA) to coordinate the activities of existing community organizations in the city to lobby for change.[54] COCA's initial efforts to engage in a dialogue with the white business community met with little success. To exert further pressure, on March 8, 1962, twenty-two members of COCA filed suit in the U.S. District Court for the desegregation of "public parks, recreational facilities . . . and all other public facilities" in the city.[55] Although conceding the probable eventual success of the COCA lawsuit, the white business community still insisted that it would draw out the process of desegregation for the longest possible amount of time.[56]

The student sit-ins had earlier failed without the backing of a unified African American community leadership. Now the efforts of COCA, in the absence of immediate pressure exerted by direct-action protests, met with little success. Only through a two-pronged approach of direct action coupled with the support of a wider community network that could help sustain such protests and articulate the demands of African Americans in the city would whites respond. Yet with the student movement at Philander Smith ravaged by harsh sentences and fines and their cases left dangling by the courts, a potential base for direct action was missing. In an effort to revive the sit-ins, the ACHR asked the SNCC head office in Atlanta, Georgia, if they could lend assistance in revitalizing protest in the city.[57]

In response to the ACHR's plea, SNCC sent white volunteer Bill Hansen, twenty-three, to Little Rock on October 24, 1962. Hansen was already a seasoned activist who had previously participated in Freedom Rides and sit-ins and in demonstrations in Albany, Georgia, earlier that year.[58] Hansen contacted Philander Smith student Worth Long, whom he had already met at several national SNCC conferences.[59] Long took Hansen to a meeting of student activists on campus that evening. At the meeting, Hansen witnessed firsthand the threadbare state of the student movement. Only seven people attended. Among those present he failed to detect any "ground-swell of . . . enthusiasm." Attempting to generate some interest, he explained the work of SNCC and what the organization had already accomplished. Hansen persuaded a couple of the students present to accompany him downtown the following day to try to gain service at a segregated lunch counter.[60]

Hansen used the sit-in to gauge community feeling among whites in Little Rock. Accompanied by the Arsnick chair Rev. William E. Bush, Hansen went into Woolworth's at noon, sat at the lunch counter, and ordered a coffee. When the waitress refused to serve Bush, Hansen went to see the store manager and asked if it was the policy of his store not to serve blacks. The manager replied that it was not store policy but rather city policy. Hansen noted "the absolute lack of tension at the counter when Bush was sitting there" in contrast to the hysteria and violence that similar demonstrations had encountered in other communities. He concluded that "the whole incident gives an indication that there would be no widespread consternation among the white community if Negroes were served at the lunch counters." Hansen advised students to avoid demonstrations, which might risk a white backlash, and instead encouraged them to talk with the managers of downtown stores to persuade them that it would be in their best interests to desegregate without any fuss.[61]

The following Monday, November 5, four black students went to Woolworth's to talk to the store manager. In an attempt to stall the students, he asked them to return in a couple of weeks' time. The students demanded an answer by Wednesday and left the store. On Wednesday, November 7, the manager told students that he was trying to work out a solution to the problem with other downtown merchants. When pressed to reveal further details he refused to set a specific date for desegregation. In response, the students sat down at the lunch counter, which the manager promptly closed. Hansen called newspapers, television stations, and radio stations to publicize the event as a way of bringing further pressure on the business community to meet the students' demands. When the police arrived, the manager refused to press charges. By midafternoon the students left of their own accord.[62]

This time the sit-ins had the intended impact on the business community. Shortly after the outbreak of new demonstrations, Willard A. Hawkins, the executive director of Downtown Little Rock Limited, representing a group of influential downtown business interests, contacted Worth Long. Hawkins informed Long that a group of businessmen had formed a Downtown Negotiating Committee (DNC), headed by James Penick, president of Worthen Bank and Trust Company, and were willing to meet with students. Penick, a well-respected and powerful figure in the Little Rock business community, had discussed the situation with other downtown merchants who agreed that desegregation was now preferable to ongoing disruption to businesses. During the following two weeks a delegation from the African American community met with the DNC to discuss the practicalities of desegregation. However, talks stalled over timing, with the African American delegation pressing for change within a matter of weeks and white merchants talking about gradual desegregation over a number of years.[63]

On November 28, disillusioned with the results of the negotiations, Philander Smith students expanded sit-in demonstrations to Walgreen's, McLellan's, and Blass's stores. At Walgreen's nine students asked for service at a segregated lunch counter. The manager closed the counter, but the students refused to leave. Hansen left the lunch counter and returned an hour later with Worth Long. When Hansen and Long tried to take seats at the lunch counter, the store manager asked them to leave. When they refused, the manager called the police and had them arrested. The two were arrested under Act 14. The arrests helped to muster more support from campus, with over one hundred Philander Smith students holding a march downtown the following day.[64] On December 7, Judge Quinn Glover added the new cases to the November 1960 cases that were still awaiting a decision in the Little Rock Municipal Court.[65]

The new burst of demonstrations brought the city's businessmen back to the negotiating table. Rather than go through a prolonged battle over desegregation, they made a decision to broker a compromise. An agreement was reached to desegregate downtown lunch counters in the early months of 1963. Penick worked to arrive at a consensus with downtown merchants about the process of desegregation.[66] In agreement with African American community representatives, a limited and controlled program of desegregation was agreed upon whereby a small number of African Americans would ask for service at particular stores at a set date and time. Over the course of a few weeks the numbers of those served and the length of their stay would increase. Each side agreed to notify both the local police and the staff at lunch counters in advance to avoid any confusion.[67] On January 2, 1963, Woolworth's, McLellan's, Walgreen's, and Blass's all desegregated their lunch counters.[68]

The successful desegregation of the major lunch counters prompted many other smaller businesses to follow suit. By the end of January several major hotels, motels, and a downtown bowling alley had also desegregated.[69] On February 15, federal judge J. Smith Henley ruled in favor of the COCA desegregation lawsuit filed in March 1962. The ruling ordered an end to racial segregation in all public facilities.[70] In June, the city's movie theaters and Robinson Auditorium admitted African Americans for the first time on an equal basis. By October, most of the city's restaurants had desegregated, as, by the end of the year, had all city parks, playgrounds, golf courses, the Little Rock Zoo, and the downtown Little Rock Arts Center. At the end of 1963, with little drama or fuss, Little Rock had desegregated most of its public and many of its private facilities.[71]

The desegregation of downtown Little Rock did not, however, bring an end to the saga of the sit-ins. In the 1962 term of the U.S. Supreme Court more sit-in cases arrived. In the first group of cases, decided under *Peterson v. City of Greenville*, sit-in participants had their convictions overturned on the basis that local ordinances required segregation in restaurants, demonstrating, the Court majority said, a clear link between state action and racial discrimination. In the second group of cases, decided under *Lombard v. Louisiana,* sit-in convictions were overturned because city officials had made it clear prior to the sit-ins that participants would be prosecuted. This, the Court majority ruled, gave explicit state sanction to uphold segregation. In *Griffin v. Maryland,* the Court majority looked to stretch the idea of state action even further. Those justices supporting a liberal interpretation of state action relied on the fact that it was a deputized county sheriff who also happened to work for the company where the sit-ins had taken place, and who had asked the students to leave, to overturn convictions. The case proved so divisive that the justices decided to hear rearguments in the case in the 1963 term before handing down a ruling.[72]

The Court's 1962 term came to an end with the justices still dismissing convictions without tackling the thorny constitutional question of extending the provisions of the equal protection clause. On May 13, 1963, the Arkansas Supreme Court handed down its ruling in the Little Rock sit-in cases. Chief Justice James D. Johnson, a former president of the Associated Citizens' Councils of Arkansas, an organization dedicated to resisting school desegregation, declared in his written opinion, surely not without some sense of irony given his previous opposition to *Brown* that "We do not feel that we can properly delay [the sit-in cases] longer to await a decision of the United States Supreme Court," since the state court ascribed "to the theory that justice delayed is justice denied." The convictions of all students arrested under Act 226 were overturned. The court accepted Wiley Branton's argument that there was insufficient evidence to support the convictions. Echoing the reasoning of the U.S. Supreme Court in its sit-in cases, the Arkansas Supreme Court pointed out that the students had been asked to leave the stores by local police who lacked the authority to make such a request. In any case, the state court ruled, there was no evidence of a breach of the peace in any of the incidents.[73]

The court viewed the cases of Frank James Lupper and Thomas B. Robinson, who were both charged under Act 14 in addition to Act 226, very differently. By dismissing one set of cases on the grounds of insufficient evidence, the court opened the way to focus on and press home a specific principle of law in these cases. Since the two students had refused to leave the premises at the direct request of a store official, the court held that Lupper and Robinson were guilty of trespass. This did not violate their Fourteenth Amendment rights, the state court ruled, since "By its terms and on its face, the statute applies to all who refuse to leave and it is not restricted to negroes. There is nothing uncertain, indefinite or vague about Act 14. It prohibits trespass." The court also held that the students had no inherent right to service at lunch counters and that store owners could legitimately choose to serve or not to serve customers at their discretion.

Moreover, the court felt that there was indeed sufficient evidence presented at the circuit court jury trial to demonstrate that Lupper and Robinson had refused to leave the store premises when asked to do so. Finally, on the question of the harshness and excessiveness of the fines and sentences imposed, the court noted that they did not exceed the penalties provided for by the state in Act 14. The convictions of Lupper and Robinson were affirmed.[74] The state supreme court's ruling effectively upheld the right of private businesses to discriminate, the very issue that the U.S. Supreme Court had been at pains to avoid addressing. When the state court refused a rehearing of the case, it went on appeal to the U.S. Supreme Court.[75]

Bill Hansen and Worth Long fared better when their cases were heard in Little Rock's municipal court on June 13, 1963. Hansen was not present but Long was, sporting a black armband in mourning for Mississippi NAACP field secretary Medgar Evers, who had been murdered in the driveway to his house in Jackson the previous day by white racist Byron De La Beckwith. When the case was called, attorney Harold Anderson immediately moved for a dismissal. In consultation with assistant city attorney Perry Whitmore, Judge Quinn Glover agreed to the request. It transpired that the store manager of Walgreen's, having resolved to desegregate lunch counters, was no longer interested in prosecuting the students. Since the store refused to prosecute, Glover had no option but to dismiss the cases.[76] On June 25, Glover, following the Act 226 sit-in cases dismissed by the Arkansas Supreme Court, dismissed all of the similar cases arising from the November 1960 sit-in.[77]

The one outstanding matter remaining from the Little Rock sit-in cases were the convictions of Lupper and Robinson. In its 1963 term, the U.S. Supreme Court found it increasingly difficult to extend the reach of state action. In the case of *Bell v. Maryland,* and the two South Carolina cases of *Barr v. City of Columbia* and *Bouie v. City of Columbia,* none of the previous caveats for state action appeared to apply. Amid much internal debate and dissent, in June 1964 the Court majority agreed to dismiss all of the convictions. In *Bell* the Court remanded the case back to the Maryland state courts for reassessment in the light of recently passed city and state laws that forbade discrimination in places of public accommodation. In *Barr* and *Bouie,* the Court overturned sit-in convictions on the basis that South Carolina's supreme court had misconstrued the state trespass statue to mean not just unauthorized entry into an establishment but also an unauthorized refusal to leave the property.[78]

Just as the U.S. Supreme Court appeared stretched to the limits of its judicial authority in the sit-in cases, developments in the U.S. Congress intervened. On July 2, Congress passed the 1964 Civil Rights Act, which, among other measures, outlawed segregation in public facilities and accommodations. Much as the Supreme Court had done, the act dissembled on the question of state action. Title II of the act, Section 201 (a), stated that, "All persons shall be entitled to the full and equal enjoyment of the goods, services, facilities, and privileges, advantages, and accommodations of any place of public accommodation, as defined in this section, without discrimination or segregation on the ground of race, color, religion, or national origin." It went on in Section 201 (b) to list a number of places covered by the act, and it defined "public accommodation within the meaning of this title if its operations affect commerce, or if discrimination or segregation by it is supported by State action." But what exactly constituted state action? Section 201 (d) of the act said that it meant "if such discrimination or segregation (1) is carried on under color of any law, statute, ordinance, or regulation; or (2) is carried on under color of any custom or usage required or enforced by officials of the State or political subdivision thereof; or (3) is required by action of the State or political subdivision thereof." Following the Supreme Court's lead, this constituted a very liberal reading of what state action meant.[79]

The Little Rock cases of Lupper and Robinson, consolidated with the South Carolina case of *Hamm v. City of Rock Hill,* were the first to be heard by the U.S. Supreme Court after the passage of the 1964 Civil Rights Act. The legislation introduced another pressing constitutional question: Could the act be applied retrospectively and thereby used to quash all of the convictions of those charged with defying the segregation laws that Congress had now made illegal? The Court employed the doctrine of abatement to rule that it could. The doctrine allowed the setting aside of pending judgments due to a change in the law that rendered invalid the laws under which the original charges were brought. Although the doctrine had never before been used to annul state criminal convictions because of a change in federal statutes, it expeditiously achieved what the Court had leaned toward throughout the sit-in cases: the reversal of convictions. Over three thousand sit-in cases pending before the courts were dismissed as a result of the ruling.[80]

The plight of Lupper and Robinson highlights the many factors that underlay the deceptively simple and straightforward direct-action tactic of sitting at a lunch counter and asking for service. The dramatic point of conflict that the action embodied was just one component in a far-reaching process. The sit-ins could not be successful without the effective mobilization of local African American community resources, which in turn proved impossible without a strong sense of community solidarity. Only then would influential figures in the white community take seriously demands for change and even consider taking action to end segregation and discrimination.

The Little Rock sit-ins likewise demonstrate the extent to which many local African American communities were dependent on outside help and assistance in their struggle for civil rights. Without the NAACP to provide lawyers and bail money, sit-in participants could not have effectively navigated the legal system. Without SNCC's ability to provide the expertise of seasoned activists such as Bill Hansen, the sit-ins may well not have ultimately achieved the success that they did. Without CORE and the Freedom Rides, and the Freedom Ride Coordinating Committee (in which CORE, SNCC, and Martin Luther King's Southern Christian Leadership Conference [SCLC] cooperated jointly) additional pressure would not have been put on the local white community to act and the local African American community to address discrimination in the city. Without the support of the U.S. Supreme Court, the U.S. Congress, and President Johnson's political skill in pushing through the Civil Rights Bill, all spurred by ongoing African American protests, the legal and political framework for change would not have existed. Examining the effectiveness of the sit-ins means unraveling the media-friendly and enduring popular images of those protests to reveal the nexus of local, regional, and national factors that contributed to their eventual success.

In two landmark rulings after the 1964 Civil Rights Act, the Supreme Court upheld congressional power to pass desegregation law that applied to accommodations involved in interstate commerce. This marked a new direction away from using the provisions of the Fourteenth Amendment's equal protection clause, a direction that had been encouraged by the Kennedy and Johnson presidential administrations. In *Heart of Atlanta Motel, Inc. v. United States,* the Court ruled that the motel was obliged to accommodate African American patrons since a failure to do so would interfere with interstate commerce. In *Katzenberg v. McClung,* the Court ruled that Ollie's Barbecue in Birmingham, Alabama, could not refuse to serve African American customers since the food cooked in the restaurant originated out of state.[81]

Nevertheless, some legal scholars still lament the fact that the Court did not extend the equal protection clause to cover private discrimination in the sit-in cases when it had the opportunity, and some believe the will, to do so. The question of state action, as well as the use of the commerce clause, has resurfaced in recent years as the Court under Chief Justice William Rehnquist narrowed the scope of both considerably. In *United States v. Morrison* (2000), the Court invalidated a section of the Violence against Women Act of 1994 that gave victims of gender-motivated violence the right to sue their attackers in federal court. The Court relied on its earlier ruling in *United States v. Lopez* (1995) that limited the commerce clause only to activities that had direct economic consequences. It also revisited the *Civil Rights Cases* to limit the definition of state action in favor of private individuals, moving in precisely the opposite direction of the Court in the sit-in cases. While the immediate issues of segregation and discrimination that the sit-ins addressed have now been consigned to the past, the fundamental questions of law that they raised remain as contested today as they were then.[82]

By the time that the U.S. Supreme Court ruling was handed down in *Lupper,* the immediate aims of the April 1960 sit-in that Frank James Lupper and Thomas B. Robinson participated in, the desegregation of Little Rock's downtown facilities, had already been realized. Both students had already graduated Philander Smith College. Few working in SNCC in Arkansas in 1964 probably even remembered their sit-in or the original court case. But the case still made a contribution to the civil rights struggle in the city and state from which it originated and indeed well beyond. In winning the abatement of other sit-in convictions, the victory freed up resources and personnel to reinvest back into the movement's efforts. The collective pressures of the sit-in court cases helped to shape and influence the federal legislation in the 1964 Civil Rights Act, which in turn provided strong support for SNCC's ongoing efforts for desegregation in local areas. It also paved the way to step up pressure on other issues, most notably the pursuit of voting rights. Thus, the Little Rock sit-in and its results fed back into the continuing local and state efforts of SNCC in Arkansas. One earlier wave of protest and demonstrations helped to set the context for the next wave of protests and demonstrations in the state. Even if they were not conscious of it at the time, the SNCC activists, old and new, were, as Martin Luther King Jr. put it in his 1963 Letter from Birmingham City Jail, "caught in an inescapable network of mutuality, tied in a single garment of destiny. Whatever affects one directly, affects all indirectly."[83] Or as SNCC appropriated it from King in a more succinct phrase, they formed part of the larger "beloved community" of the organization.[84]

2.

In the Storm

William Hansen and the Student Nonviolent Coordinating Committee in Arkansas, 1962–1967

BRENT RIFFEL

Stuck inside a cell in Albany, Georgia, in July 1962, civil rights activist William Hansen was having trouble meeting with his attorney. He had been arrested for participating in a demonstration, but when the attorney, C. B. King, insisted on seeing his client, Dougherty County sheriff "Cull" Campbell became enraged. "Nigger, haven't I told you to wait outside?" he said.[1] Campbell then picked up a cane and began beating the attorney. The next day the *New York Times* published a photograph of King, his head bandaged, leaving the hospital.[2] Hansen, however, had met with even harsher treatment. He had been thrown into a cell full of whites who were by no means sympathetic to the cause of civil rights and even less sympathetic toward a northern agitator like Hansen. He was savagely beaten, with his jaw shattered and several of his ribs broken. Only twenty-one years old at the time, Hansen had a long career as a political activist ahead of him.

Hansen arrived in Little Rock, Arkansas, later that year to head up a new branch of the Student Nonviolent Coordinating Committee, a grassroots organization that sought to harness the rising tide of black political consciousness in the South. Hansen's organizational skills earned him appointment to the post, but his interest in civil rights and his desire to fight racism dated to his childhood. Born in Cincinnati in 1939, Hansen grew up in a strict working-class Catholic family. His religious upbringing helped propel him toward a life as a political activist. "The extreme moral rigidity of American Catholicism in the pre-Vatican II days," he later recalled, "had a way of leading in the direction I went with regard to race and politics. . . . Its rigid moral doctrine, if accepted, would lead logically toward a certain set of actions."[3]

Hansen's direct experience with African Americans also shaped his political outlook. He recalled how attending baseball games—sitting in the cheap bleacher seats at Crosley Field to see the Cincinnati Reds play—allowed positive interactions with black people:

> I was a ten- to sixteen-year-old kid who made acquaintances with many of these older black men who, it seemed to me, knew everything about baseball. They took a liking to [me]. I remember at first not being able to figure out why all these Cincinnatians supported the Brooklyn Dodgers over their hometown team. I finally figured out it was because of Jackie Robinson. That realization told me something about the society I was being raised in.

Like many people of his generation, Hansen also watched the aftermath of the 1954 *Brown v. Board of Education* decision, as well as the 1956 Montgomery Bus Boycott, with rapt attention. He quickly found himself siding with civil rights activists, thinking "it was dumb to be arrested for sitting in the wrong seat in a bus."[4]

Personal relationships with blacks also played a role in the development of Hansen's political consciousness. When he was seventeen years old, he became friends with Bill Mason, a young black man with whom he often played basketball. This was Hansen's first friendship with someone from outside of his working-class neighborhood. Mason often invited Hansen back to his home, where Hansen found he was treated as a member of Mason's family. Two years later, the Masons took Hansen in, and he lived with them for a year. Their warmth offered a stark contrast to how he had imagined blacks and whites normally interacted with one another.[5]

Hansen made his first foray into the civil rights movement in the fall of 1957 while attending Xavier University in Cincinnati. He became associated with David McCarthy, a local priest who had become active in the cause. Along with Bill Mason, Hansen and McCarthy formed the Xavier Interracial Council. Hansen later downplayed its significance, arguing that it was never more than "a venue for getting to know other people."[6] But the council allowed Hansen to make important contacts with other civil rights organizations such as the Congress of Racial Equality. Hansen quickly helped set up a Cincinnati branch of CORE and also joined a local branch of the National Association for the Advancement of Colored People.

After dropping out of Xavier, Hansen fully devoted himself to the movement. By the time of his 1962 arrest in Albany, Georgia, he had been involved in a number of protests and demonstrations across the South. He had become an active member of SNCC, which at the time represented the vanguard of the civil rights movement.

While many groups, including CORE and the Martin Luther King Jr.–led Southern Christian Leadership Conference, played a major part in the movement, the "shock troops" of SNCC quite often broke down the first barriers of resistance.[7] Concentrating on the rural Deep South, SNCC met with far more violence than these other groups. But the more violence SNCC staffers endured, the greater their devotion to the cause. As SNCC grew in size and strength, its members often felt that time was on their side and that eventually dramatic social change would occur. SNCC staffers internalized this commitment to change, seeking to transform themselves as well. Combating racism, many believed, began in the individual's heart. Violence and arrest gave them a shared experience and indicated to many that they were on a righteous mission. As Hansen recalled, "the times were very intense, and most of us lived close to the edge."[8]

The rise and fall of SNCC has been extensively examined.[9] But much of this scholarship has focused on SNCC's voter registration drives and protests against segregation in rural Mississippi. There are obvious reasons for this. For one, many civil rights activists considered Mississippi the linchpin of the movement and, indeed, the symbol of Jim Crow. Forcing change there, they believed, would cause a chain reaction in which less intensely racist states (or at least states perceived as less intensely racist) would follow suit, enforcing integration and ending black disfranchisement. Yet, a more complete picture of the successes and failures of SNCC, its strengths and weaknesses, requires examination of its experience in other states. The case of Arkansas might be particularly instructive, considering that far fewer black people lived in Arkansas than in Mississippi and the considerable attention already drawn to the state by the Central High crisis of 1957. While the history of SNCC in Arkansas cannot be encompassed in any single article, William Hansen's story reveals much about the organization's career in the state and suggests something of the diversity within SNCC and the civil rights movement as a whole.

SNCC arrived in Arkansas at the request of the Arkansas Council on Human Relations, a local minority rights group, in October 1962.[10] The history of SNCC's Arkansas field office unfolded under the shadow of the Central High crisis. Many Arkansans were embarrassed by the national attention their state had received during the crisis. Sympathetic moderates often met civil rights groups more than halfway, seeking to appease the activists before another media onslaught cast the state in a negative light. Thus, many of the gains made by SNCC in Arkansas were achieved behind the scenes, even though, as Hansen noted, "a major tactic was to secure as much media attention as possible." This markedly differed from SNCC activities in Mississippi, where civil rights workers acted in the constant glare of community and media attention.[11]

Hansen had been appointed by the national SNCC office to be director of what became known as the Arkansas Project. Following Bob Zellner—one of the first white activists in SNCC—Hansen became the second white person to serve as a field organizer. Hansen's credibility among SNCC members was unquestionable. He had participated in a number of signal episodes of the civil rights movement over the previous five years. The violent attacks he had endured cemented his reputation as a committed activist. Yet, while nominally the leader of the local SNCC office, Hansen later insisted that he was not the group's sole leader, just the person the media came to first. SNCC prided itself on its lack of leaders and tended to avoid hierarchy in its organization.[12]

By the time Hansen arrived in Little Rock, a number of young activists were already at work. As sit-ins and demonstrations spread across the South in 1960–1961, all-black Philander Smith College had emerged as the center of Arkansas's student civil rights movement. On March 10, 1960, student activists held a demonstration in downtown Little Rock, at which a number of students were arrested. In other southern cities, whites had often responded to black demonstrations with violence and jeers. In Little Rock, the sit-ins and demonstrations produced a much different response. The white community, having perhaps learned some lessons from the 1957 crisis, proved more accommodating than in many other spots around the South. To quietly negotiate desegregation of the city, a secret committee was formed in early 1961. White businessman Grainger Williams served on the committee and acted as a liaison between the civil rights community and the white business owners of Little Rock: "I don't know whether it was formed by the Chamber of Commerce or who formed it, but somebody called me and asked me if I'd serve on this committee . . . and I said, 'certainly.' I think they wanted it secret 'cause they didn't want anybody to know they were working on it. They just wanted it to occur."[13]

According to Hansen, the invitation extended to SNCC was part of a strategy to make integration appear as if it were occurring naturally and the city changing on its own, without the federal government having to get involved. Hansen suggested local white liberals saw SNCC as something of a lightning rod, helping advance desegregation while deflecting backlash away from local white supporters:

That's the reason they called SNCC in the first place in 1962 and asked for an organizer, precisely because they were too afraid for their reputations and their nice suburban lifestyles: "Call SNCC and have them take the heat. They'll do what we're afraid to do and then we'll step in later as the voice of reason and moderation and take the credit." And that's exactly what they did.[14]

Scholarly accounts of desegregation in Little Rock have highlighted the role that a wave of sit-ins Hansen helped orchestrate at Woolworth's and other businesses played in speeding the integration in 1963 of local lunch counters, restaurants, theaters, and municipal recreational facilities.[15] Yet Hansen later downplayed his own role, giving the greatest credit to Philander Smith students in pushing the business community and the city to end Jim Crow.[16]

If SNCC, by Hansen's account, played a small role in Little Rock racial politics, it focused considerable attention on eastern Arkansas, where a good portion of the state's black population lived. The Arkansas delta resembled Mississippi in many ways, with its sharecropping and rigidly hierarchical divisions of race and class. Carrie Young, at the time a teen-aged black woman from Helena, summed up the delta society of this era. "I got whippings every day," she recalled. "I mean that was your life. A hundred pounds of cotton brought $3.00. And back then, I was glad to see SNCC and anything else that looked like 'em because that was my ticket out of the cotton field."[17] Young became involved in the movement at age sixteen, joining SNCC and taking part in voter registration drives in Phillips County.[18] One of the things about SNCC that appealed to delta blacks was its informality, according to Frank James. He recalled that "[SNCC] was loosely put [together] so that any student could belong and you didn't have to have a card to belong. So if you say you were a part of the Student Nonviolent Coordinating Committee, you were."[19] Black Arkansans also responded to the organization's lack of dogma, as well as its ambivalent stance toward techniques of political action. According to Perlesta Hollingsworth, "[SNCC wasn't] sold on [Dr. Martin Luther] King's approach completely. It was a little divergence. They were thinking about—you know—striking back."[20] SNCC obviously adhered to the tenets of nonviolence, but some within the movement were moving toward embracing armed self-defense. As SNCC developed, it became increasingly split between activists like Hansen, who preferred grassroots organizing, and men like Stokely Carmichael, who instead employed fiery separatist rhetoric and ultimately endorsed violence as a viable means of political action.[21]

Historian John A. Kirk suggests that many locals in the Arkansas delta—both black and white—resented SNCC's presence in the area. SNCC ignored local opinion, he argues, and simply imposed its ideas on the people there. Many black clergymen, in particular, actively opposed SNCC because it threatened their church's authority.[22] But Hansen insisted most blacks responded to SNCC's arrival with enthusiasm. "It was normal, everyday black folk who took us in, enfolded us, energized us, and took care of us."[23] He added, "some ministers held us at arm's length because they thought we threatened their political control. We probably did. On the other hand, many ministers supported us strongly. Where in the world did we hold those weekly mass meetings, but in churches?"[24]

Hansen vividly remembered the day in fall 1963 that SNCC arrived in Phillips County:

> We announced our presence with a sit-in at a Helena downtown lunch counter. As per usual, I was arrested along with a half dozen or so locals, mainly teenagers . . . I was still in jail from this arrest on the day [John F. Kennedy was assassinated]. . . . I thought it was all over. Who would pay any attention to the murder of a nobody civil rights organizer after what happened in Dallas?[25]

According to Hansen, a lack of adequate staff and "a lot of trouble with police" forced SNCC to leave the city.[26] But SNCC returned three months later. Helena would become, along with Pine Bluff, a focal point of its work in eastern Arkansas.

With SNCC's encouragement, a young black factory worker ran for Helena's city council as an independent. With only one ballot box left uncounted, he led by forty-eight votes. Two days later, when all of the votes had been tallied, he lost by over two hundred votes. According to Hansen, voter fraud had obviously occurred:

> From our investigation, we have found that much of this fraud was perpetrated by . . . the local Uncle Tom and his wife . . . who runs a beauty salon. Representing Sheriff Hickey, the most feared man among Negroes in Helena, [the Uncle Tom] approached many Negroes and told them to vote "absentee" at [the] beauty salon to avoid the crowds at the polls. Those that came were told to vote . . . and they would take care of the rest. [They] also voted for those who never came. By the way, [this man] is the president of the new Phillips County chapter of the NAACP.[27]

Thus by Hansen's account, blacks as well as whites were complicit in electoral fraud. Mitchell Zimmerman, another white organizer who, like Hansen, had come to Arkansas to get involved with SNCC's voter registration drives, wrote to the Justice Department's Civil Rights Division, demanding an investigation into election rigging and harassment of black voters in eastern Arkansas.[28]

In Pine Bluff, SNCC focused on increasing voter registration among the city's black population. According to the field reports Hansen frequently sent to the organization's national office in Atlanta, these efforts succeeded in doubling the number of registered black voters to roughly 40 percent of the entire black population of Pine Bluff.[29] SNCC also made strides in encouraging blacks to run for political office. In Pine Bluff, one black candidate narrowly won a seat on the local school board.[30] Two other blacks, Ben Grinage and James A. Bagby (both SNCC organizers), ran for state representative. As Hansen reported, "they both lost but we were encouraged by the voter turnout."[31]

SNCC's eastern Arkansas project occasionally met with intense resistance from the white community. Hansen reported to the national office that in Helena in the summer of 1964 "several houses were fired into by marauding whites and there was an unsuccessful attempt to bomb the Freedom House," SNCC's community center.[32] Later that fall, SNCC organizer Frank T. Cieciorka was beaten in front of a polling place on election day.[33] According to Hansen, many locals who had been supportive of SNCC's efforts were threatened and harassed.[34]

SNCC organizers in the Arkansas delta found that their early attempts at integrating public spaces were "mostly unsuccessful," according to SNCC's newspaper, the *Student Voice*.[35] Yet internal reports tell a different story, suggesting that the organization made considerable strides. SNCC had proved to local blacks that it would remain in the area in the face of widespread opposition. It showed them that they were not alone and that enormous political change was afoot. Beyond demonstrating its resolve, SNCC also achieved tangible results, helping, according to Hansen, over two thousand blacks in the delta to register to vote.[36]

Yet the organization could do little to ease the endemic poverty and racism facing eastern Arkansas blacks. Its experience in the delta suggested to many activists that the real battle had to be fought against the economic oppression that underlay race relations. Hansen later remarked that as SNCC grew larger its core leadership became more politically sophisticated, recognizing the systemic problems that perpetuated racial discord. He realized the challenge that this presented to the status quo:

[SNCC] began questioning the nature of wealth and property in the United States: Who holds it? Why? How did they get it? By what right? Why are people poor? And what does the "system" have to do with it? These are questions one is not allowed to ask in America. Certainly not questions one is allowed to act on. Arguing that all Americans should be allowed to eat hamburgers wherever they wish, go to school wherever they wish, vote just like white people, are issues America is willing to discuss. Questioning the nature of American capitalism is beyond what is considered legitimate discourse. [Because of this] SNCC and other organizations had to be destroyed . . . and they were.[37]

Such perceptions, together with the fact that the passage of the Civil Rights Act of 1964 and the Voting Rights Act of 1965 had effectively ended de jure segregation and disfranchisement, moved civil rights activism in radical new directions. While the civil rights movement might have faded away following its legislative victories, the movement actually heightened its assault on the status quo. This was certainly the case in Arkansas, where the cooperation of the early 1960s gave way to misunderstandings and violent confrontations. Hansen and other SNCC activists had been met with violence in rural parts of the South, but events in Little Rock had been comparatively peaceful. This changed in 1965 with a march on the state capitol. The capitol building was one of the last public holdouts to integration in the city. Local civil rights activist Howard Love participated in the march, and he later recalled the intense resistance with which they were met. "We had gone out to the Capitol and tried to eat," he remembered. "Well, they refused to serve us out there. The state police herded us out and back up the stairs. And that was a trap. They got us on the stairs and started spraying mustard gas."[38] Clearly, some Little Rock whites felt they had accommodated black activists enough. According to Roy Reed, who worked as a reporter for the *Arkansas Gazette* and then the *New York Times,* "there was a feeling that these are kids, why should we deal with them? . . . Why do they have to [protest]? Why don't they go to court? Let's don't have all of this disturbance. It's not good for our image here in the town, or, it's bad for business, or, people will get hurt."[39]

While violent eruptions like those at the 1965 march on the capitol were an anomaly, the tumult of this protest signaled the emergence of a new element in the Little Rock civil rights scene. Many local SNCC members coalesced into a radicalized militant bloc. Nationally, SNCC underwent a similar change in its ranks as the Black Power movement developed. Leaders like Stokely Carmichael and H. Rap Brown began pushing for a more aggressive approach. They felt that SNCC's insistence on nonviolence had been a practical necessity. But, as race riots erupted throughout the United States in the summer of 1965, many within SNCC argued that non-violence no longer had a place in the movement. With this radicalization came a new current, one that sought to expel white members from SNCC. The call for separatism within the organization initially fell on deaf ears but soon became an irresistible force.[40]

Arkansas's move toward Black Power came in 1966, with the emergence of the Black United Youth (BUY) as a new civil rights group in Little Rock. Many of its members had splintered off from SNCC. Indeed, there probably would never have been a BUY had SNCC not arrived first. BUY offered an implicit critique of SNCC's more moderate philosophy of non-violence and its cooperation—at least in Arkansas—with white authorities. Led by Bobby Brown, BUY combined radical political action with a new Afro-centric cultural awareness that typified Black Power groups. As the local SNCC activist Lottie Shackleford, who would serve as mayor of Little Rock in the 1980s, recalled, "[BUY was] considered the rough guys. In fact, if you knew that BUY was going to be conducting some kind of activity some place, you probably avoided that area."[41] BUY continued the process of integration begun by SNCC, focusing on grocery stores, which at the time remained segregated on a *de facto* basis. At the same time young activists shifted toward Black Power, leaders like Hansen began questioning the new ideological directions of the movement. Thus, the Arkansas Project's membership began eroding from both ends.

Though he continued to work in Arkansas, William Hansen resigned from his SNCC directorship in 1964, citing the need for black leaders to take over the Arkansas Project.[42] He left the organization altogether in 1966. His departure broke all ties between the Arkansas Project and the early SNCC members who had been in the organization since 1960–1961. Different rationales have been offered for Hansen's leaving SNCC. In his general history of SNCC, Clayborne Carson suggested that Hansen's departure stemmed from his unwillingness, in contrast to most Arkansas SNCC staffers, to toe the emerging party line of Black Power, a clearly untenable course for a white activist.[43] By this time, the Arkansas Project's staff had dwindled to an almost all-black membership. In 1962, Hansen had been the only white staffer in Arkansas. A number of white northern activists, including Mitchell Zimmerman, joined SNCC in 1963–1964, yet by 1966 Hansen was one of only a handful of whites still involved in the project.[44]

Hansen has offered more pragmatic reasons for leaving, citing the need to earn more money for his wife (he had married a black female activist from Pine Bluff during his days as director) and their newborn child. But Hansen has also given other reasons for resigning more in keeping with

Carson's account. He felt that by the time of his resignation SNCC's programs "were dying on the vine with no resources and people leaving. I
thought the way the Black Power slogan was being articulated was inco-
herent and confusing, thus undermining what we were trying to do."
Hansen continued:

> I knew the expulsion of whites was coming. Those who wanted to
> get rid of whites in the organization came to every meeting and
> had been doing so for several years. . . . [This] led SNCC into an
> endless internal cycle of recrimination. For me, I did not want to
> undergo the indignity of being expelled from an organization that
> had consumed my life for the previous six, seven years. Particu-
> larly as the people who were demanding our expulsion were rela-
> tive newcomers who hadn't even been there during the really
> tough years of the early sixties. For the most part, they had been
> on nice white campuses up North.[45]

Still, Hansen's recollections suggest internal racial tensions did not play
as large a role in the state field office as some historians have suggested
they did nationally. Hansen argued that racial tension within the group was
nonexistent until after 1964 and the influx of many new, mostly white,
members: "SNCC grew too fast after the summer of 1964, and tried to
absorb a large group of people (largely white, largely educated, largely
northern, and often quite aggressive) who were new to the organization,
often overly romantic about what the 'movement' actually was." But even
after 1964, whatever tensions did exist were, as Hansen recalled, "a very
minor part of our collective relationship."[46]

In many ways, William Hansen symbolizes the evolution of SNCC,
from the boundless, idealistic energy of its early days to the fractured, internal struggles of its final period. Ironically, both in Arkansas and nationally,
it became politically irrelevant almost as soon as it had become a powerful
force. SNCC ultimately collapsed under its own weight, following the
imposition of militant dogma on an organization founded on the notion of
not having an ideology or hierarchy. The *Arkansas Gazette* reported in
May 1966 that Pine Bluff SNCC leader Benjamin Grinage had threatened
to resign if the Arkansas Project adopted the national office's new platform.[47] In July 1966, Grinage carried out his threat (at virtually the same
time Hansen resigned), though he cited the need to earn more money, not
ideology, as his motive for leaving the Arkansas Project.[48]

The need to earn money that both Grinage and Hansen cited in leaving
SNCC could itself be traced back to the organization's ideological shift,
which caused a dramatic drop-off in funding that began around 1965. The

lack of funds filtered down to the state level, sending the organization into disarray. Hansen cited two specific reasons why funding came to a virtual standstill: SNCC's vehement opposition to the Vietnam War and support for Palestinian nationalism. SNCC had usually avoided international politics, but, by 1966, members of the organization began traveling to controversial political hot spots such as Havana and Hanoi. Its support for the Palestinian movement caused the most significant reaction against SNCC, because much of the group's support came from sympathetic Jewish liberals. According to Hansen, the desertion of the Jewish community had a devastating effect:

> Virtually overnight we were deprived of funds. Without at least some money the field programs began to wither and die. Organizers, needing to eat, left to find jobs, causing more decline in the field programs. As the organization shrank it left the door open to the loony ultra-nationalist fringe who were, I think, in large part, the infiltrators. We were vulnerable, and they got us.[49]

In referring to "infiltrators," Hansen was alluding to COINTELPRO, a highly controversial, secret program headed by the Federal Bureau of Investigation director J. Edgar Hoover. This program investigated, and hindered the actions of, political groups that certain elements of the government considered dangerous. Hansen believed infiltrators played a major role in SNCC's collapse, and he suspected certain Arkansas Project staffers of being involved in subterfuge. As Hansen recalled, "there is no question in my mind—virtually all SNCC veterans agree with me here—that we were infiltrated. . . . Often those who claimed to be the 'blackest' (and I am definitely not talking about Stokely Carmichael here) were the ones I suspect of being agents provocateurs."[50] However, like everything associated with COINTELPRO, the evidence remains murky. Only as documents concerning COINTELPRO become more available through declassification will the effect this program had on SNCC become clearer.[51]

After leaving SNCC, Hansen moved to Atlanta where he worked for a number of organizations that sought to combat rural poverty: the National Sharecroppers Fund, the Southern Rural Project, and the Westinghouse Learning Corporation's Vista Training Project. By 1969, he had come to believe that these organizations were accomplishing little. Moreover, he had become increasingly disillusioned with the direction of the civil rights movement, which he considered to be, at the close of the 1960s, mired in "self-absorption and self-delusion with its ultra-romantic notions of armed revolution succeeding in urban America."[52] Accordingly, Hansen moved with his wife and two young children to West Germany and, then, West

Africa. In the mid-1970s, he returned to Germany, where he took a job writing for a weekly English-language newspaper, but his leftist politics quickly got him fired. He then moved to London to pursue graduate work in African politics. In 1979, he returned to the United States to begin work on a Ph.D. at Boston University. Shortly afterward, Ronald Reagan ascended to the White House and became, by Hansen's estimation, "the first president to come to office with the explicit intent to roll back the sixties."[53] During the 1980s, Hansen's political activism focused on two major issues: opposing nuclear proliferation and the arms race and the growing solidarity movement in South Africa.

Hansen remained active in various political causes during the 1990s and in 1997 took a teaching position at the American University-Central Asia, in Bishkek, Kyrgyzstan. He kept in contact with many of the civil rights leaders that he had worked with in the 1960s. In the spring of 1998, he took his son to meet former colleague Stokely Carmichael (by then known as Kwame Ture), two months before Carmichael would succumb to cancer. For Hansen, this encounter illustrated how SNCC still lived on:

> My son and I spent the day with Stokely Carmichael in an apartment in New York City . . . and talked about the old days, about Africa, about the continuing struggle, about his impending death. My white, freckle-faced, red-haired son [from Hansen's second marriage] was in awe as Brother Carmichael treated him with respect and as a member of the collective struggle. His friendship with me was forged in countless places and countless instances over those short years of SNCC.[54]

To Hansen, SNCC represented a "circle of trust, a band of brothers" that continued to exist and have meaning long after the organization ceased its activities.[55]

William Hansen played an important, if overlooked, role in the history of the American civil rights movement and the history of Arkansas. SNCC's willingness to work with white civic leaders in Little Rock helped the city to integrate quietly and with relative peace. In the Arkansas delta, SNCC's presence probably did little to affect the larger social divisions there. But during his brief time as head of the Arkansas Project, Hansen helped delta blacks to develop greater political consciousness through his efforts at voter registration. And, through his leadership, William Hansen provided a model for young white activists, showing how sympathy for the plight of African Americans could be translated into overt political action.

3.

"It Was the Wrong Time, and They Just Weren't Ready"

Direct-Action Protest in Pine Bluff, 1963

HOLLY Y. MCGEE

Whether by design or fate, the first sit-in conducted by the Pine Bluff Student Movement (PBSM) occurred on February 1, 1963, the first day of Black History Month, established thirty-seven years earlier, as well as the third anniversary of the Greensboro, North Carolina, student sit-in. Thirteen students of Arkansas Agricultural, Mechanical & Normal College (AM&N) entered the F. W. Woolworth store in downtown Pine Bluff a little after 2:00 P.M., carrying textbooks and dressed in their Sunday best. As soon as the students sat down at the lunch counter, a waitress—apparently by prior arrangement—turned off the lights, closing the counter for business. For more than two hours, the thirteen students silently sat in the semidarkness as word spread through downtown that a sit-in was in progress. Curious onlookers filed into the Woolworth store to watch. After being identified by the police as the leader of the PBSM, Robert Whitfield, an AM&N junior from Little Rock, was approached by store manager T. W. Harper and asked into Harper's office for a private meeting. As the other students continued the demonstration, Whitfield spoke with Harper for more than one hour, no doubt trying to reach an amicable compromise.[1]

At 5:30 P.M., when Harper announced the store was closing more than two hours early, the A&MN students quietly rose from the lunch counter and left the store. This sit-in, the first in Pine Bluff history, broke a number of barriers. The city's black community was large and vigorous but existed apart from white institutions. Situated in the heart of the black section of Pine Bluff, the campus of AM&N and its students were largely self-sufficient. More generally, black entrepreneurs—operating everything from financial institutions to eateries and beauty shops—offered a range of services unavailable to the black citizenry via most white owned establishments in the city. The sit-in, however, bridged this divide. The city's daily newspaper, the *Pine Bluff Commercial,* placed a photograph of three unidentified protesters —two men and one woman—on its front page. Prior to the publication of the photograph, pictures of African Americans had rarely appeared on the front page of the *Commercial.* Certainly, pictures of black ministers, university officials, and community leaders had appeared, but they were buried deep within the newspaper. Most important, prior to the student sit-ins, news relating to the black community had not appeared on the paper's front page. Instead, the *Commercial* largely confined its coverage to basketball games between historically black colleges, a segregated obituary column entitled "Negro Deaths," and infrequent, token articles about presumably good race relations. Henceforth, stories associated with the AM&N sit-ins would regularly appear on the front page. Over the course of a few months, a small group of student activists changed the face of race relations in their community.

There is much more to the story of Arkansas during the civil rights movement than Little Rock alone, but the events in 1957 have long overshadowed other episodes that changed lives and entire communities. The painful birth of the PBSM is one such episode. Newspapers across the world did not headline the events in Pine Bluff. The president did not federalize troops to ensure PBSM members could continue their education at AM&N. But examining events that led to the expulsion of fifteen students, the bitter split within the black community over AM&N chancellor Lawrence A. Davis's decision to oust them, and the consequences individual students faced is instructive, for it suggests the inadequacy of narratives that manage to portray Arkansas's civil right movement as a success story —largely by cutting that story short at the reopening of Little Rock high schools in 1959.[2]

Pine Bluff held an important place in Arkansas's civil rights history. Two African American attorneys based there, W. H. Flowers and Wiley Branton, had been central to the struggle in the courts, but grassroots activism had been slower to develop. Yet the city's demographics seemed to favor action. The U.S. Census reported that in 1960 Jefferson County, where the city of Pine Bluff is located, African Americans numbered

35,365—approximately 43 percent of the county population.[3] Benjamin Grinage of SNCC recalled that although blacks in Pine Bluff were not as well organized as those other parts of the South, "whites knew that [blacks had] enough people to raise hell."[4]

In 1960, during the first wave of student sit-ins across the South, a small group of AM&N students organized a meeting to discuss the possibility of such actions in Pine Bluff. But, according to a Student Nonviolent Coordinating Committee report filed two years later, the AM&N administration "got wind of" the meeting and promptly expelled three students it identified as the "ringleaders."[5] Three years would pass before activism returned to the campus. This time the students were determined to exact tangible social gains for local blacks.

By early 1963, news of recent civil rights gains in Little Rock had filtered into nearby Pine Bluff.[6] Many students had simply been waiting for an opportunity to join the struggle. Dr. Joanna Edwards, a sophomore at AM&N in 1963, recalled that after hearing about the Greensboro sit-in she "had tried to get some students to go down with me to demonstrate, but I think they thought I was just joking." Two years later, as a student at AM&N, Edwards finally felt she was a part of a community capable of demanding and securing substantive political and social gains for black citizens. Many AM&N students appreciated the open, intellectual atmosphere the campus seemed to offer. AM&N provided most black students —predominantly from small towns in less densely populated regions of the state—with opportunities they never would have enjoyed had they not attended the historically black college. Campaigning for student office, organizing campus activities, and having a sense of a campus "community" offered black students what they felt was a revolutionary view of the world —a world in which they had a voice.[7]

Local events also galvanized many students' emerging activist consciousness. When William Howard, a black Pine Bluff resident, attempted to pick up his niece one day after school, he became involved in an altercation that resulted in him stabbing eighteen-year-old Johnny Irvin Jr., a white student at Dollarway. Howard's niece, Sarah, was a high school student and one of only four blacks who had enrolled at Dollarway in the previous two years. Sarah also just happened to be the daughter of George Howard, a local attorney and president of the state chapter of the National Association for the Advancement of Colored People. Before the incident, George Howard himself had appealed to both U.S. attorney general Robert Kennedy and Governor Orval Faubus for protection for Sarah and second-grader Samuel Wayne Cato, who at the time was the only other black student in Dollarway. Though both Sarah and Samuel were routinely taunted and threatened at school, Howard's requests went unheeded. One afternoon in late January 1963, after his brother, William, had collected both Sarah and Samuel and driven away, according to the local paper, "he heard something hit the car and he stopped." William Howard later maintained that the *something* he and the children heard strike the vehicle actually broke a window, which forced him to stop. Jefferson County sheriff Harold Norton, however, refused to accept this as a precipitating factor in the events that followed, since, according to Norton, "there was no indication that the window on Howard's car was broken *prior* to the knifing . . . it could [have been] that the window was broken *after* Howard left the car."[8] Though the catalyst was in dispute, all parties acknowledged that the real trouble began when Howard locked the children in the car and exited the vehicle "to find a telephone and call [his] insurance company." As Howard proceeded down the street, a white youth ran up to him from behind and when he reached Howard, grabbed his shoulder. No doubt believing he was in imminent danger after having had an object hurled through the window of his car, Howard turned and stabbed his would-be attacker in the side. The white youth later claimed "a Negro was chasing his younger brother" and when he'd run to the aid of his sibling he saw Howard walking down the street and made the *logical* conclusion that Howard was the mythical Negro. William Howard, meanwhile, was arrested on charges of assault with intent to kill, despite the fact that the youth's wound "was not considered serious."[9]

No doubt this incident and the arrests the same month of William "Bill" Hansen and Benjamin F. Grinage, an ordained minister and native of Little Rock, added to the burgeoning desire of blacks in Pine Bluff—particularly students to become active in the civil rights movement. Hansen had recently been assigned to work in Arkansas by James Forman of SNCC following an incident in Albany, Georgia, where Hansen was jailed and beaten so severely by police officers that his jaw was broken. It had to be wired shut in order to heal properly.[10] After seeing demonstrations in Little Rock suppressed by whites during negotiation stages, Hansen and Grinage, who met through their work on the campus of Philander Smith College, decided to go to Pine Bluff, only forty-four miles to the southeast. In town a scant few days, Hansen and Grinage were arrested near the AM&N campus and charged with vagrancy when it was suspected they were "attempting to organize sit-in demonstrations" in the city. The sit-in at Woolworth's quickly followed.[11]

In order to sustain this demonstration past February 1 and continue attending classes at AM&N, students organized subsequent sit-ins so that participants could sit in two- or three-hour shifts. This tactic heavily depended on the participation of area high school students, whose numbers greatly added to the AM&N forces. Joanna Edwards recalled the ways in which schoolchildren helped members of the college community stage effective sit-ins:

> [The high school students] were faithful. When they got out of high school during the day, they would come down to Woolworth's immediately . . . of course all you needed was one [black] person down there to keep [the counters] closed. But what [we] would do was go in shifts [during the day] . . . of course, when the high school students got out [of school in the afternoons] the whole store would be full of children (laughter).[12]

The participation of high school students highlights the fact that the direct-action demonstrations were led and sustained by the city's younger black generation. In the coming months, the young people of Pine Bluff would become clearly divided—with previously sympathetic students taking a surprising stance. For now, however, the presence of high school students allowed PBSM leaders to organize Woolworth sit-ins on six consecutive workdays during the first week of February.[13]

Elsewhere, black student protesters may have received a well-timed beating from white onlookers, but their position as AM&N students connected these particular youths to a larger community, which initially protected them from arrest and physical assault. Pine Bluff residents were intrigued that something of that magnitude was happening in their relatively small city, leading many to venture downtown and simply stare. Business leaders adopted the practice of immediately closing either the counter or the store when AM&N students appeared for a sit-in. Undoubtedly, this reduced profits for businesses, and, on February 5, the manager of the Woolworth lunch counter chose not to close the counter when ten students arrived at 11:00 A.M. for what had become the daily sit-in. The manager likely believed the students would just go away if he allowed the counter to remain open and simply instructed waitresses to ignore them. The tactic backfired when the students continued the sit-in until the close of business, six and one-half hours later.[14]

If AM&N students initially escaped arrest or violent reprisal, their white allies were not so lucky. During the third week of the sit-ins, the *Commercial* reported that "one white man," more than likely Hansen, was participating in the sit-ins.[15] As a white man and an outsider, Hansen became one of the most easily identifiable targets associated with the AM&N student movement. On February 14, after staging another sit-in,

Hansen and two companions were attacked by a mob of white youths in the middle of a city street. Although Hansen had previously contacted the police department and requested protection, officials informed him "that Pine Bluff has too few policemen to assign them to protect sit-in groups" (the city evidently had enough officers to have stationed some inside the Woolworth store since the second day of protests). Defenseless and committed to SNCC's nonviolent tactics, Hansen was kicked as he and fellow protesters left downtown heading to St. James Missionary Baptist Church where the group regularly met following demonstrations. "Armed with belts and a pole," the white gang then beat Hansen and two other protesters. For the duration of the beating, a freight train blocked police cars from reaching the scene. By the time they arrived, the officers claimed "no one was in the area except the demonstrators." On February 24, Hansen was sitting at a lunch counter when a white teenager approached him and yanked him from the stool. As Hansen lay curled on the floor, the white youth "beat and kicked Hansen for what [Robert] Whitfield said seemed to be about three minutes" before policemen stationed in the store intervened. It took three policemen to pull the youth off of Hansen. Eventually, the assailant was arrested. Pine Bluff police chief Norman Young declared, however, that Whitfield's estimate of the duration of the beating was "exaggerated." Eight days earlier, Pine Bluff police had arrested another white resident, fifty-seven-year-old W. R. Lemmons, and charged him with disturbing the peace following an altercation with Hansen.[16]

The sit-ins also brought less violent countermeasures. One morning around 9:00 A.M., white youngsters kept members of the PBSM from sitting in by occupying the seats activists normally took. The white youths mockingly employed PBSM methods. For more than seven hours, they sat in shifts at the Woolworth lunch counter, one sitting down as another stood. Around 4:30 P.M., PBSM members finally took seats at the counter when the white youngsters called it a day, and sat in until closing time. In an article entitled, "Negroes Stage Less Than Hour-Long Sit-in," the *Commercial* portrayed the event as a defeat for activists. The article ignored the fact that while white youngsters played musical chairs at the lunch counter to prevent blacks from sitting down, AM&N students determinedly waited (presumably in shifts) for their opportunity. White youths had not ended the student-led sit-ins, as the *Commercial* suggested, they had only postponed one.[17]

At the beginning of March, PBSM leader Robert Whitfield hinted that AM&N students might soon "start another integration effort," targeting other establishments. Demonstrations ended at their initial target—F. W. Woolworth. When AM&N students had arrived at Woolworth around

10:30 A.M. on February 28 to begin the twenty-eighth day of demonstrations, they found every stool at the lunch counter—more than thirty—had been removed. Plastic bags covered the metal stands on which the stools had previously rested, and buckets of artificial flowers lined the entire lunch counter. The *Arkansas Democrat* reported, "A policeman at the store said the group walked in, looked at the counter and left the store." Who had won? Woolworth management thwarted student efforts by cleverly removing the very instruments needed for a demonstration, but the students had forced store officials to change standard operating procedures.[18]

If the college setting had helped galvanize activism and if students' status as privileged members of the black community had afforded them some protection in this initial round of protests, AM&N had, from its own perspective, been placed in a delicate position. Chancellor Lawrence A. Davis Sr. had issued a statement as soon as Hansen and Grinage appeared, disavowing any knowledge or support of student-led protests.

We had no prior knowledge that the men were coming to the campus. We certainly don't want to get into anything that would disturb the community in this manner. We—the faculty and our students—have worked hard to build this school, and we'll have nothing to do with anything that would hurt our college. My interest is in protecting the college and not to do anything [that] would [jeopardize] it in any way.[19]

Davis's interest in protecting the college, and presumably his career, were indeed put to the test in the coming weeks. William Chafe's *Civilities and Civil Rights* portrays student activists of North Carolina Agricultural & Technical College and Bennett College as being supported and even protected by university administrators. The experiences of AM&N students would be decidedly different, and their futures would be threatened by the very administrators whose rights the students felt they were fighting for.[20]

AM&N began its institutional life as Branch Normal College for Negroes. Founded in Pine Bluff in 1873 as the only state-supported institution of higher education for former slaves in Arkansas, Branch Normal initially struggled both financially and educationally. It was not until 1929 that the institution became a four-year college, more nearly meeting Congress's requirement that "agricultural and the mechanic arts," "scientific and classical studies," and "military tactics" be taught at all universities created pursuant to federal land-grant legislation.[21]

When students at AM&N began their sit-in in February 1963, they had to have been aware that the state legislature had convened several weeks earlier. They were knowingly demonstrating right in the middle of a session that would appropriate funds to all state-supported educational institutions. The possibility of fiscal reprisal at the hands of the Arkansas General Assembly raised very real concerns for the future of AM&N. The legislature did not have to zero-fund AM&N; it simply could have under-funded the institution and allowed it to die a slow death. Chancellor Davis made plain his concerns to student activist Ruthie Buffington, telling her that the university was attempting to secure its appropriation and the legis-lature "probably wouldn't like having [students] demonstrate." Two years' worth of operating funds were at stake. Further, with the end of the session looming, AM&N might have had no timely recourse in the event of adverse legislative decisions. Chancellor Davis committed himself to a course he felt would prevent financial crisis.[22]

Davis's quick disavowal of student actions caused a painful break in what had been a tightly knit AM&N community. With "extreme reluc-tance" but under extraordinary pressure to preserve what he felt was the "security and safety of the larger college family," Davis immediately assumed a defensive posture, issuing an open letter to the students of AM&N in which he denounced the actions of protest participants. Dated February 11, a little more than a week after the sit-ins began, the missive thrust those participating outside of the protective sphere of the "AM&N family" and threatened future participants with suspension from the uni-versity. It also documented the chancellor's attempts to discourage the protests:

> On at least three distinct occasions in an assembly of students and on several other occasions in smaller groups and individual stu-dent conferences, I have emphasized that "this would be the worst time possible for students of AM&N College to participate in sit-in demonstrations in the Pine Bluff community . . . therefore, I can assume in good conscience that my position as President of the college is clearly and widely known and was known before any student of AM&N College participated in the sit-in at the Woolworth store."[23]

Privately, however, Chancellor Davis seems to have had taken a different position. More than thirty years later, Joanna Edwards distinctly recalled that on multiple occasions she had heard Chancellor Davis state that his "bags [were] packed and [he would] leave [the university] before [he would] suspend a student for participating in the sit-in demonstration." Davis told Ruthie Buffington that while he would not "go along" with the protesters, "he would not expel anyone if they did demonstrate." Unfortunately, if Davis believed that students had a right to oppose a racist system, this belief could not stand up against pressure from those responsible for determining the university's fiscal budget.[24]

Still, despite his very vocal and well-publicized denunciation of student actions, Chancellor Davis continued to feel responsible for the educational welfare of "his" students. Davis issued a private last-minute warning to sit-in leaders. Edwards recalled:

> [Chancellor Davis] had someone call us at home one Sunday afternoon, and told us he wanted to meet with us [at] 8:00 Monday morning. We all met in Caldera Hall Auditorium [the next morning] and he told us that if we went [downtown to Woolworth] after 10:00 that morning we would be automatically and indefinitely suspended.[25]

Davis attempted to persuade students to save their educational futures and warned them of the impossible position their actions placed him in. Hours after the brief, clandestine meeting, Davis released a lengthy statement to the local newspaper:

> [Any] and all students who plan to participate in sit-in demonstrations after Monday, February 11, 1963, at 10:00 A.M. are requested to withdraw voluntarily from the college. Students who participate in the sit-ins after said time and who do not withdraw voluntarily are automatically and immediately suspended from the college indefinitely, forfeiting all rights and privileges as students of AM&N College.[26]

Some members of the black community lambasted Davis for his "cowardly act." Rev. Arthur A. Robinson, pastor of the St. James Methodist Church, called him a hypocrite and reminded reporters that "Davis previously told the demonstrators that he would resign his position before taking action against them." Meanwhile, PBSM leader Robert Whitfield defiantly announced that the sit-ins would continue, though it was unclear how many students would remain committed to the movement in the face of possible suspension. Prior to Davis's campus letter and press statement, the college demonstrators had received widespread encouragement from the black community, easily counting their supporters one week into the protests as at least one hundred. Following Davis's statement, the number of student supporters dwindled. Only ten students—Janet Broome, Hazel

Crofton, Joanna P. Edwards, Charles Jackson, James O. Jones, Nexton Marshall, Mildred Neal, Robert Whitfield, William Whitfield, and Herman Wilson—ventured downtown after their morning classes, staging what would be their final sit-ins as members of the AM&N community. Surprisingly, despite their suspension, in the coming weeks five additional students would protest alongside these former classmates. Subsequent disciplinary actions against Shirley Baker, Ruthie Buffington, Spurgel Hicks, Leon Jones, and Leon Nash raised the total number of students suspended for participating in sit-in protests to fifteen.[27]

Then and now, questions regarding Davis's decision seem to center on the lack of race solidarity and leadership in the black community. Why would a black college president suspend students who, in part, were fighting for his civil rights? Why did he essentially abandon an entire community of students who loved and trusted him? How could he, as the product of a tightly knit black community himself, be responsible for rending Pine Bluff's black community in two?

Chancellor Lawrence A. Davis Jr., the current president of what is now the University of Arkansas at Pine Bluff, was six years old when his father became president of AM&N College in 1945. The younger Davis, who would earn an M.A. in mathematics from the University of Arkansas, Fayetteville, and a Ph.D. in engineering mechanics from Iowa State, became an instructor at AM&N in 1961. In an interview, he recalled that his father had a difficult time reconciling his suspension of the students with his conscience, but Davis Sr. could not help but be mindful of the proud history of AM&N, a history he was not willing to let end on his watch.[28]

The elder Davis had fostered a family atmosphere on campus. He believed in a high level of academic engagement, which included exposing students to speakers with whom Pine Bluff's white business and civic elites may not have agreed. In 1958, following the Montgomery Bus Boycott and the emergence of Martin Luther King Jr. as a leader in the civil rights movement, Davis invited King to be the commencement speaker at AM&N—a bold and courageous action that, in the words of Chancellor Davis Jr., would have been "tantamount to inviting Louis Farrakhan" to speak today.[29] Race relations in 1958 were in turmoil throughout the state, particularly in central Arkansas. Gov. Orval Faubus was preparing to close public schools in Little Rock to prevent further desegregation. In this atmosphere, according to the younger Davis, the invitation to King was not undertaken lightly:

Dad either had to compromise on his philosophy that students have a right to hear or allow Martin Luther King to come. But by allowing Martin Luther King to speak here, [my father] incurred the wrath of both black and white citizens. The attitude was that he was bringing in a "rabble-rouser" who would disturb the good relationship between the races . . . [but] what's a good relationship if I'm in prison and you're my jailer (laughter)? We get along fine, long as I don't break out.[30]

Delivering a fiery address to more than one thousand blacks from Pine Bluff and surrounding areas at the 1958 commencement, King urged attendees to "revolt against segregation and discrimination everywhere." By 1958, King's mere presence in cities across the United States had already begun to arouse the ire of white civic leaders, and his incendiary address at AM&N was quoted again and again in both local and state papers.[31]

Davis's vocal assertions that King was "a new type of mass leader" probably contributed to the perception among politicians in Little Rock that he and, by extension, AM&N were aligned with King and what he represented. Lawrence Davis Jr. recalled the particularly scornful reception his father faced when he ventured to the state capitol the next year to lobby for the school's biennial appropriation. Chancellor Davis became, in the words of his son, the victim of a "verbal lynching" led by a prominent Faulkner County legislator.[32] Faulkner County had a black population in 1960 of slightly over 10 percent of the total county population—nowhere near the numbers in Jefferson County—and its legislators were likely unaccustomed to outspokenness on the part of black leaders.[33] According to Davis Jr., his father's position did not keep the Faulkner County statesman from speaking to him as if he were a child rather than a lettered man who headed a university: "'Lawrence! You double-crossed us.' To which Dad said, 'Well, sir, he made an excellent speech, I wish you could have heard it.'"[34]

Many legislators probably agreed that Chancellor Davis had "double-crossed" them. Having been made to realize in 1959 how vulnerable any embrace of the movement could make his institution, Davis probably felt he had no choice but to issue the threat of expulsion in February 1963. Chancellor Davis was under tremendous pressure from a number of entities to help resolve the tensions caused by student sit-ins, but none needed to be satisfied more quickly than the Arkansas General Assembly. An official display of punitive aggression by Chancellor Davis was necessary for the survival of his black-managed institution.[35] Davis's action was not unusual. Historian Charles Payne has noted that "black colleges . . . frequently dependent on white economic or political support, were not always free to support the burgeoning movement. Protesting students were often suspended or expelled from publicly supported black colleges."[36]

If AM&N had been placed in a precarious position, that of the expelled students was even more so. Surprisingly, when questioned about their reactions, former students recall being more saddened by the fact that it was Davis who expelled them than by the expulsion itself. Joanna Edwards lamented, "The thing that was so tragic for most of us was that we loved this man. We called him 'Prexy,' fondly, we just loved him to death."[37] Three years after the Pine Bluff sit-ins, Ruthie Buffington, a member of the second group of expelled students, echoed Edwards's claims of a deep and abiding respect harbored by AM&N students:

> The thing you have to understand about [AM&N] is that President Davis was a tight man who had done so much for some of the students that if he said, "kneel," they knelt. It was just that type of history and background at the campus, and years before he had been threatened [with being fired], and a lot of students demonstrated against his being put out. . . . they felt, I guess, that they owed allegiance to him.[38]

In the spring of 1963, Buffington, a second-semester senior, was a well-liked student government officer. On February 2, the morning after the first downtown sit-in, Davis summoned Buffington to his office to ask if she had participated in the previous day's demonstration. Buffington denied having done so, truthfully stating she had, in fact, been on campus all day, nowhere near Woolworth. Despite her denials, Chancellor Davis told Buffington that it was "not the time" and he did not want students demonstrating. Buffington recalled, "At the time, no one wanted [Hansen] to be on campus because people said they weren't ready for this. It was the wrong time, and they just weren't ready." With graduation only months away, Buffington's initial reluctance to join the movement in Pine Bluff is not surprising, especially when rumors of suspensions began circulating around campus. For the next two weeks, Buffington labored daily over the question of whether or not to join her classmates downtown at the Woolworth counter.[39]

After attending numerous on-campus forums at which Davis expressly asked students not to participate, Buffington felt compelled to join the sit-ins. There remained two people she had to speak with regarding her decision—the aunt with whom she lived and Davis. Buffington sought out the chancellor, wanting to reconcile her desire to protest with respect for his wishes. Davis informed Buffington that despite her status as a second-semester senior, he would have no choice but to expel her if she joined her classmates downtown, an action that would prevent her from graduating.

When Buffington asked for her aunt's opinion, she was bluntly informed: "If you do it, you'll have to leave home because I can't allow you to stay at home and [protest]."[40] Buffington ultimately deemed the cause of civil rights worth the sacrifice of both her education and home. She joined her classmates downtown at the Woolworth counter and was summarily suspended from AM&N. Eventually expelled and cast out of her home, Buffington chose to continue her activist work in Arkansas at the side of the man who would become her husband, William Hansen.[41]

Other students had to figure out whether to remain in Pine Bluff or leave and start anew. Some were not native Arkansans and faced having to return home. Hansen reported that six of the expelled students had left Pine Bluff at the insistence of "irate parents," and two others who lived in town "had been told by their parents to get out." Edwards, a double major in art and mathematics, attended AM&N on a Lawrence A. Davis Scholarship, which she lost when suspended. Most students at AM&N received some type of scholarship, without which they never could have afforded to earn a college degree. The stigma of their suspensions followed many of them and threatened to ruin future opportunities. But as Ben Grinage proudly claimed, some local families stepped into the void by providing the expelled students with places to live. A surprising number of former students decided to stay in Pine Bluff, remaining activist thorns in the side of business and civic leaders.[42]

Less than one month after the suspensions, administrators informed former students that they would be allowed to return to school on the condition that each write a letter apologizing for participating in the sit-ins. AM&N administrators were giving the suspended students one last opportunity to rejoin the "AM&N Family." The students had made their point and suffered the consequences, and now, the administrators seemed to be saying, it was time for the students to swallow their pride and come home. With tangible proof of the students' remorse, administrators, if need be, could assure members of the General Assembly that the students had learned their lesson.

Evidently, the right decision for a small number of the suspended students—Hazel Crofton, Spurgel Hicks, Charles Jackson, Leon Jones, and Nexton Marshall—was to make the requisite apology and be reinstated. Interestingly, while the *Commercial* printed news of the reinstatements, it never mentioned the letters of apology. According to Edwards, she was never sure to whom the letters were to be addressed, only that they had to express regret at participating in the movement.[43]

Shortly after the suspensions, Ben Grinage, head of the Pine Bluff Freedom School, angrily spoke out on behalf of Edwards and her fellow activists:

The "leaders" couldn't stop us because they weren't leading. We were tired of waiting for the Negro "leaders," so we organized a group of students and went down to eat at Woolworth's. The "leaders" tried to stop us. They said we were hurting relations between the races in Pine Bluff. But the students kept on demonstrating. . . . The leaders are the people who do things.[44]

Ministers, lay leaders, and student organization leaders took very vocal—and opposite—sides in the days following the publicized suspensions, but the lines of demarcation are not necessarily what one would have expected in this community with a large population of educated, affluent African Americans and a decades-old tradition of resistance to white supremacy. While some student leaders urged their colleagues to stop participating in the sit-ins, believing that grievances were being addressed through negotiations, area pastors continued to vilify Chancellor Davis's decision to suspend the fifteen students. A loosely knit citizens' group, led by Rev. Arthur Robinson, announced plans to appeal the students' suspensions directly to Gov. Orval Faubus. To Robinson, the lack of support from black elites in Pine Bluff was reason enough for the city's NAACP chapter to step up the frequency of meetings. "We are going to have different speakers each week, and we are going to bring Dr. Martin Luther King to this community," Robinson said. William Dove, president of the Pine Bluff chapter, claimed it supported the students and that "NAACP money was in a Pine Bluff bank with which to fight any legal battles that might result from the sit-ins."[45]

On February 24, 1963, Southern Christian Leadership Conference field secretary James Bevel visited Pine Bluff where he chided AM&N before a large crowd at Allen Temple A.M.L. Church. The *Pine Bluff Commercial* reported:

[Bevel] said they are not truly the leaders of the Negro population. He put Arkansas AM&N College President Lawrence Davis into this category. . . . [Bevel] blamed part of the problem on state-supported Negro colleges. "They're teaching your child about agriculture," he said. "But your child doesn't own any land to farm if he does learn anything. This is the space age, and they are still teaching horseshoeing in the Negro colleges."[46]

Three weeks after the suspensions, a period during which the former students had continued protesting, the Pine Bluff Movement (PBM) was born. In a March 4 interview, Robert Whitfield, chairman of the new organization, stated "the Pine Bluff Movement was formed today out of the Pine Bluff Student Movement, which was essentially comprised of students at Arkansas AM&N College." Six of the ten original students who were suspended and refused to write apologies served as members of the organization's executive committee: Robert Whitfield, chairman; James O. Jones, second vice chairman; Janet Broome, secretary; Joanna Edwards, financial secretary; William Whitfield; and Mildred Neal. The suspensions, it seems, only encouraged the former AM&N students to expand their activism. They also seemed to prompt action by other groups in the black community. By the middle of March, sit-ins, boycotts, and pickets were popping up all over Pine Bluff. The city's NAACP chapter mobilized boycotts of two downtown stores, much to the chagrin of business leaders who had dismissed the original protests in February as only a fad.[47]

The PBM quickly began to win small victories. On March 5, the restaurant at the local Holiday Inn broke custom and, to the shock and surprise of white patrons, served four PBM demonstrators. Before going to the restaurant, Robert Whitfield had telephoned the Holiday Inn manager, informed him that four demonstrators would attempt to integrate the hotel's restaurant, and asked if they would be served. When the manager, Bruce Hugo, said they would be, Whitfield and three other demonstrators went there and ate dinner—a first for blacks in Pine Bluff.[48]

On March 15, five members of the PBM entered the Magnolia Cafeteria at 7:45 P.M. asking for service. Employees told Whitfield and four other activists that the restaurant was closing and that the group could therefore not be served. Apparently testing the assertion that the denial of service was due to the lateness of the hour, the very next night around 5:30, two members of the PBM returned to the Magnolia Cafeteria and were served. A third establishment targeted by the PBM, the Keese restaurant, accepted black patrons the same evening as the Magnolia. Not surprisingly, given white backlash against the movement, the managers of the Keese, Magnolia, and Holiday Inn were not available for comment regarding their decisions to desegregate.[49]

When Woolworth closed its lunch counters after almost a month of sit-ins, the PBM began to picket the Walgreen Drug Store, which promptly closed its counter rather than suffer through sit-ins. When the counter reopened on March 18, the PBM resumed the sit-ins. When Walgreen once again closed its lunchroom and used display cases to block the counter, PBM members picketed the store instead. Rev. Arthur Robinson urged Pine Bluff's black community to participate in "selective buying" campaigns, aimed at local businesses. "If you can't hold jobs as salesmen and clerks," Robinson asserted, "you ought not spend your money there." Even with successes under its belt, the PBM continued sit-ins at numerous cafeterias, hotels, and businesses, and began hinting its members might want to worship at white churches.[50]

Prompted by the "very strong rumors" of protests, South Side Baptist Church in March voted 237 to 59 in favor of seating blacks who wished to attend services. Similarly, the board of deacons at Immanuel Baptist Church voted to seat blacks—but only in the balcony. Lakeside Methodist, Trinity Episcopal Church, Central Presbyterian, and First Baptist—all-white congregations—claimed they would admit any individual who elected to attend Sunday services. Integration was already well underway in the Catholic Church. For more than twenty years, black families had attended St. Joseph's, and two black churches, St. Raphael's and St. Peter's, consistently served large numbers of white families.[51]

But these weeks of progress also saw a toughening of the official response. Prior to the suspensions, AM&N students existed under a partial umbrella of protection offered by their association with the college. Davis's casting them out of the "AM&N Family" did not go unnoticed by the white community. In publishing the addresses of suspended students, the *Pine Bluff Commercial* left both the students and their families open to reprisals.

Nearly two months after the first sit-in, and only after the suspensions-turned-expulsions from AM&N, the police began arresting PBM members. On March 26, Shirley Baker, Ruthie Buffington, Mildred Neal, Spurgel Hicks, James Jones, and Leon Nash were taken into custody at the hotel Pines after a three-hour sit-in. The six had made reservations for six single rooms. When they arrived and attempted to check in, the manager informed them "Negro guests" were not accepted. Instead of leaving immediately, the group took seats in the Pines lobby. After three hours, and probably to irk the sensibilities of Pines employees, some of the men in the group removed their socks and shoes and stretched out on the recliners in the lobby. They were subsequently taken to jail, where, the *Commercial* reported, they "refused to accept bail and planned to remain in jail until tried" or the charges were dropped.

The Pines arrests marked a new chapter in the development of the PBM. After fifty-three days of constant protest, Pine Bluff police arrested movement participants for actions directly linked to a sit-in. Before the week's end, the number of arrests would more than quadruple. An important point to keep in mind is the stigma and danger once attached to arrest within black communities. "It was the worst, the absolute worst thing that could happen to you," Edwards recalled. Nationwide, tales of beatings and torture within the walls of city or county jails were common. Obituaries of blacks citing deaths behind bars due to self-inflicted wounds or resisting police force were all too familiar. Overwhelmingly, during the mid-twentieth century, blacks in America viewed jail as a destination from which blacks rarely returned unmolested. Nonetheless, many of Pine Bluff's black youths accepted these and other risks.[52]

The police had opened a new door in dealing with protesters. Suddenly, every infraction of civil disobedience on the part of the PBM became a ticket to the city jail. Six days before the incident at the Pines, a group of ten PBM members had been refused admittance to the white section of the downtown Saenger Theater. One by one, PBM members tried to purchase tickets at the main (i.e., white) ticket window and were turned away. The group left, returned thirty minutes later, and were, again, denied tickets. Two days after the Pines arrests, twenty-seven protesters returned to the Saenger and attempted to purchase tickets at the white ticket window. This time, when they were refused, the group staged a stand-in, effectively blocking numerous doorways. The manager of the Saenger then called the police, who arrived with a paddy wagon and—after giving each protester one last chance to go free, a chance each refused—arrested all twenty-seven. The next day, police arrested sixteen more demonstrators at the Saenger for the same violation. All refused bail. By the end of March, the PBM packed the Pine Bluff jail with forty-four protesters (five individuals had been released on bail), far exceeding both the jail's capacity and resources. It would take the efforts of Helen Hughes Jackson, the mother of an arrested PBM member, to keep the jailed youngsters fed—a burden Pine Bluff police claimed was not their responsibility because the arrests had placed an undue burden on them.[53]

Leon Nash had introduced his mother, Helen Hughes Jackson, to Bill Hansen and Ben Grinage shortly after their arrival in Pine Bluff. When Nash, Grinage, and Hansen asked to use the Jackson home as a head-quarters for the PBSM, the mother of six agreed for several reasons. First, she was eager to help a movement aimed at fighting against the way blacks in Pine Bluff were treated. Second, as a self-employed hairdresser in the black community, Jackson was financially independent from whites—a cir-cumstance she recalled as "vital." Financial independence freed her from the fears of economic reprisal harbored by many blacks in the civil rights era. Without this freedom, she "never would have considered becoming involved." Third, Leon Nash was adamant in his support of Hansen and Grinage, and Jackson felt it her duty to support her son. Without Leon, Jackson states that, "being a black woman and a widow," she would not have joined the cause.[54]

Jackson was one of a growing number of adults who became active after the PBSM became the PBM. Jackson, a graduate of AM&N, was hurt by Davis's decision to suspend the students and could not understand why the chancellor did not share the sentiment harbored by so many of Pine Bluff's black residents of "only wanting to be recognized as a human, not an animal." Jackson regularly participated in the daily sit-ins. One day, however, Nash asked his mother not to accompany the group, because he had a feeling something was going to happen. That afternoon, Nash and five others were arrested at the hotel Pines. After being informed that the Pine Bluff Police Department would not feed any arrested protester, Jackson asked if she could provide meals for the young people, to which the police department agreed.

> I made a plea to the different churches and some of the food stores that I knew would help me. They gave us food and I picked it up, but then I wondered how I was going to get the food prepared. I went to some of my [church] members and friends, and solicited help. I was able to put someone in charge of the kitchen who I knew would be responsible. She [in turn] solicited other people to help her prepare food for those children for one week.[55]

Organizing the meals was never simple, but the Pine Bluff police compounded Jackson's work by stipulating the exact time and manner meals had to be delivered to the jail. The department required Jackson to have the meals, each individually wrapped, at the jail promptly at 11:30 A.M. This was the single meal allowed protesters by the Pine Bluff Police Department. Weeks later when the last protester was released, Jackson learned that it had become a joke inside the jail that some of the protesters felt so well taken care of that they did not want to get out. Through the support she organized within the black community—mobilizing women to cook and prepare plates of food for incarcerated students—Jackson helped the PBM adjust to changing tactics on the part of the police.[56]

Over the next several years, the PBM would successfully integrate public swimming pools, organize "don't buy where you can't eat" campaigns, coordinate intensive voter registration drives, pressure local business to hire black workers, and establish a Freedom Program in which children of all ages could enjoy everything from afterschool sporting activities and art sessions to reading and freedom song lessons.[57]

The work of the Pine Bluff Movement spanned more than three years, but even this brief glimpse into its beginnings demonstrates the need to rethink the state's civil rights history. The "master narrative" of the movement in Arkansas has been reduced to a seemingly simple, yet clichéd, theme of an eventual triumph over unbeatable odds, leaving little room for failure or defeat.[58] For all the progress ultimately made toward the desegregation of public accommodations, the initial stages of the Pine Bluff struggle had seen fifteen students expelled from AM&N and a vibrant black community left badly divided. Making the situation even more tragic, Lawrence Davis Sr. and other figures at AM&N who opposed the protests seem to have been driven not by mere acquiescence to racism but by the desire to protect one of the few institutions in Arkansas (aside from churches) under the day-to-day control of African Americans.[59]

The civil rights movement in Arkansas did not begin in Little Rock in 1957 nor did it end when high schools there were desegregated on a permanent basis. It is equally important to analyze lesser-known events, the ways in which they affected and challenged the racial status quo, and the impact they had on their communities. If vital yet unexplored episodes continued to be ignored, the movement's history in Arkansas will remain distorted, and Arkansas will face the very real possibility of becoming, in the words of Charles Payne, "alienated" from its historical self, leaving contemporary black activists unable to "recognize its theft."[60]

4.

Crossing the White Line

SNCC in Three Delta Towns, 1963–1967

RANDY FINLEY

In November 1965, the red lights of a Gould, Arkansas, police car pulled over a vehicle driven by Dwight Williams, a black activist accompanied by a white female. The constable charged Williams with "crossing the white line." Although describing a driving infraction, the phrase could also have referred to the repeated violations of racial etiquette that occurred in Arkansas in the 1960s. In that decade, black and white Arkansans witnessed the dismantling of Jim Crow—a system of laws, customs, mores, and values that had encrusted the South since the Civil War. "The Negro population has been waiting for years for this movement and it has finally arrived. It's a rather incredible experience," noted one black in the Arkansas delta. Another African American insisted that it was not so much that dreams had suddenly come alive, but rather that life finally approximated "the ways things should have been."[1]

Some Arkansas whites, on the other hand, dreaded change. Congressman E. C. (Took) Gathings of West Memphis told the House Rules Committee in 1964 that the "lot of the southern Negro isn't as bad as it is sometimes painted. He understands the members of the white race and they understand him." "We know our niggers a little better than you," a West Helena realtor assured an "outside agitator." But John Bradford, one such "agitator" who came to Helena, did not see the same delta as Gathings and the realtor. "The housing is so bad that when you're inside, you're still outside. We were renting a room and every time it rained, we got wet.

There were no bathroom facilities. They [delta blacks] aren't living. They're just existing. They have nothing to be happy about." A black activist in Gould agreed: "We were being oppressed, depressed, held back, kept down. . . . When you got out of school, you had to migrate to the North or just be stuck in a rut here." A white former resident of Helena returned for a visit in 1963 and sensed the conflict brewing: "The Negro is bearing more on the mind of southerners today than at any time in history. The white southerner is worried. He knows the Negro is seeking his rights but does not know where the next move will be."[2] The black and white activists of the Student Nonviolent Coordinating Committee were among those plotting these moves.

SNCC was founded at an April 1960 conference at Shaw University in Raleigh, North Carolina, after students used sit-ins to integrate Woolworth lunch counters in nearby Greensboro and Nashville, Tennessee. Although no Arkansan attended the April meetings, SNCC leaders immediately recruited students from Philander Smith College, an African Methodist Episcopal (AME) Church institution founded in 1877 in Little Rock. These new recruits joined veteran Little Rock civil rights activists and began sit-ins at downtown Woolworths in March 1960. Intra-group rivalries, poor planning, and fear of police reprisals resulted in failure; seating at Woolworth remained segregated.[3]

For the next two and half years, relatively little protest occurred in Arkansas. Ruth Arnold of the Arkansas Council on Human Relations wrote SNCC national headquarters in September 1962 asking for someone to be sent to revitalize the movement in the state. A SNCC secretary promised that James Forman, the organization's executive secretary, or Charles McDew, SNCC's chairman, were on their way. "They are unpredictable," she warned, "but they do seem to be moving in your direction. They descend like acts of God over which neither you nor I have any control." Instead of Forman or McDew, a young white activist from the North, William Hansen, arrived at the campus of Philander Smith on October 24, 1962. Labeled a "professional agitator" by Arkansas governor Orval Faubus, Hansen was, in the words of the *Arkansas Gazette,* a "lean, intense young man."[4]

Hansen immediately contacted SNCC leaders at Philander Smith and Shorter Junior College and organized a strategy session attended by seven students. A renewed attempt at integration of downtown Little Rock public eateries was much better planned than the 1960 failure and was undertaken by a more united black community. By New Year's Day 1963, black and white community leaders had brokered deals that integrated many department stores, restaurants, and bowling alleys.[5]

In early 1963, SNCC leaders scouted new territory—Pine Bluff, in the south central part of the state. Facing stiffer white resistance than in Little Rock, black and white civil rights activists pushed to integrate Pine Bluff's public facilities through large demonstrations. Boycotts and mass protests revealed the readiness of local blacks for change. "The good white folks are beginning to hurt," Hansen observed. As a result of the agitation, city officials drew up timetables for integration of public parks, restaurants, swimming pools, and schools.[6]

Successes in Little Rock and Pine Bluff directed SNCC's attention toward areas of more hard-core racism. Leaving what the SNCC activist and historian Martha Prescod Norman called the "beachhead project" of Pine Bluff, activists decided to roil the Arkansas delta. The largest delta county, Phillips County, suggests the challenges they faced. It was home to 25,308 blacks (57.5 percent of the population) and 18,552 whites (42.2 percent) in 1960. But less than one-fourth of those registered to vote in 1963 were black. Sixty-five percent of the black population had less than a sixth-grade formal education, compared to only 14 percent of whites. Three percent of blacks had high school diplomas, while 28 percent of whites did. Blacks earned an annual median income of $616, with 1,923 black households earning less than $1,000 in 1960 and only 147 earning more than $5,000.[7]

A survey of SNCC's activity in three towns—Helena (the county seat of Phillips), Forrest City, and Gould—can illustrate the range of the group's activities and experience in the Arkansas delta. SNCC activists pursued a multifaceted agenda: integrating public accommodations, registering African American voters and encouraging them to become politically active, improving educational opportunities for black Arkansans, assuring that civil rights were protected, and providing more economic opportunities in the poverty-stricken delta.

Activists John Bradford, Bruce Jordan, and Noah Washington arrived in Helena in late October 1963, after cotton-picking season. Using contacts nurtured by Pine Bluff veterans Hansen and Ben Grinage, SNCC workers visited Mary Johnson of the Helena Life Insurance Company. Rochester Johnson, secretary of the International Woodworkers of America local, whose membership was 20 percent black, was not nearly as enthusiastic as the activists hoped. By contrast, when they met at a local barbershop with Bobby O'Neale, a twenty-six-year-old with a pregnant wife, the activists found a man who "wanted to be in the first march down the main street of town." Several black businessmen and professionals received them warmly. George Miller, a twenty-five-year-old black teacher and Michigan State graduate who owned the movie house, twenty rent houses, a cafe, and a barbershop, provided their principal support. "He said that he is ready, when we are ready," Bradford reported. Frank Jordan, funeral home director, would contribute bail for those arrested. Two local dentists named Miller and Profitt and a pair of physicians, a Dr. Douglas and a Dr. Connor, supported the movement, though only behind the scenes.[8]

But other members of the black elite were not as wholehearted in welcoming the young activists. The pastor of King Solomon Baptist Church warmly greeted SNCC organizers James O. Jones and Joseph Wright and insisted that "we are capable of turning this town upside down." But private promises did not mean public support. Three leading black ministers in Helena, in fact, opposed SNCC's activities and urged their congregations to stay away from the protests it led. "The preachers are holding us back," lamented Bradford in a report to national headquarters. Still, a number of clergymen did rally to the cause. Rev. J. H. Price of Alien Temple AME opened his church to SNCC rallies, as would Rev. Raymond Lyles, pastor of the Pettis Memorial Christian Methodist Episcopal Church, who also participated in at least one SNCC action.[9]

While one black activist declared, "It's about time that someone has come to Helena," many local whites, of course, disagreed. Arkansas attorney general Bruce Bennett, raised in the delta, warned that "whoever is pulling the strings that make William Hansen jump does not know the facts of life of the people of Helena or Phillips County. I remember my father telling me about the Elaine incident." Bennett seemed to be making a veiled threat in referring to the 1919 race riot in Phillips County that crushed a black union and left scores murdered. Helena police chief Roy Ross warned SNCC workers that "whenever you come across that Phillips County line, we've got you. Take that station wagon, that literature and all that SNICK stuff and get out of here if you know what's good for you. Be sure to tell your buddy Hansen that everything I've told you goes for him."[10]

In January 1964, during testimony before the Arkansas Advisory Committee of the U.S. Commission on Civil Rights, John Bradford and William Hansen described the climate of fear cultivated by whites in Helena. "At the beginning of the Helena movement," Bradford noted, blacks "were very much afraid. I think a lot of fear was based on what was happening elsewhere in the world. Most of the people would say, 'I'm glad you're here—we need you and we've been waiting for you. But we're afraid.'" Hansen agreed that "a general systematic aura of fear permeates the county. . . . The people are doing what 'Mr. Charlie' wants them to— or what they think he wants them to do." He described an "obnoxious" harangue by Helena judge D. S. Heslep about how blacks "should wash

inside as well as outside, stop having illegitimate children and so forth."
Whites knew, he concluded, that "their little monolithic empire is subject
to elimination if and when the Negro decide to get together and do something." Organizer James Jones concurred: "Helena is very much a
Mississippi type of town. . . . When we first came to Helena people were
completely afraid of anything that was connected or related to freedom."[11]

Nevertheless, though white resistance would lead to a brief early suspension of SNCC activities in Helena, activists lost little time in pursuing
one of their chief goals—integration of public places. Efforts to desegregate
Helena's Henry Drug Store and Habib's Cafeteria began in mid-November
1963. Police incarcerated over thirty demonstrators, including leaders Noah
Washington, John Bradford, Curtis Grady of Pine Bluff, and Granville Miller
of the Phillips County Movement, an organization containing SNCC members as well as other activists. Police charged Hansen, Bradford, Bruce
Jordan, and Rev. Raymond Lyles with "inciting to riot." Insisting that their
constitutional right to peacefully assemble had been denied, SNCC leaders
demanded an FBI investigation, which resulted in their being interviewed
by an FBI agent stationed in Arkansas.[12]

The following June, Joseph Wright, a black twenty-year-old activist
son of a Methodist minister from Cincinnati, Ohio; Thomas Alien, an
eighteen-year-old black Arkansas AM&N student; and Ellis Ford, a local
black high school student, peacefully integrated the Helena Public Library.
Trailed by police chief Ross, they then peacefully ate in the "whites only"
section in Habib's Cafeteria. An attempt to integrate the swimming pool,
though, proved too much for Ross to bear. White and black adolescents
would not mingle, scantily clad, in the pools of Helena as long as he was
chief of police. He arrested the three young men. Ford and Alien were
beaten while in jail.[13]

That July, Wright, Allen, Ford, Robert Blockum, and Larry Siegal, a
New Yorker, tested the Civil Rights Act of 1964 within days of its becoming law. White business owners seemed unsure of what to do. Some refused
service one day but offered it the next. The local library, Habib's Cafeteria,
and Henry's Restaurant served both races peacefully on Monday, July 6.
On the next day, however, Henry's manager closed the fountain. On
Friday, July 10, the bowling alley, In-Between Grill, and Ben and Rose's
Restaurant refused to serve SNCC workers. On Saturday, Nick's refused to
wait on blacks, Henry's served black students without incident, and the
bowling alley demanded a membership fee of $5 and recommendations
from two leading citizens of the town. No whites reacted violently, however, and no blood was shed.[14] Responses to similar actions in March 1965
were more menacing. SNCC workers peacefully integrated a bowling alley

and several cafes and were "cordially served," but upon leaving the bowling alley they found their car's windshield cracked. At a Helena truck stop, they received rude service and a bottle whizzed by their heads, exploding on the wall, as they left.[15]

Amid all this, the Helena hospital remained basically untouched. Black doctors could not practice in the hospital, black nurses could not work on floors with white patients, and black patients could not use the first floor eating facilities. Although in some places change seemed tangible, in the Helena hospital, 1965 seemed much like 1935.[16]

SNCC similarly tested enforcement of the Civil Rights Act in Forrest City, forty miles north of Helena and home to 10,554 people, and Gould, a Lincoln County community of 1,210 people. On Sunday, February 28, 1965, black SNCC workers entered an all-white restaurant in Forrest City. Although they received many stares, they dined peacefully. Throughout the year, integrated SNCC teams ate at restaurants that previously had served only whites. Often, waitresses served blacks but ignored the white SNCC workers. Owners felt the law forced them to accommodate blacks, but they could not bring themselves to serve the ultimate betrayers—whites who helped blacks dismantle Jim Crow. At times, patrons fought with activists as when Simon Kahu, a twenty-one-year-old white student from Maryland, was beaten when he joined black activists for lunch.[17] In Gould, summer volunteers forced Holthoff's Restaurant and Knight's Dixie Queen to integrate peacefully.[18] Each community set its own pattern of compliance.

SNCC activists understood that mobilization of black political power would best ensure enforcement of civil rights legislation and make African Americans a force that could not be ignored. By early 1964, 77,714 blacks had paid their Arkansas poll taxes, compared to 68,970 in 1961, heartening SNCC activists. By spring 1964, SNCC leaders James Jones and Joseph Wright were canvassing black neighborhoods, knocking on hundreds of doors to discuss the importance of voter registration. They hoped to register 100,000 of the 190,000 eligible voters by the summer primaries. But their success brought difficulties. They moved from house to house as no one considered it safe to permanently lodge them.[19]

As temperatures sizzled in August, voter registration efforts brought Helena close to the boiling point. As bus loads of blacks arrived at the Phillips County Courthouse to register, SNCC workers exulted. Joseph Wright observed, "progress has been slow, but it's come along pretty good now. When we first came here, people were very pessimistic about the movement, but now they are beginning to realize that something can happen here." At night, cars driven by whites encircled Freedom House, a meeting place for SNCC volunteers and community activists. A young black woman active in SNCC had her house peppered with shot five times. Two whites firebombed a dwelling in West Helena that housed a SNCC worker. Hansen described the situation as "very tense. They've got some angry young Negroes over there." Police arrested three SNCC workers—Wright, Larry Siegal, and Robert Blockum—on "vagrancy" charges. Siegal and Wright received fines of $250 and three-month jail terms, and Blockum received a thirty-day sentence and a fine of $150, further infuriating many blacks. Sensing the town's fears, a *Helena World* editorial headlined "Rumors, Rumors, Rumors" urged all to stay calm. The editor wanted to make sure that Helena did not become another Birmingham, Alabama, complete with national media exposure. Helena and West Helena white and black business owners and ministers created the Good Will Movement pledged to interracial dialogue and improved race relations. Although the black business owners and ministers disavowed the activism of SNCC, they did capitalize on agitation, demanding that the city hire a Negro for the police force, another for the fire department, and black workers at city hall. Hansen insisted, "Gestapo tactics . . . are not going to stop us from our voting registration drive. This is a very tense, angry Negro community and I just hope that the police have more sense than to push something until there is an explosion."[20]

SNCC also pursued black empowerment in Forrest City and Gould. In early January 1964, James Jones and Pearlie Sneed launched an attack in Forrest City. At first, local blacks refused to direct SNCC workers to the home of a Reverend Keys, a Methodist pastor, but the activists eventually located him, and he allowed them to speak at his church. Jones and Sneed also talked to people in barbershops and cafes, urging them to register to vote. They attended the quorum court to better understand the county and its white power structure. They cultivated the support of Mrs. J. O. Clay, a black funeral home owner, whom they hoped would help them. In Gould, Mayor A. L. Butcher believed the two SNCC workers who enrolled voters intended "to stir up trouble." The mayor acknowledged SNCC's right to work in the area, but he warned the students that "if they broke any laws, blocked the streets or anything, we'd throw them in jail. We'd stick it to them just like we do the local people who break the law." Seven black teachers, with an average of three years of experience, lost their jobs at Lincoln County High School when they joined SNCC voter registration drives.[21]

The fruits of SNCC's labors became apparent with the 1964 school board, city council, legislative, and presidential elections. The percentage of eligible black citizens registered to vote rose from thirty-four to forty-nine. In many cases, they overcame violence, psychological intimidation, and apathy. One black woman in Helena wondered if women over sixty-five could vote. Ninety-four-year-old Anna Clay registered, noting, "I went down to register to vote to see what that equality was all about." Harassment continued until election day, though. Sheriff Edgar P. Hickey of Phillips County placed a black poll at the beauty shop of what SNCC workers believed to be one of the county's biggest Uncle Toms, infuriating activists and intimidating countless black voters. By November, whites accepted blacks transporting other blacks to the polls, but whites performing the same task infuriated them. White bullies in Helena beat white SNCC activist Frank Cieciorka, a twenty-five-year-old native of San Jose, California, as he drove black voters to polls.[22]

Eight black candidates sought seats in the state legislature in 1964, including one from Lincoln County. SNCC leader Rev. Ben Grinage lost, but Arthur Miller won his Pine Bluff School Board race when the white vote divided. Florence Clay, a black woman from Helena, lost to incumbent E. C. Gathings in a race for a seat in Congress. That she, Ethel Dawson from Pine Bluff, and Velma Hamilton from Marvell campaigned suggests how not only racial equality but gender equality had become a dream to be realized. In Helena, Rev. James D. Alexander appeared to have won a city council seat, but a precinct box mysteriously arrived three days late and negated his forty-eight-vote lead. He "officially" lost by two hundred votes. Although black Arkansans counted only one electoral win in local elections, they gained a better sense of their potential. Countless others decided that they could run and win in the future. The following July, Julian Bond and John Lewis, national SNCC leaders, spoke at West Helena and inspired two hundred people to go to the courthouse the next day to register to vote.[23]

Voter registration accelerated after Congress passed the Voting Rights Act of 1965. Arkansas Project director Ben Grinage urged the U.S. Civil Rights Commission to send observers to the delta to prevent the fraud he knew to be pervasive. "Continued denial of effective suffrage," he warned, "can be expected to erode people's faith in social justice." The Civil Rights Commission scheduled hearings in Forrest City on April 23, 1966, to investigate Grinage's concerns. As the hearings approached, Grinage decided SNCC would not attend because the commission refused to hear from citizens of several counties who could attest to past election fraud. "We are refusing," he insisted, "to participate in any parody of a meaningful investigation." But Grinage changed his mind and appeared before the commission. He eloquently described an election process that "systematically disfranchised Negroes." He revealed scores of irregularities involving absentee voting and recounted how white officials took much longer to process blacks' voter registration forms than those of whites, causing blacks to leave in frustration after interminable waits. Ultimately, the commission sent two fieldworkers to the delta to supervise absentee voting and elections. This action represented the first federal intrusion in an Arkansas election in the twentieth century.[24]

SNCC's empowerment campaign contributed to a turn in Arkansas's political history in 1966. In the August Democratic primaries, SNCC operatives campaigned for gubernatorial candidates Sam Boyce and Brooks Hays, recognizing that Hays pushed hard for black votes. But after segregationist Jim Johnson won the nomination, SNCC activists backed Republican Winthrop Rockefeller, urging blacks to vote en bloc for him. He won, receiving 80 percent of the black vote and becoming the state's first Republican governor since Reconstruction. But in Gould, Carrie Dilworth, a black activist since the 1930s, failed in her bid for mayor.[25]

In addition to desegregation of public accommodations and enfranchisement, SNCC sought to improve educational facilities for black Arkansans. Before the Elementary and Secondary Education Act of 1965, which used the prospect of massive federal aid to encourage southern public schools to integrate, blacks and SNCC activists pushed for implementation of *Brown v. Board of Education* (1954). SNCC leaders James Jones and Joseph Wright encouraged black parents in Helena to send their children to previously all-white schools, and, by mid-April 1964, thirty-five black students had registered to integrate Helena schools in August. Activists in Gould pushed for a new school. "We're working to get one," Mayor A. L. Butcher insisted. But neither he nor SNCC could figure out how to fund it.[26]

The most significant confrontation over schools in these years exploded in Forrest City. Local blacks loathed the "freedom of choice" plan, which allowed whites to sidestep the *Brown* decision by permitting students to attend the community school of their choice. Most blacks considered "freedom of choice" an illusion. Enormous pressure was exerted on black parents to keep their children in all-black schools, and, in any case, some blacks preferred equitable funding for their racially separate schools to integration. When a handful of black students entered the previously all-white junior high school, they were forced to eat lunch in a separate room. School officials insisted this deterred violence, but many blacks believed it but a façade for continued segregation. Other black parents vehemently protested the inferior facilities assigned to predominantly black schools. They charged that schools were rat infested and lacked adequate science laboratories and libraries. Over one thousand students and five hundred parents petitioned black principal C. T. Cobb, demanding better facilities. After the principal stonewalled, a boycott of schools began in mid-September, with 90 percent of the black students participating.[27]

On September 16, police arrested nearly two hundred students and SNCC workers for disturbing the peace. The arrests overwhelmed the St. Francis County jail, forcing authorities to hold many protesters at the swimming pool, the civic center, or the dog pound. The jail included the "Bullroom," a filthy, dark cell teeming with lice and chiggers. Toilets overflowed. Meals consisted of peanut butter sandwiches. As parents and SNCC leaders scurried to come up with the $25,000 bail, city officials reportedly told parents that charges would be dropped if they signed documents promising to keep their children away from SNCC's Freedom Center and out of future demonstrations. On September 20, the school board broke off discussions with local black leaders. The next night, police broke into the Freedom Center at 1:30 A.M. to harass workers. By September 22, the town "crawled with state troopers."[28]

Blacks refused to back down. Over two hundred protesters maintained a silent vigil outside the courthouse when SNCC worker Tex Lowe was sentenced to a year in jail and fined $1,000 for "contributing to the delinquency of a minor." Prison officials at the Mississippi County Penal Farm in Luxora beat him severely. The boycott continued throughout late September. Fourteen Forrest City blacks journeyed to Washington, D.C., to provide Justice Department official John Doar with eyewitness accounts of the events transpiring in their hometown. White officials expelled two black students and arrested nine for planning to hold a "learnin'" at the white high school. Three state education department officials toured the community in November and warned students: "Be glad nothing worse has happened to you; people in Mississippi and Alabama have been beaten."[29] L. C. Bates of the National Association for the Advancement of Colored People and Dr. Earl Evans of the state Office of Economic Opportunity eventually brokered a deal between the school board and black parents. The board dropped all charges and promised to investigate the complaints brought by blacks.[30] An uneasy peace had come to Forrest City, but four years later the firing of a teacher by the all-white school board prompted a black boycott of local businesses. Subsequent racial unrest prompted the dispatch of National Guardsmen to the city.[31]

In 1965, African American parents in West Helena and Gould joined those in Forrest City in protesting the inequities of "separate but equal" school systems and the façades of choice in freedom-of-choice plans. In West Helena, parents documented that only eighteen black students opted to attend the "integrated" grades of one, four, seven, and ten. They also complained that they only received a week's notice about the freedom-of-choice plan, that whites paid smaller book fees, and that some black teachers had not finished high school. A West Helena delegation lobbied their congressman in Washington for improvements to their children's schools. Gould parents organized a black Parent-Teacher Association to pressure school officials, but white leaders locked the high school to prevent their meeting.[32]

In an effort to gain more control of the educational process, SNCC workers in Helena encouraged local women to join the Women Voters' League to prepare for the upcoming school elections. Over thirty black candidates ran in Arkansas school board elections held on September 28, 1965. SNCC activists encouraged voter turnout and black candidates. Rampant voter fraud revealed whites' fears that blacks would at long last win. Policemen, often accompanied by dogs, used excessive force in monitoring black voting precincts. At Forrest City, according to a SNCC report, a white man marked ballots for illiterate blacks, casting their votes for the white candidate regardless of blacks' preferences. Temporary deputies in West Helena warned blacks not to vote for SNCC-backed candidates. As if white intimidation and fraud were not enough, blacks in Helena fragmented when Joel Hines, supported by SNCC as a "new kind of Negro," was spurned by the black elite because of his working-class background. The elite at first proposed their own candidate, Henry Jordan of Helena Insurance and Real Estate, but he quickly withdrew.[33]

Twenty-nine of the thirty black candidates who ran for school boards in 1965 went down to defeat. In Gould with a black population of 82 percent and in Helena with a 56 percent black population, black candidates lost decidedly. SNCC workers quickly attributed the mysterious voting patterns to white fraud and demanded Justice Department investigations.[34]

Whether pushing for civil rights, political empowerment, or improved educational opportunities, SNCC activists knew that raising political consciousness and stoking racial pride were critical if Jim Crow was to be breached. They focused on schoolchildren and young adults in establishing Freedom Houses or Freedom Centers as places where youths could meet with friends and hear SNCC workers explain their next moves. Helena leaders established a Freedom House in that city in 1964. Two cars, two typewriters, and one mimeograph machine helped spread the message of social justice, but the work was slow. A mob of 150 menaced the Freedom House in early 1964, forcing SNCC workers to spend the night in a cornfield. Paint peeled from the Gould Freedom Center, located in a dilapidated house owned by a local black. Cardboard boxes covered broken windows, cracks in the walls allowed the cold winter air in, and the bathroom fixtures needed repair. But each afternoon and night scores of African Americans entered to prepare themselves for new opportunities they knew they would soon grasp. Workers helped youngsters prepare for college entrance exams. They studied Negroes in *American History: A Freedom Primer,* which, one student insisted, "is a history book about us. It is about a history that has been denied us by lies about what we are and what we have been." The Freedom Center in Forrest City, originally a funeral home, consisted of eleven rooms—two of which could seat one hundred people each and four of which housed workers. Two local teachers and two SNCC activists worked with from fifteen to thirty students twice daily. Such centers allowed black people the necessary physical and psychological space to construct new identities and envision new dreams.[35]

With this sort of encouragement, many stripped off the mask of acquiescence they had worn so long. One Helena youth questioned the gradualism of the movement and wondered, "When are we going to start shooting?" One SNCC worker complained that local retailers sold blacks only shotguns and prohibited them from purchasing rifles. When a note, "a Klansman was here," surfaced at the Helena home of black activist Cornelius Perkins, people from the community armed themselves and guarded the house around the clock.[36]

As Dr. Martin Luther King Jr. and other civil rights activists were discovering in Chicago and elsewhere in 1965, Jim Crow could be defied more readily than systemic economic changes could be brought about. By that year, African Americans were pressing beyond voting rights and desegregation, publicly linking equality to economic opportunities. After a series of meetings organized by the integrated St. Francis County Achievement Committee that involved SNCC activists, blacks picketed downtown Forrest City stores that hired only whites, using Title Seven of the Civil Rights Act of 1964, which dealt with fair employment practices, to gain federal government support. Hearing that whites planned to shoot up a strategy session, two FBI agents and scores of armed black residents guarded the meeting place. Picketing began in late June 1965. The city council countered by prohibiting demonstrations of over fifteen protesters. The Achievement Committee responded by limiting the picketing to groups of ten. In Phillips County, SNCC encouraged black citizens to sue Mohawk Tire Company and Mobil Corporation for discriminatory hiring practices. SNCC activist Myrtle Glascoe trekked through Phillips County, urging blacks to build up black-owned businesses. Rich white farmers of Phillips County controlled the region, and an economic boycott of white businesses, she argued, could bring justice and economic opportunity to the region. In Gould, activists protested disparity in agricultural pay, poor neighborhood roads, lack of job training, and whites' refusal to hire blacks in downtown stores.[37]

SNCC activists paid a price for their efforts to bring equal access, political power, and educational and economic opportunities to black residents of the Arkansas delta. From late 1963 until 1966, local police constantly beleaguered activists and arrested them capriciously. Police often invaded protesters' homes to see what they could discover. Activists asserted that the Phillips County sheriff ordered landlords not to rent office space to SNCC, making finding a workplace difficult. In Gould, two SNCC workers hid at night to escape the police. The town's police also raided five black activists' homes and monitored even the smallest activities, as when Gould's chief of police, Harold Pierce, arrested deaf sixteen-year-old Tee Harvis Cox for wearing a t-shirt that proclaimed: "Harold Pierce I'm Going to Kick Your Ass."[38] Gould's chief warned Laura Foner, a white SNCC worker, that whites would cut her head off and throw it in the river. When SNCC protesters sought help from the FBI, agents seemed more interested in the nineteen-year-old Foner's New York father, historian Philip S. Foner. FBI Arkansas agents received warnings from national headquarters to monitor the younger Foner since her father had spoken at a Fair Play for Cuba rally in New York City in November 1963 and taught at the New York School for Marxist Studies.[39]

The plight of Noah Washington, a nineteen-year-old SNCC field secretary from Pine Bluff who was an Arkansas AM&N student and one of the first activists to arrive in Helena, illustrates the dilemmas young blacks in the movement confronted. Believing the activities of SNCC far more important than calculus or literature, Washington, Bruce Jordan, and James Jones spent much of September 1963 in Lincoln County urging blacks to register to vote and encouraging student participation. In November, he joined other SNCC activists and secretly planned demonstrations to desegregate public eateries in downtown Helena. After Washington was arrested with thirty others and placed in the Helena jail, something in the young man snapped. Facing Judge D. S. Heslep on charges of "inciting a riot," he pleaded with the judge that "had I known what this was all about I would never have participated." The *Arkansas Gazette* headline, "Negro Youth Begs Forgiveness in Helena Sit-In," must have elated many whites. Washington also admitted that he had been "brainwashed" and "duped" (key Cold War motifs), descriptions sure to please many local whites, confident as they were that outside agitators had stirred up the trouble. Pleading guilty and receiving a sixty-day suspended sentence and fine, he swore, "I just want to get this over and forget about it. I want to start my life over." Doubtlessly, pressure from his parents, his youthfulness, the nightmare of a winter's night in a delta jail, and the prospect of many more such nights of incarceration wore down the young activist.[40]

Class conflict exacerbated tension among African Americans. A Helena black voter's league shunned the black working class and student activists, negotiating instead directly with the white power structure. The black community, facing violence and loss of jobs, seemed hopelessly divided, and, as James Jones lamented, "they tell the white people everything." Lost jobs were no abstract threat for many activists. For instance, officials fired Cornelius Perkins, a black employee at the Helena City Water Company, after he housed SNCC workers. Office space proved difficult to obtain. "I get the impression," Jones observed, "that nobody wants us to have an office near them."[41]

As much resistance as SNCC faced in Helena, Forrest City, and Gould, the demise of its efforts in those places had more to do with the disintegration of the national organization. SNCC head John Lewis apologized to Arkansas activists in late 1965 when national headquarters omitted Arkansas from their new four-year plan. Also, racial tensions among SNCC activists were becoming more prevalent as the Black Power movement emerged.[42] This impulse filtered down to the local level. In Helena, Myrtle Glascoe began pushing for "books by Negroes, about Negroes." "This is not a Panther-Party type thing," she insisted, but many whites feared their imminent expulsion from SNCC. In February 1966, white Helena worker Howard Himmelbaum instructed the national SNCC office that "we will not accept any white people except under unusual circumstances." The growing racial tension among state and national activists, coupled with burgeoning financial difficulties, forced a disillusioned Ben Grinage to admit to Vernon Jordan in early 1966 that "our financial state suggests that it would not be unduly pessimistic to expect the liquidation or collapse of Arkansas SNCC within the next few weeks."[43]

Grinage's despair deepened after a May coup at a national SNCC conclave near Nashville, Tennessee, replaced John Lewis with the firebrand Stokely Carmichael. The conference voted to allow whites to work only in white communities.[44] Grinage, who attended this conference, strongly objected to Carmichael's insistence that "racial integration is irrelevant," declaring:

It is our position that the announced new emphasis of SNCC will not ultimately be in the best interests of the deprived Negro in Arkansas. We are committed to the dignity of all mankind, black and non-black alike. We don't feel that integration is irrelevant, but is vital if this country is concerned with showing the rest of the world that peaceful coexistence is really what we are trying to achieve.

He sadly surmised that "we as individuals may no longer be able to work under the banner of SNCC, but our commitment is to the people of this state and this country, not to any particular organizations." Carmichael journeyed to Arkansas in early July to stop the hemorrhaging and to solidify his control over the organization. He denounced Grinage's management of SNCC's financial affairs in Arkansas and attacked Grinage and Hansen for criticizing the organization in the national media. Grinage resigned as the Arkansas Project director. Hansen also stepped down.[45]

The new leadership of SNCC thought investment in rural areas non-productive; Los Angeles and Chicago, not Gould or Forrest City, needed attention. Arkansas SNCC, which had received one-third of the paltry $12,000 operating budget of the entire organization from January to March 1966, could expect far less money and support from national head-quarters.[46]

Only a handful of SNCC workers remained in Arkansas by early 1967, as money and volunteers evaporated. Robert Cableton, still working in Gould in January 1967, observed that the defeat of Carrie Dilworth's may-oral campaign had further demoralized the movement. Since 82 percent of the town's voters were black, large numbers of them had obviously voted for her white opponent. He urged more political education classes but added that SNCC workers had distributed clothes and toys to the few needy families he could help. Icy weather reflected the gloomy spirits of the activists in the death-rattle days of SNCC in Arkansas.[47]

Although SNCC ended its work in Arkansas not with a bang but a whimper, it instigated staggering changes. An Arkansan absent from the state for the mere thousand days spanning 1963 to 1966 would not believe that in January 1967 blacks voted in large numbers and ran and elected African American school and government officials, black and white chil-dren sat peacefully in the same classrooms, people of all colors dined together at McDonald's and in cafes across the state, or that blacks and whites might work together for roughly equal pay. Tangible signs of the death of Jim Crow appeared everywhere—in Helena, Forrest City, Gould, and across the state. The young activists of SNCC, playing the role of Socratic gadflies, challenged white Arkansans to accept as inevitable the relatively peaceful dismantling of Jim Crow in Arkansas and emboldened African Americans to demand justice and equality. SNCC helped blacks cross the previously uncrossed white line and move, at long last, toward genuine freedom.

5.

Replicating History in a Bad Way?

White Activists and Black Power in SNCC's Arkansas Project

JENNIFER JENSEN WALLACH

Stokley Carmichael, chairman of the Student Nonviolent Coordinating Committee from 1966 to 1967, derided what he viewed as the "media-driven" version of the civil rights organization's history, which suggested that "SNCC began as an 'integrated' group devoted to a mystical Christian vision of a communal 'beloved society' before the rise of an intolerant 'black nationalism' ruined this interracial Eden."[1] This simplistic version of the organization's trajectory has become a crucial part of what Brian Ward has identified as the "master narrative" of the movement, which is found "not just in the pages of many popular high school and college surveys of postwar American history, but also in public celebrations . . . journalistic accounts, memoirs of activists, novels set in Movement days, Hollywood feature films, popular songs, and television dramas and documentaries on the subject."[2] Analyses of this kind hinge upon a turning point, after which the noble ideals of the movement were supposedly irrevocably lost.[3] Writing in 1967, historian C. Vann Woodward, in answering "what happened to the civil rights movement," decried the black nationalist politics of the era as having "the unmistakable quality of fantasy and a tenuous contact with reality."[4]

This "media-driven" interpretation, which glorifies early, integrationist civil rights leaders and vilifies black nationalists as white-hating separatists, has often been accompanied by much hand wringing over the fate of the white activists who, as the story goes, enthusiastically and at great personal risk joined the organization only to be asked to leave as SNCC assumed a more black nationalist posture from 1966 onward. The 2008 documentary film, *The Jewish Americans,* after highlighting the extraordinary and numerically disproportionate involvement of Jews in the freedom struggle, recounts the expulsion of whites from SNCC. A fiery speech by Stokely Carmichael is juxtaposed with footage of some middle-aged Jewish women emotionally describing their sadness at being "asked . . . to leave the movement." Rabbi Rachel Cowen recalls, "We wanted to be loved in return, and we weren't, and that was painful."[5]

Other SNCC activists remembered being similarly pained. Abbie Hoffman claimed that the expulsion of whites from SNCC made him feel "like a schmuck."[6] Casey Hayden recalled, "To me [the movement] was everything: home and family, food and work, love and a reason to live. When I was no longer welcome there, and then when it was no longer there at all, it was hard to go on."[7] For their part, some of the black SNCC members who, for a variety of reasons, began to favor black separatism later expressed a sense of guilt. For example, Ethel Minor remembered feeling torn about the decision afterward, particularly as it pertained to Bob Zellner, the first white to join SNCC. She recalled, "Here was someone who had been on the front lines before I came into the organization. No one wanted to look at Bob afterwards."[8]

A close examination of the activities of the Student Nonviolent Coordinating Committee in Arkansas, however, reveals a more complex narrative. Although some white SNCC activists there also felt devalued and discarded, there was a far broader range of responses among white members of the Arkansas Project to the system of beliefs identified with the phrase "Black Power." Some white SNCC staffers in Arkansas came to understand that they had inadvertently reinforced the racial order they were seeking to unravel. Many underwent profound political changes as they sought ways to dismantle and disavow white privilege. Some even began to move toward a political position that can best be described as black nationalism and had to redefine their relationships to the civil rights movement as a result.

From its founding in 1960 onward, SNCC was a predominantly black organization. Whites were not involved in significant numbers until what has become known as the "Freedom Summer" of 1964, when over eight hundred volunteers—three-quarters of them white, northern, college students—streamed into Mississippi to aid in voter registration drives.[9] Legendary SNCC organizer Bob Moses's tactical gamble that the presence of middle- and upper-middle-class whites in Mississippi would garner media interest and national sympathy for the movement paid off. However, the infusion of a large number of white volunteers, many of whom wanted to continue their service beyond the summer, created interracial tensions, fomenting debates about the role of whites in the movement even before the doctrine of Black Power explicitly emerged.[10]

As political scientist Emily Stoper has observed, these tensions arose over a number of issues. Many white volunteers were better educated and certainly more affluent than southern blacks, and they often exhibited the confidence associated with their class position and had the tendency to take over office tasks and to be vocal at meetings, often drowning out black voices. The presence of these white volunteers in southern communities may also have "reinforce[d] the tendency of local blacks to defer to white people." Furthermore, because whites themselves would not directly benefit from a change in the racial order, many black SNCC members harbored suspicions about the sincerity of their decision to volunteer, speculating that some had motivations that were not purely altruistic. For example, Stoper suggests that some "seemed to have come to learn about life or to find themselves, to help the poor benighted black people and earn their gratitude, to act on an ideology . . . to atone for guilt, [and] to escape themselves," among other things.[11]

Because of the sheer number of whites present in Mississippi, what happened there has been most thoroughly chronicled and been made to appear as *the* representative SNCC experience almost by default.[12] But, the SNCC project in Arkansas offers a marked contrast to the Mississippi experience. The SNCC staff in Arkansas had always been integrated, and the organization remained so throughout its duration. In fact, the Arkansas Project initially had a white director. As in Mississippi though, the percentage of white volunteers increased over time.[13] In April 1965, half of eight full-time workers in the state were white.[14] That summer Arkansas hosted sixty to seventy volunteers, half of whom were white, but the project never faced the same kind of dramatic shift in its demographic make-up as seen in Mississippi.[15] Although some of the same tensions may have existed in Arkansas, they were more manageable, being on a much smaller scale.

The permanent staff of the Arkansas Project was relatively small, as was the number of summer volunteers who entered the state, and SNCC members in Arkansas were likely more intimately acquainted with one another than was possible in Mississippi during Freedom Summer. This familiarity may have occasionally bred contempt, but it also seems to have resulted in a relatively harmonious working environment.[16] White Arkansas staffers were never completely alienated by the calls for "Black Power" that intensified throughout the life of the organization. Arkansas is fertile ground, then, for constructing an alternative narrative of the white experience in SNCC.

SNCC entered Arkansas in 1962 at the invitation of the Arkansas Council on Human Relations, an organization affiliated with the Southern Regional Council that was devoted to improving race relations, and at the behest of politically active students at historically black Philander Smith College. Bill Hansen, a white member of SNCC, initially organized sit-ins in Little Rock and later helped establish a SNCC presence in Pine Bluff, Helena, Forrest City, and Gould.[17] In spite of these efforts, the local activities of SNCC were somewhat overlooked by the national media and also by the SNCC leadership in Atlanta. In 1965, SNCC headquarters in Atlanta inadvertently omitted Arkansas from their four-year strategic plan.[18] Robert Cableton, an organizer active in Gould, complained bitterly about feeling marginalized by the Atlanta office: "People would ask me, well, you never get a call from the national office? What's happening in Atlanta? So it put me in a position of having to lie for Atlanta, until I got tired of lying."[19]

Despite this marginalization, the SNCC story in Arkansas is not completely unlike the SNCC story elsewhere. The organization played a significant role in desegregating local facilities, increasing black voter registration, and supporting the development of homegrown political leadership. The group's direct-action campaigns and voter registration drives were met with white hostility and violence throughout the areas where it operated. Indeed, in Arkansas, as elsewhere in the South, SNCC members were beaten, threatened, and arrested, meeting resistance not only from the white community but also from some middle-class black Arkansans who were unsettled by the student-led challenge to their authority in the community.[20]

Notwithstanding this, there was a modicum of interracial cooperation in Arkansas that did not exist in many other parts of the South. Much of this relative calm was attributable to fallout from the Little Rock school integration crisis of 1957–1958. After his showdown with federal authority finally ended, Gov. Orval Faubus appeared satisfied that he had proved his white supremacist mettle. This allowed him to make concessions to the black community, particularly to members of the NAACP, whose goals appeared modest in comparison to the young radicals in SNCC. For example, Faubus engaged in a series of negotiations with NAACP field secretary L. C. Bates that resulted in more than one hundred black appointments to positions in state agencies. Local business leaders sought to avoid a repeat of the international humiliation wrought by the events at Central High, which had adversely affected the economic prospects of this ambitious southern state.

Members of the Little Rock civic leadership tardily engaged in secret negotiations with the black community, quietly desegregating Little Rock's downtown stores in 1963.[21]

During the 1960s, certain pressures, then, probably worked to rein in the forces of massive resistance in the state, making the situation for SNCC workers somewhat safer. White volunteer Mitchell Zimmerman wanted to work with the Arkansas Project, "primarily because my parents . . . would . . . be likely to worry about me slightly less if I were there [instead of in Mississippi or Alabama]."[22] This relative degree of safety had a large impact on the internal dynamics of the Arkansas Project. Black Arkansas volunteer Kwame Shaw speculates that racial friction was kept at a minimum within the organization in part because "tensions were not as high" as they were elsewhere.[23]

The Arkansas Project did suffer, though, from some of the same growing pains that affected the national organization as SNCC struggled to redefine itself in the wake of what historian Adam Fairclough has called the "crisis of victory" spawned by the passage of the Voting Rights Act of 1965.[24] After the movement had achieved its goals of ending formal segregation and restoring the franchise to black voters, organizers struggled with the fact that these changes in policy did not end economic disparities or fundamentally change the distribution of power in the United States. They were then left with the challenge of redefining and reorienting the movement to fight against injustice of a more amorphous variety. Stokely Carmichael and Willie Ricks began to popularize the "Black Power" slogan in June 1966 as part of an attempt to articulate a new direction for SNCC. In Arkansas, as elsewhere, members of SNCC had to try to elucidate the meaning of this rhetorical posture and to chart a new path for the organization to follow.

The words "Black Power" proved to be inspirational to some, infuriatingly cryptic to others, and somewhat frightening to still others. The phrase contained multiple meanings. It could be a cry for black political representation as African Americans seized upon the promises implicit in the Voting Rights Act and began electing their own representatives. It could also be a statement conveying racial pride, a critique of the method of nonviolent protest, a call for Pan-African unity, or an articulation of frustration with the slow pace of change. Increasingly, for some, it became entangled with a desire for black separatism and a reassessment of integration as the primary goal of the movement. The expression had a different combination of meanings depending upon who uttered it. This vagueness made the slogan remarkably adaptable to a wide variety of circumstances, while fostering a kind of superficial consensus among those who embraced it. But the lack of a coherent, fixed meaning meant that in any crowd in which the phrase was heard, those shouting "Black Power" likely intended a number of different things.[25]

The challenges faced by SNCC in Arkansas to define "Black Power" began to intensify as the cries for black empowerment and black control within the organization nationally began to take a markedly separatist turn. The tension between the extreme integrationist and extreme nationalist positions within the national organization escalated throughout 1966, coming to a head in December when members expelled whites from the organization altogether. As Clayborne Carson emphasizes in his seminal study of SNCC, the expulsion vote was a narrow one. Nineteen staff members voted for expulsion, eighteen against, and twenty-four abstained from voting on the painful issue.[26] The lack of a mandate for the extreme black nationalist position continued to plague the remaining SNCC members, who could not even agree on what the decision meant, some claiming that white members were completely expelled from the organization, others arguing that whites could continue to work behind the scenes or on a contractual basis, with still others declaring that whites could continue to work under SNCC auspices but must confine their organizing efforts to white communities. Carson claims that the issue was not definitively resolved until May 1967, when the Central Committee refused white SNCC veteran Bob Zellner's request for support for a white project in New Orleans and continued voting rights in SNCC.[27]

In the Arkansas Project, white ties to SNCC were never severed as neatly as the master narrative of white expulsion might imply. Most white SNCC members were not insensitive to calls for black control of the organization, and many resigned preemptively before the official exclusion of whites, making the term "expulsion" something of a misnomer. But, because the tenets of Black Power ultimately called into question white participation in SNCC, whites had no choice but to reflect on the meanings of the philosophy and upon their personal relationship to the organization. Black members of the SNCC Arkansas Project, by contrast, were not forced to come to terms with Black Power in the same dramatic fashion. African Americans had the choice of embracing the idea of Black Power, renouncing it, or simply not overtly engaging the idea.[28]

Bill Hansen, the first director of the SNCC Arkansas Project, anticipated the discussions about black empowerment and black leadership that would begin to dominate ideological debate within the organization. Early on, it became clear that Hansen would receive a disproportionate amount of press coverage, partially because he was an anomaly, a white leader in a black organization, and an outsider and "race traitor" to boot. Hansen received a great deal of publicity, for example, after his marriage to Ruth Buffington, a black Arkansan, in 1963. Because interracial marriage was illegal in Arkansas, the couple married in Hansen's native Ohio, creating a media sensation in both states.[29] Hansen later complained to a reporter at the *Arkansas Gazette*, "Too many stories about Snick wind up being stories about William W. Hansen. . . . I could go out and join the Citizens' Council now and the movement would continue."[30] In 1964, in part to combat this tendency, Hansen publicly resigned from sole leadership of the Arkansas Project, becoming instead a co-director with a native black Arkansan, James Jones.[31] Hansen recalls, "I had been thinking about it for awhile. . . . I realized I was replicating history in a bad way. . . . it became apparent to me that this was a role I had simply used up."[32]

Sharing the directorship did not diminish Hansen's commitment to SNCC or his role in the organization. Leadership of the Arkansas Project was conducted on the group-centered model favored by SNCC. Thus, Jones had played a large part in decision-making long before he was officially named co-director.[33] However, Hansen's action showed his sensitivity toward the political implications of white leadership. He told the media that whites should play a "significant part" in the freedom struggle but that "it is the Negro's place to take the leading responsibility."[34] In retrospect, this decision represented the first step toward Hansen's separation from SNCC. In the fall of 1966, he resigned in anticipation of the forthcoming expulsion vote, recalling, "I didn't want to go through an expulsion with an organization that I helped build."[35]

Hansen understood by 1966 that SNCC was not the same organization it had been when he first arrived in Arkansas four years earlier. Although he clearly agreed with the ideas of black empowerment and black leadership, he remained ambivalent about the phrase "Black Power," which he thought lacked coherent meaning and a specific political program. In Hansen's estimation, the "Black Power" slogan became an unnecessarily divisive distraction, preventing members of the organization from doing the hard work of making a transformation "from being reformists to being revolutionaries."[36]

On a personal level, Hansen would come to admit that the cries for black separatism "hurt a lot."[37] Understandably, it was an emotionally wrenching experience to separate himself from SNCC, an organization that had defined him during the crucial coming-of-age years of his twenties. He had been only the second white to join the organization as a field organizer. Before his arrival in Arkansas, he had served time in jails in Mississippi, Maryland, and Georgia due to his movement activities. In 1962, in Albany, Georgia, he had been the victim of a brutal beating by a prison trusty told that Hansen needed to be "straightened out."[38] In contrast, other white members did not arrive in Arkansas having already spent extensive time in southern jails. Instead, most arrived directly from northern colleges and became involved with the organization only briefly. Unlike Hansen, they joined in 1964 or later.[39] As a veteran of the struggle, Hansen was irked that "the people who were demanding our expulsion were relative newcomers who hadn't even been there during the really tough years of the early sixties. For the most part, they had been on nice white campuses up North."[40]

Historian Brent Riffel asserts that Hansen's departure "broke all ties between the Arkansas Project and the early SNCC members who had been in the organization since 1960–61."[41] Although technically Hansen's ties to the organization were broken, his decision to resign in the face of expulsion did not necessarily signal an end to his civil rights activities or to his association with other SNCC members. The informal power structure of SNCC meant that personal relationships and past accomplishments (such as time spent in jail, a badge of honor to civil rights activists) were of greater consequence than formal titles or being on the SNCC payroll, which was being met only sporadically by 1966 anyway.[42] Hansen's marriage to a black Arkansan ensured that he had strong ties to the local black community, which were not severed when his job description changed. In fact, he felt so firmly integrated into that community that he longed to stay in Arkansas, but his reputation as a radical and a race traitor left him a "marked man" and made securing employment impossible.[43] Hansen also maintained a lifelong friendship with Stokely Carmichael, chairman of the organization during the tumultuous period when the sometimes vicious debate about the roles of whites in the organization began to dominate many organizational conversations.[44]

During the summer of 1967, six months after the supposed expulsion vote, Hansen moved to Atlanta where he began volunteering at the SNCC office doing clerical work. Although some new SNCC members, particularly northerners, were hostile to his presence in the office, the vast majority of SNCC workers tolerated, even welcomed, his assistance, indicating the trend toward black separatism was not without nuances and exceptions. Rather than feeling rejected on a personal level by the black radicals, in Hansen's estimation "the ultra black power people . . . were friends of mine." After Martin Luther King's assassination, Hansen's former SNCC colleagues lifted him and passed him out of an angry crowd of mourners in order to ensure his safety.[45]

In fact, some of Hansen's staunchest critics when he led the Arkansas Project had been not black but white members of the organization. Arlene

Wilgoren and Nancy Stoller believed that he was not sufficiently aware of his own white, male privilege.[46] Others recall attempting to, in effect, expel Hansen from SNCC because of the general perception that he was not adequately embracing the new direction of the movement, namely the adoption of Black Power ideology.[47] Reflecting upon his SNCC experience, Howard Himmelbaum found it difficult to remember the precise contours of some of the white members' grievances against Hansen. Trying to recapture that forgotten moment, he speculated, "I think it was because we were so much more radical than Bill and believed that his activities and behavior were destructive to what we were trying to build."[48]

But some of these other white SNCC members also left the organization in the months leading up to the December 1966 vote. Arlene Wilgoren, a white Brandeis graduate, had begun working for the SNCC Arkansas Project in June 1964. Her involvement in the civil rights movement began in 1960, when, as a college student, she picketed a Woolworth's on Harvard Square in support of the sit-ins going on in the South. She then moved to New York where she volunteered at the Friends of SNCC office. Wilgoren did not plan to travel South to continue her activism until she heard the news that three activists, James Chaney, Andrew Goodman, and Michael Schwerner, had gone missing in Mississippi during Freedom Summer. She recalls, "That was it for me. I quit my job, packed my things, and got on a bus to Atlanta." Soon she found herself stationed in Pine Bluff, Arkansas, where she performed mostly office work but also canvassed, urging people to register to vote.[49]

After continuing in that capacity for over a year, she recalled one pivotal meeting that cemented her decision to leave SNCC. Wilgoren remembered, "A local southern black woman stood in front and said that she wanted to work in the movement. She wanted to type the newsletters and print the leaflets and it shouldn't matter that she could not type as fast as the white girls from the north."[50]After hearing this testimony from a black Arkansan seeking a larger role in the liberation movement, Wilgoren became convinced that she had outlived her usefulness in that particular aspect of the struggle. She left the project in part because she was afraid that the combination of her own "personality flaws" and her socialization as a white person meant that she might have trouble stepping aside and letting local people assume leadership over tasks she had become familiar with and could do well. The best solution, she decided, was to leave Arkansas altogether.[51]

Wilgoren returned to Boston to work with People against Racism, educating the white community about racial issues. Interestingly, in leaving the southern civil rights struggle to organize whites, she was, in effect, simultaneously coming to the same conclusion as many advocates of white expulsion. Wilgoren's actions anticipated, for example, a 1968 statement by the SNCC Central Committee declaring, "it should be the conscious effort of SNCC organizers to encourage white radicals to organize against American racism."[52] In fact, Wilgoren was so devoted to the idea that whites should organize other whites and blacks should organize other blacks that after leaving Arkansas she wrote a letter to a fellow white volunteer in Arkansas, Howard Himmelbaum, asking why he and Mitchell Zimmerman, another white staff member, were still in the state working with the black community. Wilgoren went so far as to make an offer to raise funds for the Arkansas Project contingent upon a satisfactory answer to that question, writing, "frankly, your being there does seem inconsistent with the new policy—right?"[53]

Nancy Stoller's story was similar to Wilgoren's. While an undergraduate at Wellesley, she also picketed the Woolworth's in Cambridge, Massachusetts, and later became active in the Nonviolent Action Group before traveling to Arkansas. After several months in Arkansas performing clerical work and writing for the project's paper, the *Arkansas Voice,* she too left the organization voluntarily. She had never planned to stay in Arkansas permanently, believing as she did that "community organizing, leadership should be in the hands of people from the communities involved as much as possible."[54]

Although some whites became ardent defenders of Black Power, belief in the principle was by no means universal. White volunteer Vincent O'Connor, like Wilgoren and Stoller, decided to leave the organization as it began to shift in the direction of Black Power. But O'Connor, a native Californian and the son of a San Francisco superior court judge, did not leave SNCC in deference to the new agenda but rather because he disagreed with it. An ardent dissenter, O'Connor was not only a civil rights crusader but also an antiwar protester. After being drafted to serve in Vietnam, he became a conscientious objector, a decision that ultimately earned him a fourteen-month sentence in a California prison.[55] Although the fervor of his convictions never wavered, his belief in the SNCC program ultimately faltered. In a letter written in August 1966, O'Connor claimed that he was "in the process of resigning from SNCC because of its financial irresponsibility toward its workers and the continuing drift of its policies towards violence, separatism, and the eventual destruction of the American left."[56] After leaving the organization, O'Connor remained in Arkansas doing what he described as "free-lance peace and civil rights work."[57] His correspondence reveals ongoing contact with active SNCC members in the state even after his official resignation, indicating that his uneasiness about the direction being taken by the national SNCC organization did not necessarily translate into a desire to distance himself from local SNCC workers.[58]

Even those white SNCC staffers who claimed to support Black Power differed in their feelings about how the doctrine applied to them and to their relationship with the organization. While Wilgoren and Stoller knew, for a variety of political and personal reasons, when it was time for them to leave, white staffer Mitchell Zimmerman did not immediately see his own involvement in SNCC as contrary to the Black Power principle. Zimmerman was a graduate student in political science at Princeton University when he became involved with SNCC. Although his "initial interest in Arkansas was political, not academic," he arrived in Arkansas in September 1965 on the pretense of conducting dissertation research on SNCC's style of community organizing.[59] Zimmerman spent most of his time in Arkansas serving as communications director in the Little Rock office, though he also conducted fieldwork in West Memphis, where he was arrested after local police discovered that he was living in a black neighborhood.[60]

In June and July 1966, Zimmerman wrote letters to the editor of the *Arkansas Gazette* vigorously defending black nationalism, claiming, "Black power does not mean hating white people—I am a white man and I feel no anomaly in working for black power. Nor does it mean the total exclusion of white persons from the struggle. Nor is it separatism."[61] That same year Zimmerman, along with Howard Himmelbaum and black Arkansan Jim Jones, defended and described the concept of Black Power to a group of high school students attending a summer college preparatory program, indicating that white staff members felt comfortable assuming the role of ambassadors for Black Power.[62] Zimmerman, in fact, voted for Stokely Carmichael as chairman of the organization in the 1966 election, effectively helping to solidify the nationalistic direction of the movement.

Yet, the increasing tilt toward black separatism was not something that even Zimmerman could accept with complete equanimity. As early as September 1965, he wrote, "I find myself becoming particularly short with the anti-white shit."[63] As the voices of separatism began to challenge his more integrationist vision of Black Power, Zimmerman left the organization. By September 1966 it was clear to him that "white people where neither desired . . . nor . . . had any role to play in its evolving direction."[64] Although the voices of separatism became at least temporarily dominant in the organization, other SNCC members continued to adhere to Zimmerman's more inclusive vision of Black Power long after the notorious expulsion vote. For example, Michael Thelwell did not view white expulsion as inevitable, thinking instead that it was "possible theoretically for the organization to define itself in a firm, aggressive, militant nationalist posture and say anybody who is in the organization will accept and work in that discipline."[65]

Indeed, this was the position taken by white SNCC field director Howard Himmelbaum, who, like Zimmerman, voted for Stokely Carmichael. Himmelbaum initially became involved with SNCC by volunteering in the New York office while attending college at the Bronx division of Hunter College (now Lehman College). By the time he arrived in Arkansas in February 1965, he acknowledged that "things were getting messy in Mississippi and Alabama regarding white volunteers." He credited his ability to secure a position to a recommendation from venerable SNCC advisor Ella Baker. He spent nearly two years with the Arkansas Project, working as a field secretary out of West Helena and earning $20.00 a week "when [SNCC] had the funds."[66]

Himmelbaum found ways to embrace the ideology of Black Power, never seeing a conflict between it and his own involvement with SNCC. In fact, the infamous December 1966 expulsion meeting never affected Himmelbaum directly. He claims, "No one kicked me out. No one said a bad word. I mean Stokely . . . all those folks coming through Arkansas, Cleve Sellers, they knocked on my door and said, 'Hey, we need a place to stay.' They were the people who were supposed to be kicking all the whites out. . . . I don't know . . . if it was because it was Arkansas and no one gave a shit. . . . they were never mad at me."[67] Himmelbaum continued to work in Arkansas under SNCC auspices long after the organization had stopped meaningfully functioning in the state. In West Helena, where he operated, he became a one-man representative of the group, often sending out press releases under the name of SNCC.[68] He recalls not sending in his resignation to the national office until December 1967, and even then he continued his civil rights activities in the state under a research grant from the Southern Regional Council.[69] In fact, only Bob Cableton, a black SNCC worker active in Gould, outlasted Himmelbaum as a SNCC affiliate in the state.[70]

Obviously Himmelbaum's failure to sever ties with the organization or to be forced out complicates the SNCC expulsion story. His embrace of Black Power ideology also adds a layer of complexity to the narrative of black separatism during the late SNCC years. Himmelbaum recalls being so "radicalized" that "I didn't trust anyone white. . . . I found I didn't like their styles. . . . They were so paternalistic. They were patronizing."[71] Himmelbaum was uniquely able to negotiate the racial divide in a way that did not alienate black radicals, and, unlike Wilgoren and Stoller, he managed to support Black Power by remaining in the organization rather than by leaving. Black Arkansas organizer Kwame Shaw attributes this to Himmelbaum's unique personal attributes, comparing his style and charisma to that of Bill Clinton, whose background and special relationship with the black community prompted Toni Morrison to somewhat playfully label him the nation's "first black president."[72]

Himmelbaum's SNCC experiences also mirror Carmichael's observation that whites who joined SNCC, in a sense, stopped being white, that "whatever class and color privileges they might have taken for granted were immediately suspended." Their status as "race traitors" often earned them the special ire of the white establishment, making them particularly vulnerable when incarcerated in the white sections of southern jails. Of course, for many white SNCC members, this process of, to use Carmichael's phrase, "becoming black" was a gradual one.[73] Many were not aware of unconscious behaviors that were the residue of backgrounds of class and racial privilege. Zimmerman recalls, much to his chagrin, inadvertently antagonizing local blacks by his "highhandedness," by "taking over things . . . and elbowing aside blacks who were doing them." This is a dynamic that Zimmerman was best able to appreciate only in retrospect, but he recalls having conversations with fellow white volunteer Laura Foner, who was already sensitive to the possibility that "in light of decades of subordination [there was] a risk that local people would automatically defer to the white civil rights worker . . . and that this undermined the point of the struggle."[74]

In the end, only one SNCC Arkansas staff member publicly criticized the Black Power position—Ben Grinage, an African American. Serving as project director when Stokely Carmichael publicly declared that integration was "irrelevant," Grinage issued a public statement arguing that the "new emphasis of Snick will not ultimately be in the best interests of the deprived Negro in Arkansas. . . . We are committed to the dignity of all mankind. . . . We have symbolized this not only in our philosophy but in the composition of our staff."[75] Inadvertently, Grinage's decision to hold a press conference and to speak out against Black Power affected Hansen too, who felt torn between his loyalty to SNCC and his loyalty to Grinage. While leery of the Black Power slogan and believing that its meaning needed to be clarified, Hansen was determined not to publicly renounce it and did not agree with Grinage's assertion that it amounted to "reverse racism."[76] He managed his conflicting impulses by attempting to skirt the issue. Hansen attended the press conference held by Grinage, thereby implicitly appearing to agree with him, but he offered no statement himself. He did, however, later tell the press, "I don't think Carmichael used good judgment."[77] However, he remained deliberately vague about which aspects of Carmichael's behavior he was criticizing.

Shortly thereafter, due to personal convictions as well as to implied pressure from Carmichael and others in the organization, Grinage resigned as project director, publicly citing personal reasons for leaving.[78] He left behind an integrated staff almost universally devoted to supporting Black Power, although theories about what this nationalism should look like varied from member to member.

Other African Americans who had been active in the Arkansas Project embraced the separation that Grinage rejected. Michael Simmons, a young Temple University student, decided to become a member of SNCC in the spring of 1965, at which time he was "so upset with myself for not joining sooner." He was first drawn to Mississippi due to the "romanticism" of working in one of the most notoriously racist southern states, but he was advised that the SNCC operation there was in organizational disarray. Simmons chose the Arkansas Project on the recommendation of Jimmie Travis, a member of the Mississippi Project, who claimed that the SNCC operation in Arkansas was "well organized and focused," a claim that Simmons's experiences substantiated.[79] Simmons describes being "starry eyed" in the presence of Bill Hansen, who was a seasoned political activist when Simmons met him in the summer of 1965. Nonetheless, in a matter of months, Simmons had left Arkansas to become a founding member of the SNCC Atlanta Project, the most outspokenly separatist contingent of the organization. Simmons became one of the most forthright advocates of white expulsion, a position that he still maintains was politically necessary and the natural outgrowth of civil rights struggle.

Simmons cited racism in the organization as a justification for white expulsion, claiming that just because "somebody opposed slavery doesn't mean they thought black people were equal." But he also claimed that the presence of middle-class white people in the movement had an almost stupefying effect on some members of the black population who were not used to being around "good white people." The adulation of local blacks enforced the white sense of superiority and lulled some local blacks into allowing whites to assume control of the direction of the movement. If black people were to lead the movement for their own liberation, Simmons argued, whites had to be removed and their efforts channeled toward organizing against racism in the white community.[80] But even Simmons recalled feeling "sheepish" around former SNCC comrades like Bill Hansen in the aftermath of the expulsion vote, because they were "nice people," people he admired.[81]

Other black Arkansas Project members seem to have adhered broadly to the doctrine of Black Power but were far more ambivalent regarding the role of whites in the movement. Jim Jones, who succeeded Hansen as project director, proved to be more than willing to cooperate with white activists like Zimmerman and Himmelbaum, but he also wished to limit the number of white volunteers in Arkansas. He remarked, "if you notice during the SNCC development Arkansas never had the big influx of whites from the North and that's why, because I specifically say that if I'm going to direct this program I have to have some freedom of decision making. One of the decisions I made is that I'm interested in blacks. If there are a number of blacks in the North interested in coming down, I'll accept all of them, but as far as whites, I've seen too many problems that came out of the Mississippi situation [to want] to repeat that."[82] Millard Lowe, who was recruited to the Arkansas Project while a student at Texas Southern University, likely represents the sentiments of most black Arkansas staff members and volunteers. Initially, he recalls being "indifferent" to white leadership of SNCC in Arkansas. His later experiences in the struggle convinced him that "a black should be in charge." This, however, was not an endorsement of black separatism, and he continually regarded Bill Hansen as a "close personal friend."[83]

Black member Bob Cableton was critical of Hansen's leadership, claiming "Bill Hanson [sic] could not accept the fact of working under . . . black leadership . . . he was able to maneuver in such a way that he could fold or twist the minds."[84] As a whole, however, Arkansas was notable for its harmonious race relations rather than for racial dissension. This was due, in large part, to the fact that there was a strong basis of support among its white members for the doctrine of Black Power. A research report produced by the Arkansas Council on Human Relations asserted that "some SNCC workers remain in Arkansas, most of them white from non-southern states. Some of these proclaim their loyalty to the new SNCC and its goals, including the concept of 'Black Power' and denial of the relevance of integration." But, the report concluded, "Being white they have a dubious role in an organization now committed to a movement of, for and by Negroes."[85]

By the time the much-needed discussion about white involvement in the movement came to the fore, SNCC was on the verge of dissolution. Historian Randy Finley has argued that the demise of SNCC in Arkansas can be linked to the "disintegration of the national organization," an assertion that is likely true. The Arkansas Project certainly suffered as funding from Atlanta began to disappear.[86] Fundraising became a more difficult challenge after the passage of the Civil Rights Act of 1964 and the Voting Rights Act of 1965. Furthermore, SNCC's 1965 statement against the Vietnam War and 1967 position paper critiquing Zionism alienated many of SNCC's staunchest supporters and irreparably damaged fundraising efforts. The movement toward Black Power also served to weaken SNCC's traditional base of financial support as the media caricatured the proponents of this ideology, instilling fear in some former supporters.

In assessing the demise of SNCC, Finley also asserts that "racial tensions among SNCC activists were becoming more prevalent as the Black Power movement emerged. This impulse filtered down to the local level." As evidence for increasing racial tension, Finley refers to a letter written by Howard Himmelbaum indicating that the Arkansas Project would "not accept any white people except under unusual circumstances."[87] However, something more complicated than interracial animosity seemed to be going on. A white man himself (as Finley acknowledges), Himmelbaum was sensitive to calls for black empowerment and honored that principle as he recruited new SNCC volunteers. He was also committed to elevating local blacks to positions of leadership, indicating, "What we really want are Black Arkansans who can work for a long period of time."[88]

Although emotions ran high on both sides and many veteran SNCC members like Hansen felt somewhat betrayed after the expulsion vote of December 1966, some white SNCC members in Arkansas experienced political evolutions that were not unlike the ones undergone by black counterparts like Michael Simmons, indicating—at least in Arkansas—more widespread agreement about the direction the struggle should take than the simplistic narrative of integrationism versus nationalism would indicate.

II.

Firsthand Accounts

6.

Arkansas Daze

BILL HANSEN

Bill Hansen, the founding director of the SNCC Arkansas Project,
served the project between 1962 and 1966. After leaving SNCC,
he was employed by the National Sharecroppers Fund and as an
organizer training VISTA volunteers. Since then he has worked
as an educator on four continents, teaching at the Connecticut
State University, the American University of Central Asia, and
the European Division of the University of Maryland. Today he
holds the position of assistant dean and professor of interna-
tional and comparative politics at the American University of
Nigeria.

I first came to Arkansas in October 1962. I was twenty-three years old.[1]
With more than a little trepidation I drove alone from Atlanta across
Georgia, Alabama, and Mississippi in a battered 1954 Pontiac. What was
I getting myself into? I knew nothing about Arkansas except for the lurid
headlines and TV news I had seen half a decade earlier as a teenager in
Cincinnati.

My family was white, Catholic, and working class; lunch bucket, beer,
and bowling alley. My parents voted for FDR and had, more or less, the
same political views as did most others of their race and class. They supported unions, social security, an active public sector, and most of the rest
of the New Deal. Racial separation and the fact that whites should be privileged and take precedence was something they accepted as being part of
the natural order of things.

My neighborhood was white only and working class. The parochial
schools I attended were the same. There were only a handful of African

and African American students at Xavier University when I arrived in 1957. One of those exceptions was Bill Mason and we soon became fast friends, a friendship that lasted for almost fifty years until his death a few years ago. As my friendship with Bill grew, my relationships with my old friends from high school, male and female, withered. No one could understand what in the world had gone "wrong" with me. In the course of, perhaps, eighteen months, my "social community" went from being 99 percent white to 99 percent black. Eventually, sometime in 1958 or thereabouts, my mother gave me an ultimatum. I had seen it coming. My mother's antipathy toward blacks and Jews was palpable. Unacceptable, I moved out of my parents' home for good. I was nineteen.

As the fifties came to an end I had become a political activist in Cincinnati, sometimes referred to as a "northern city facing south." Both Bill Mason and I worked with the NAACP and even became board members of the Cincinnati branch. With other younger activists we also organized the Cincinnati chapter of the Congress of Racial Equality of which I became vice chair. I spent a good bit of 1960 on picket lines in front of Woolworth's and other such dime store chains in support of the southern student sit-in movement that had erupted in February 1960. I first came to the South in the summer of '61 as a Freedom Rider and spent a couple of months as guest of the state of Mississippi in that salubrious Delta tourist resort known as Parchman Penitentiary.

Leaving Mississippi after my sojourn at Parchman I went home to Cincinnati with the intention of resuming my education. However, I had been bitten by the adventurous lure of the burgeoning southern civil rights movement. After several weeks of flat-out boredom I took off for New York and the national office of CORE, the organization that had initiated, if not completed, the Freedom Rides. CORE's national office was a chaotic maelstrom in the fall of 1961. I was asked to go to Baltimore and Washington to give a series of talks about being a Freedom Rider. In the course of these events I became acquainted with a pool of student activists, virtually all black, the likes of which I had never experienced before: Stokely Carmichael (Kwame Toure), Ed Brown (Rap's older brother), Bill Mahoney, Peggy Dammond, Reggie Robinson, Kathy Conwell, and a host of others, many of whose names have faded from my memories.

In his early twenties, Reggie Robinson, a Maryland native, was a field secretary for SNCC, an outfit I had never heard of before. He recruited me. Reggie and I began organizing in Cambridge, Maryland. The Eastern Shore was not supposed to be a permanent SNCC project, so Reggie and I both moved on in the spring of 1962 leaving behind the core of a militant organization headed by the extraordinary Gloria Richardson. I became a SNCC "campus traveler," wandering from campus to campus, both white and black, through the southeast trying to carry the SNCC message.

Late that spring I arrived in Atlanta for the first time and went to the SNCC national office at 197½ Auburn Avenue, the famous "windowless cubicle."[2] This was my initial meeting with Jim Forman and Julian Bond, who, along with Norma Collins, ran SNCC's national operation. I was immediately sent to Albany, Georgia, and SNCC's Southwest Georgia Project headed by the redoubtable Charles Melvin Sherrod.

In midsummer, Martin Luther King returned to Albany for a trial resulting from an arrest the previous winter. King's arrival, of course, was a major political and media event. A circus! A series of demonstrations ensued that summer and most of us were in and out of jail a half dozen times. On one occasion I had been shifted from the Albany City Jail across the street to the white section of the Daugherty County Jail. In the bowels of this dungeon I was sitting on the stoop in front of my cell lost in thought when a white jail trusty came in to distribute something. Suddenly the left side of my face exploded. I had been hit with something, probably a fist, but I don't know. I never saw it coming. The next thing I knew I was on the floor being stomped amid shouts of "You motherfuckin' niggerlovin' sonafabitch" fading in and out of my increasingly elusive consciousness. I passed out. Somehow I'd managed to drag myself to my bunk with blood all over my face and pieces of teeth floating around in my swollen mouth. Later on, I'm not sure how much later, the authorities decided they should get me to a hospital.

It turns out I had a broken jaw, some broken teeth and, although not discovered for another few weeks when I couldn't take a breath without searing pain, several broken ribs as well. This occasioned a "rest and rehabilitation" trip to New York City. With my jaws wired together and sipping malted milks through my clenched teeth, my breath was sufficient to keep anyone from approaching within twenty feet. After almost two months, a local New York dentist removed the wires from my mouth.

A week or so later I was back in the Atlanta SNCC office. The plans were that I'd return to southwest Georgia. But things don't always go according to plans. Forman, as usual, was at the middle of the storm. It seems he'd been being bugged for weeks—phone calls, letters, etc.—by a man named Ozell Sutton, the associate director of the Arkansas Council on Human Relations. Sutton had been pleading that SNCC send some organizers to Arkansas to reinvigorate a student movement that had erupted briefly in the heyday of the sit-ins in 1960, but had petered out soon after with minimal accomplishments.

SNCC was swamped in the fall of '62 with its two large ongoing operations in Mississippi and Georgia. Forman was not going to commit any scarce SNCC resources to what he clearly considered as a "non-priority" place like Arkansas. When another letter arrived from Sutton, Forman handed it to me and said something to the effect of, "Why don't you go over there for a few weeks, see what they want, maybe get something started. You'll be back here by Christmas."

So Forman dredged up an old Pontiac from somewhere and I packed a bag and set out in a westerly direction. What I didn't know at the time is that I was supposed to be some sort of a guinea pig. The people at ACHR and their downtown allies wanted to threaten the conservative holdouts who were still resisting Main Street desegregation. They would secretly import some crazy "SNCC radical" and brandish him in their faces with the implicit threat of Little Rock crisis redux. The radical would hold some meetings, the pot would simmer, 1957–59 would be re-imagined, the holdouts would capitulate, and the radical would be dispatched back where he came from. In hindsight, that's pretty much what happened, except for the fact of going back to Atlanta.

In Little Rock the first thing I did was go to the ACHR offices where I met the insistent Mr. Sutton and the Council's executive director Nat Griswold. The next day I met three Philander students: Worth Long, Ben Grinage, and Bert Jones, respectively from Raleigh, Louisville and, my own hometown, Cincinnati.[3] All three were slightly older than typical Philander undergrads. Affiliated with the segregated (all-black) central region of the Methodist Church, Philander in those days was an almost anachronistic example of *in loco parentis.* As I recall female students were never allowed, at any time, to leave the campus by themselves. They had to go in groups of at least three and had to be back on campus by something like 6:00 P.M. This place was pretty much in permanent lockdown. Within a couple of days we had several meetings and collected a group of, perhaps, thirty who committed themselves to nonviolent, passive resistance and, if necessary, going to jail for refusing to leave a segregated lunch counter. We had a few training workshops and within no more than two weeks began the downtown sit-ins.

We targeted a Woolworth's and a Walgreens lunch counter initially. Worth Long and I were arrested, but there was no violence whatsoever. The police were attentive and in force. There were some bystanders and catcalls, but nothing significant. My sense is that everything was *pro forma.* Before we could get our second breath the daily sit-ins and picket lines were suspended while "negotiations" with a shadowy group of downtown potentates took place. One or two of the students were involved, but mainly "our side" was represented by the ACHR and a handful of ministers and other prominent black Little Rock natives.

That was it! It was over almost before it started. A "desegregation schedule" for various downtown facilities was drawn up and, suddenly, it was time for me to go back where I came from. However, I had developed some different ideas. Several long discussions with Ben Grinage about Arkansas and civil rights led him to drop out of Philander and become Arkansas's second SNCC organizer. After a single reconnaissance trip we loaded up that old Pontiac and headed permanently forty miles south to Pine Bluff; to set up camp in a different sort of Arkansas, one far less willing to accept what Little Rock had.

In those days Pine Bluff was the center of black Arkansas. With a population of slightly less than 50,000 it was almost 50 percent black. It had the black state university, Arkansas AM&N. It had a sizeable number of black professionals. Ben and I holed up in a room at a place called "Rooms for Rent" located next door to a popular black saloon called "The Duck-Inn" and just a few hundred yards from the front gate of the college.

The next day we went to the campus trying to locate activist students. News of the presence of two SNCC organizers on campus spread rapidly. Being white on an all-black campus in 1962 was not an easily kept secret. At the student government offices we received a mixed reception. The president of student government, a young man named Dorsey, wanted nothing to do with us and suggested we go back to Little Rock; preferably further. The SGA secretary, a beautiful young woman named Ruthie Buffington, who ten months later would become my wife, introduced us to several other would-be student activists: the Whitfield brothers (Bob and Bill), Jim Jones, Janet Broome, Shirley Baker, Joanna Edwards, Mildred Neal, Leon Nash, Odell Thorne, and a number of others.

Later that evening Ben and I left the campus in the company of Leon Nash and pulled into a coin-operated laundry across the street with the intention of doing our laundry. Before we could get out of the car we were surrounded by two police cars, lights flashing. Told we were under arrest, we were bundled off to the city jail for a night of rest and relaxation. The next day, police chief Norman Young and several of his stalwarts took me out of jail for a tour of several downtown stores. In each I was marched in wearing my handcuffs. Several white clerks in each store were asked, "Is this the one?" They all answered, "Yes. He's the one."

They were all attesting to the fact that I was the one who had passed a bad check in their store in the previous week. Of course, I hadn't been in Pine Bluff the previous week. At first I was sort of surprised at the crudity of the tactic. Then I began asking them to produce the alleged checks.

Finally, I simply began laughing at the silliness of the whole event. Young realized this attempt at intimidation wasn't going to work so they took me back to the jail and told me I was free to go.

That was my introduction to Pine Bluff.

Fifteen students were expelled from AM&N that spring for their refusal to stop participating in the sit-ins we had helped organize. Several joined the SNCC staff, and several pursued their education elsewhere. One who became a SNCC organizer was James Oscar Jones, a natural community organizer and, in an organization filled with brilliant field organizers, the best I ever encountered.

As Forman and the Atlanta office gradually came to accept the fact that, intended or not, Arkansas had become the third SNCC field project, we began to establish headquarters in Pine Bluff and expand from there. Our initial efforts in Pine Bluff were aimed at desegregating public accommodations, but as the program began to look at the long term, there was a shift into more involvement in voter registration and grassroots political organizing. To this end we began running candidates for political office and block-by-block organizing. Simultaneously we moved into neighboring counties.

Our first effort in this regard was Lincoln County, immediately south of Pine Bluff. One day that spring ('63) I drove Jim to Star City, the county seat, and dropped him off. We knew no one there. We had arranged a place where I would pick him up in exactly five hours. Three hours later he was back at the Freedom House in Pine Bluff driving a car a local person had loaned him upon learning that he was a SNCC member. Jim had the unique capacity to be welcomed and trusted far quicker than anyone else.

Getting things under way in Star City, Jim moved on to the other end of the county, to Gould. There he came upon a most extraordinary woman. Carrie Dilworth must have been in her late fifties or early sixties then. A little humility can be learned in a variety of ways. Here we were, a bunch of piss and vinegar young radicals trying to motivate people to rise up and resist an oppressive system. What do we find with Ms. Dilworth? This remarkable woman had more than a few things to teach us about radical organizing. Thirty years earlier she had been a stalwart of the old Southern Tenant Farmers Union (SFTU). Her stories of interracial organizing, militant left-wing trade unionism, strikes, night riders, and vigilantes were gripping and compelling. It is, I think, the arrogance of youth to think that what one is doing for the first time is the first time that anyone has done it.

Within months of the beginning of the sit-ins in Pine Bluff negotiations had begun. From the point of view of Pine Bluff's whites I was the vilest sort of being; an odious race traitor whose betrayal represented a basic threat to civilization as heretofore known. This, of course, presaged a continuing problem for SNCC in Arkansas; that is, the image of an African American social and political upheaval "led" by a white man, and an outsider at that. The whole concept of "leadership" in SNCC was, for anyone really familiar with the internal workings of the organization, fundamentally different from the mainstream concept. From the beginning virtually all SNCC decisions were the product of collective discussion and decision. This is why SNCC meetings took so long. Scheduled for an afternoon and evening they might drag on for days and even weeks.

That October I married Ruthie (later Ruthe) Jena Buffington. The event created considerable consternation.[4] Ruthie was twenty and had been a senior at AM&N when she was expelled for participating in the sit-ins. Interracial marriage being illegal in Arkansas, we were married in Cincinnati, Ohio. Neanderthals like Governor Faubus and Attorney General Bruce Bennett grumbled, postured, fulminated, and made threats after we returned to Arkansas but did nothing tangible.

That same fall of 1963 SNCC had moved north into the Delta to begin a project in the notorious Phillips County. We set up our operations initially in West Helena, directly adjacent to Helena, the county seat. Helena was initially chosen for our first foray into the Delta in part because it had a 60 percent black population or thereabouts, because of its reputation as being racist and violent and because it seemed a linchpin of the entire eastern Arkansas area. The plans were to use Helena as a base from which to expand into places like Marianna, Forrest City, West Memphis, and Blytheville. As I recall I first went to Phillips County in the company of Jim Jones and Bruce Jordan.

Bruce was an eighteen-year-old Pine Bluff high school graduate who had been recruited onto the SNCC staff earlier that year. It was through Bruce that I was provided with one of the more remarkable experiences of my life. Bruce had a great-great-auntie who was the matriarch of the family and, as I recall, 104 years old. At least that's how old she thought she was. No one then knew for certain. In 1963 a 104-year-old would have been born in 1859. A slave! One day in the summer of 1963 Bruce and I put this elderly woman in a car and drove her to the Jefferson County Court House in Pine Bluff so she could register to vote. Here was a woman who had been born a slave registering to vote for the first time, and I was helping to escort her to the event. I was in awe. All these years later I can still remember that moment. As she was illiterate, her young nephew filled out the form for her. She marked her X.

Mostly we were welcomed in West Helena even if that welcome by many was a bit on the surreptitious side. As was typical in these sorts of situations it was the young people, high school students, who first became involved. Adult support was primarily from women. We decided, as a tactical move, that we needed to "announce" our presence through some sort of public gesture. The target was a Main Street restaurant in Helena. I forget how many of us there were at that initial sit-in in late November 1963, somewhere like a dozen perhaps. In such a case the politics of the situation required that I be a part of the first demonstration. Had I not, one could easily anticipate the accusation that some outside agitator, a white guy, had flummoxed a bunch of local teenagers into getting arrested while he stayed safely in the background.

As part of SNCC's security precautions someone was always posted near a phone to notify SNCC's Atlanta office, the local and national press, the local and the national FBI as well as the Civil Rights Division of the Justice Department. The fact that there was knowledge of our arrests at the highest levels of government acted as something of a safety blanket in that it inhibited, to some degree, that ability of the local police to act with impunity. How in the hell were we supposed to know that the president of the United States would be assassinated the next day?

The first I heard of the events in Dallas was when a white jail trusty at the Phillips County Jail came into the cell block and, looking directly at me, shouted with pure, unalloyed joy, that "They shot that nigger-loving Kennedy in Texas today." An hour or so later we were told that the president had died of his wounds. "Oh, oh," thought I, "I'm in some seriously deep shit."

In those days I was still a firm believer in Camelot and the essential rectitude of the American government; a patriot, I suppose. At the same time, even though I was only twenty-four years old, I was reasonably familiar with political and cultural realities. If the president of the United States has been assassinated the total attention of every political and cultural institution in the universe will be focused on what happened in Dallas. What happens to some obscure, unfortunate white guy in Helena, Arkansas, is of little interest. So someone dumps his carcass in the nearby Mississippi River. Who cares? Who will even know? At that moment I was probably as frightened for my life as I had ever been or ever was again.

As 1963 morphed into 1964 SNCC's entire organizational attention—Arkansas included—began to focus on the Mississippi Summer Project. The concept of bringing hundreds of summer volunteers from elsewhere in the country, mostly white and mostly young, was audacious, spectacular, and successful. The Summer Project did, however, have long-term ramifications for SNCC as an organization that were not always beneficial. Bitten, presumably, by the same bug that had bitten me after my own first summer in Mississippi; inspired, perhaps, by a creeping realization as to the historic nature of what was involved, many of those summer volunteers decided to stay on in Mississippi and elsewhere in the South.

For an organization that had grown organically over the years from a rather small cadre of a dozen or so close friends, SNCC quickly more than quadrupled in size. The newcomers were largely unfamiliar with the pre-existing organizational culture. Furthermore, black or white, they were generally far better educated than we were, far more articulate and politically sophisticated. The pre-Summer Project SNCC staff often felt overwhelmed and overshadowed by this new group. SNCC, as an organization, was never able to absorb adequately these newcomers and, as a result, the organization changed from being a close-knit band of (very) young men and women who, for the most part, knew one another personally and were largely southern in origin, to a much larger bureaucratic group that no longer had the "cultural feel" that had preceded it.

It was also sometime in 1964 that Arkansas SNCC's "white leader" image had become too important not to address. My own doubts as to the continuing efficacy of our public image had begun at least a year earlier. I discussed it constantly with both Ben Grinage and Jim Jones, as well as with my wife. Interestingly, both Ben and Jim initially thought I was exaggerating it as an issue. Capitulating to such an image and its perceived negative effect would contradict the very thing we were trying to accomplish: a society in which race and color made no difference. Eventually, however, I was able to convince Ben and Jim that a change needed to be made. At a SNCC Executive Committee meeting in Atlanta (I was an elected member of the committee) I announced my intention to resign as the Arkansas Project director although I would remain on the SNCC staff in the state.

The discussion at the Executive Committee meeting mirrored some of those that Jim, Ben, and I had had over the previous months; that is, that resigning for such a reason would defeat the very purpose for which SNCC had been created in the first place. Finally, a compromise was reached. Within SNCC, Jim Jones and I would be known as co-directors. Externally I would be identified as the deputy director. In practical terms, this change had no effect whatsoever since we had virtually from the beginning made all decisions collectively and we continued to do so.

That fall ('64) a SNCC delegation went to Africa. The trip had come about through the efforts of Harry Belafonte. Belafonte, the singer-actor with his international reputation and radical Pan-Africanist, leftist political views, knew several figures in the recently independent (1958) West African government of Guinea including its president, Sékou Touré. SNCC was at the radical forefront of the American civil rights movement so the Guinean government issued an invitation for us to send a delegation. The trip was financed by Belafonte. I was the only white member of a group that included Forman, Bob Moses, Julian Bond, John Lewis, Don Harris, and Prathia Hall. For all of us it was our first trip to Africa and for most our first time outside the United States.

It was an extraordinary experience and was also SNCC's first step into the arena of international politics. It foretold several things. First, it signified SNCC's growing understanding of the connection between domestic issues (civil rights, poverty, racism) and global affairs (imperialism, U.S. foreign policy, neocolonialism). Second, it was a distinct harbinger of SNCC's emerging radicalism that would eventually lead it, in the face of considerable opposition within the civil rights movement, to condemn the Vietnam War and, eventually, to become critical of Israeli and U.S. policy toward the Palestinians. Third, it signaled an emerging Pan-Africanism that morphed, within a few years, into nationalism and Black Power.

As 1965 began, my first child was born and SNCC in Arkansas was preparing for its own version of the Mississippi Summer Project, albeit on a much smaller scale. My memory of how many "summer volunteers" came to Arkansas later that year is vague. Prior to the summer the Arkansas SNCC staff must have been about twelve to fifteen full-time organizers. My guess is that somewhere in the neighborhood of thirty to thirty-five new people arrived that June. This significant increase in staff allowed us to move into hitherto untouched areas like Forrest City, Marianna, West Memphis, Stuttgart, and Blytheville. In retrospect I think we expanded too quickly without having adequate plans for maintaining new programs when the summer came to an end and many of the summer volunteers left to return to school.

Of course, as could have been expected, the rapid increase in the sheer number of people produced organizational strains. Having said that, however, I think to this day that far too much has been made of internal tensions. There are such tensions in any organization and they will inevitably be exacerbated under conditions of rapid and unplanned growth particularly under pressure conditions (jail, threats of violence, too few resources). I also think that the tensions that affected SNCC as a whole—often simplistically explained in terms of "racial tensions"—had their effect in Arkansas as they did throughout the organization. Perhaps a dozen of the summer volunteers stayed on as permanent staff members.

The year 1966 would effectively be the last year that Arkansas SNCC actually functioned as an organization with ongoing projects and activities. Our traditional funding sources began drying up. Those who had willingly supported us in the early years now began showing a decided reluctance.

However, the decline in resources was hardly the only cause of inner tensions in the organization.

This was the heyday of J. Edgar Hoover's COINTELPRO and SNCC, like many other progressive organizations, was a victim as well. We were infiltrated. It's as simple as that. I remain convinced that many of the internal organizational tensions, particularly those dealing with race, were instigated by Hoover's operatives who had infiltrated SNCC. I want to emphasize that I am *NOT* referring here to Stokely Carmichael. While Stokely and I might have, and did, disagree on a variety of issues, I have never had the slightest doubts as to his political and moral integrity.[5]

SNCC itself had undergone a metamorphosis. At its origins it had been a quintessentially reformist organization. America was, at its essence, what it proclaimed itself, domestically and internationally, to be; that "shining city on the hill." America's only fault was when it failed to live up to its own values and promises. The object of the civil rights movement was to hold up a mirror of America to its face, show it the ugly blotches that sometimes disfigured it, so as to hasten an epidermal improvement.

By 1966 this conception of America had changed with most of the people in SNCC. Far from being a bad skin condition, the epidermis of America concealed an extremely ugly internal reality. Far from being that shining city on the hill, America itself was at the core of the problem. In my opinion this transformation of SNCC began at Atlantic City, New Jersey, in August 1964 when the Freedom Democratic Party (FDP) challenged the seating of the "regular Democratic" convention delegates from Mississippi on the grounds that they had been chosen through a process that excluded more than 40 percent of the state's population on racial grounds.

Arriving at Atlantic City the SNCC/FDP (the FDP was the child of the Mississippi SNCC Project under Bob Moses) delegates were, for the most part, idealistic, young reformists convinced that, indeed, God, righteousness, and the U.S. Constitution was on their side. In Atlantic City they saw the crass and ugly underside of American politics and the willingness of many of their heretofore northern liberal friends to sell them out in the interest of being "realistic." They watched in disbelief as the President of the United States cynically called a press conference for the sole purpose of preempting Fannie Lou Hamer's mesmerizing speech from the convention platform. The SNCC people who had arrived in Atlantic City as reform-minded liberals left the resort as newly minted radicals.

When these domestic incidents were matched by U.S. supported coups in faraway places like the Congo, Brazil, Ghana, Guyana, and Indonesia, LBJ's invasion of the Dominican Republic and the inexorable ratcheting up of the genocide in Vietnam many SNCC organizers completed their transformation from a liberal reformist to a radical outlook. The organization, however, was still essentially a reformist one and SNCC increasingly found it impossible to make such a transition.

By the spring of 1966 SNCC in Arkansas had decided to intensify its activities in Forrest City.[6] Florence Clay, the matriarch of a local family, had welcomed SNCC organizers to the area the previous year and allowed us to use as a "Freedom Center" an abandoned building that had once been a funeral home. There had been a voter registration campaign, demonstrations, marches, picketing, and jailings for several months before that June when several people from the SNCC headquarters in Atlanta, including Cleve Sellers, came to town. One day the Forrest City Police, accompanied by St. Francis County sheriff's deputies raided the Freedom Center.

The authorities were after the leadership, figuring if they threw the book at a half dozen people and kept them locked up for a while, the momentum we'd built up would go away. As they burst into the front door Cleve and I jumped out a back window and made our way surreptitiously to Ms. Clay's house, about two hundred yards away. Inside she told us to go upstairs to the second floor where there was a ladder to a sort of trapdoor opening into a hidden attic. Sure enough, within minutes the police were at her front door inquiring as to our whereabouts. For the next week or so Cleve and I ate in the kitchen and slept in the attic. Every time the doorbell rang we'd race upstairs, pull the trapdoor, and slip into the attic.

Then we got news that James Meredith had been shot while marching through the Mississippi Delta and the entire civil rights movement began converging on that point to complete the march. Many of our staff took off immediately for Mississippi. Arkansas SNCC had a fleet of cars numbering something like fifteen. One of those was a bright yellow Dodge pickup. Cleve borrowed it to get to Mississippi and I was later told that it was from the bed of this truck that SNCC organizer, Willie Ricks, first shouted the slogan "BLACK POWER!!!" Though none of us were aware of it at the time, that moment effectively marked the end of Arkansas SNCC as it had been and, in my opinion, the end of SNCC as a whole. The slogan became the issue, setting off a media feeding frenzy. Suddenly BLACK POWER was all one could read in the news or on radio and TV.

What did Black Power mean? It was sudden and unexpected, hardly planned, discussed, or approved as a policy. Its appearance, as best I know, was the sudden, spontaneous, in the heat of an intense moment, shouted statement of a SNCC organizer known for his flamboyant rhetoric. What Black Power "meant" came to dominate the discourse. People from all parts of the political spectrum contributed their two cents' worth, most of which was pure political posturing.

Unplanned and spontaneous as it was, Black Power caught on and spread with the speed of a prairie fire. The truth is that it reflected a mood, a feeling on the part of those who'd been part of the civil rights struggle for years, an unspoken truth, as it were. This underscores my previous point with regard to a transformation from a liberal to a radical understanding of society with no place to go with this new knowledge. The late Ernest Gellner, as astute an observer of the nationalist phenomenon as I know it, has suggested that nationalism is not so much a consequence of modernity as it is of its uneven diffusion. Accepting the "peculiarities and specificities" of the African American situation, Gellner's understanding would seem to have more than a little purchase. The idea that SNCC was somehow broken in half by a conflict between the "integrationists" and the "separatists" is ultra-simplistic, not to mention completely inaccurate.

In the next few months money completely dried up. There was none! The various field projects withered away to nothing. Most of us began to look for some way to survive. It was clear that SNCC as it had been was no more. Ruthie and I had a two-year-old child to support. Ruthie got a job with John Walker, a Little Rock attorney who had, on behalf of the NAACP Legal Defense Fund, represented SNCC in various Arkansas courts.

I looked for a job but was unable to find one. My old friend Ben Grinage was by then the director of the Arkansas Council on Human Relations, the same outfit that had lured me to Arkansas in the first place. They had an advertised opening for the position of assistant director. I approached Ben about the job but was told that I was simply too controversial—anathema as it were—in Arkansas and there was no way he could give me a job. It was then that I knew, as much as I wanted to stay, that, ultimately, I would have to leave Arkansas. I was simply *persona non grata.*

I did get some funding to attend Little Rock University for a year with the intention of completing the degree that I had begun a decade earlier in Cincinnati. Then, sometime in the spring of 1967 my old friend Julian Bond called me from Atlanta to say there was a job opening with the National Sharecroppers Fund which had gotten an OEO (anti-poverty) grant. Was I interested? I leaped at the chance.

I really liked Atlanta, but it simply wasn't the same. Ruthie and I bought a house and tried to settle into a middle-class, paid-for-by-the-poverty-program existence. I organized laid-off workers from a Levi plant in north Georgia. Then I went to Augusta and worked with hospital workers there. For a while I trained VISTA volunteers. None of it worked. I had a difficult time adjusting. I missed Arkansas. I missed the work. I missed the rush of waking up every morning thinking that I was making a difference. Trying to "wind down" after the previous seven years was not that easy. Now for the first time I had a "real" job with a real income. I even had a credit card. The temptations of middle-class American life are seductive and I felt myself succumbing. So, in January 1970, Ruthie, the almost five-year-old Billy and our four-month-old second son, Malcolm, left for Europe, then Africa, then back to Europe. For most of the last fifty years I have lived outside the United States, the last five in Nigeria.

7.

Excerpts from an Interview
with Jim Jones

ROBERT WRIGHT, CIVIL RIGHTS
DOCUMENTATION PROJECT

*Jim Jones is a native Arkansan who became the second director
of the SNCC Arkansas Project. After SNCC dissolved, he
continued his activism as the training director of the Federation
of Southern Cooperatives, an organization created in 1967 to
empower African American farmers. He later moved to Texas
where he worked as the director of produce marketing for the
state's Department of Agriculture.*

WRIGHT. This is Robert Wright . . . The date is October 15, 1970. I am
in Atlanta, Georgia, interviewing Mr. Jim Jones or James Jones . . . a former head of SNCC in Arkansas. Okay, Jimmie, I thought we could start off
by getting some of your personal background like where you were born,
where you are from, where you went to school, and how you first got
involved with Arkansas SNCC . . .

JONES. I was born there in Arkansas in a small town called Louisville,
Arkansas, in south central Arkansas.[1] Grew up there on a small farm that
my father owned. Managed to finish high school and graduated from high
school and had a scholarship to Arkansas A & M College . . . After beginning there and I had been in school not a full year, in February, I believe,
there were a . . . series of meetings that was held by a few people on campus

---

Source: Civil Rights Documentation Project, Moorland-Spingarn Research Center, Howard
University

there, talking about the discriminations that existed within the city and among black people . . . I said that I was interested in seeing such segregation brought to an end and there was also another six or seven students who also expressed a similar interest.

WRIGHT. Do you remember many of the people?

JONES. In that group of people there was Bob Wickfield from Little Rock . . .[2]

JONES. There was myself. There was a gentleman named Charles Wiggins from Texarkana, Arkansas, Leon Nash from Pine Bluff, Arkansas, Ben Grenish, who is a student from Philander Smith College who would come and sit in on the meetings with us along with Bill Hansen, who at that time was a field worker with the Student Nonviolent Coordinating Committee . . .[3] So we decided we were going to sit in at Woolworth lunch counter as our beginning approach, when we did, the morning of February 1, 1960, I believe was the day.[4]

WRIGHT. You mean you had these meetings before the sit-in movement started?

JONES. Well, that was when—well, this was '61, a year later.

WRIGHT. Okay, right.

JONES. So we all, we sat in and at that time there was some discussion between us and some students at Little Rock, at Philander Smith College . . . The Chamber of Commerce and all those people and they decided to open up public accommodation facilities. About a year later we came back and decided that Pine Bluff should be a second place and this was when we began. I believe this was February '63, a little bit longer than a year and we decided that we were going to sit in at Pine Bluff . . .

WRIGHT. What did you call yourselves during this time?

JONES. We hadn't named ourselves. We just was a group of students out there doing our thing kinda. When we did start in Pine Bluff with the exact same people involved we sat in for about five days and then we was given the ultimatum by the president of the college, A & M. We had the choice of either continue to sit in at our own expense meaning we would be suspended or we could voluntarily withdraw from college or voluntarily withdraw from the sit-in and come back to school . . . We decided . . . that for those who was not willing to take the risk of being suspended from school to withdraw from the group. We had about three people to withdraw from the group and we had about five I think left . . . We were suspended from school by the president the next week and I think a big turning point was when that became known a lot of political action took place in the state around the suspension of the students . . . When my mother came up she simply wanted to know if I was hurt and I told her everything was fine. That was all she wanted to know. Same thing with my father. Some of the students were reprimanded and my mother made a statement that the press on that day, she was quite satisfied with the decision that I had made . . .

The sit-ins kept going. I think we sat in for about 21 consecutive days and then Woolworth's finally announced that its facilities would be open to all races. Then we began to move around to the Walgreens and the various motels and hotels in downtown Pine Bluff. Once we got to the motels and hotels and then the arrest began to come . . . When the arrest was made of five students, five expelled students, then we had about another 75 students on the college campus that came to protest our arrest . . . At which point we did pick up additional college students, that's when my wife became involved. She was suspended and a number of about 15 additional students . . . became involved and they all were suspended. Then we had 35 or 40 high school students that was marching and picketing. The students who was at the high school was going to be suspended from high school except from one high school which was the Towson Park High School. The principal at that high school was Elijah Coleman. He refused to suspend any student so long as a student didn't miss a class during this picketing or marching downtown . . . Over the weekends we began to try to talk about ways of getting the story of Pine Bluff told outside of Pine Bluff. We invited at that time John Lewis who was chairman of SNCC to come in and speak and we held these small mass meetings. We invited people like Dick Gregory to come in and speak. And then I think the real big turning point in our life was SNCC national office here in Atlanta decided to ask me to come to Atlanta, Georgia, to tell the office our story and they sent me to Washington, D. C.

WRIGHT. Was this one of the conferences?

JONES. Well, this was not exactly a conference but these were meetings that James Farmer organized to try and set up and had me to go and tell the story of Arkansas.[5] That was the very, very first time ever in my lifetime being exposed to . . . speaking to a group and ever traveling and going North . . . I met other organization people. I also met with people who were like rich white people who were giving money to SNCC. I met with those people and it was just one great big ball of fear for me . . . Farmer was interested in folks like myself and other people to overcome those fears and they sent me right back to Chicago . . . I went and sat with the office when they had all these meetings throughout the various white neighborhoods, black neighborhoods where I was guest speaker, you know, shaking, the whole bit . . . I went back to Atlanta. They sent me back to Arkansas and I decided in Arkansas whether or not I wanted to go back to school because it is September now and I said I think I will stay out of school until January and keep on doing this . . . After I did that with fear I had about facing groups, the fear I had about my not having a college education began to drum a little because I began to meet all these people who were running programs or were not college graduates . . . I began to kind of relate to those people and see how they did it and that kind of introduced me to the whole new concept of life and that college was not that important. That was the kind of concept these people had . . . and all these guys began to suggest books for me to read because prior to that I had absolutely no reading in my life . . . So I did this for about 5 months . . . I just didn't have that fear. I had self-confidence. I read a few books. I felt like I was pretty smart. So I really was ready to move and make some decisions on my own . . . what I wanted to learn was political science and history and economics and stuff and I went back to school that coming January and I went and enrolled at the University of Arkansas rather than back at A & M.

WRIGHT. The big school.

JONES. Right and I was specifically going for some very specific kind of things. I wasn't interested in leisure at all . . . I went to school there for one full year . . . all the other stuff was just a waste of my time and that if I could just self learn myself, continue in SNCC . . . I just go buy the book and read it . . . And I came back to Little Rock and . . . discovered where I really wanted to be and that was with the civil rights movement. At that time I was hired for $10 a week as a field representative of SNCC. I worked there five or six months and then I was voted by other field representatives, of which there was about thirteen, to become the state director. And then after that the SNCC national office located in Atlanta was interested in getting me as much exposure as possible and they started sending me to various parts of the country . . . When I came back, SNCC asked me to come work at the central office, and I said that I think what I see is that what is wrong with states like Arkansas is that when people learn certain kind of experiences, they take off . . . I was given some money under the SNCC budget . . . I went to Washington, Chicago, and various places, recruiting staff but I was also specifically concerned about recruiting staff within the state of Arkansas. And the summer of '64 even endorsed my argument on the saturation program that took place when all the northern whites come down because I thought a lot of people really got caught up in a lot of confusion . . . Many local blacks I think develop a very strong inferiority complex because the system that a lot of folks came from under, the plantation kind of thing, that had been replayed with a northern white person. And that was even worse to me because the relationship was so close between that person cause they had worked together, they stayed together and it had developed a kind of one or two year life pattern. Another thing is I think a lot of northern white were very naive to where blacks were or think they were, particularly the southern blacks where I think a lot of people withheld what they really felt because they considered these people being nice people and they were not the same kind of people. So those expressions on the part of local blacks a lot of times went unnoticed or unheard. And I was kind of on the other end of the pole in that I was specifically interested in those kind of voices being heard. And if you will notice during the SNCC development Arkansas never had the big influx of whites from the North and that's why, because I specifically saw that if I'm going to direct this program I have to have some freedom of decision making. One of the decisions that I made is that I'm interested in blacks. If there are a number of blacks in the North interested in coming down, I'll accept all of them, but as far as whites, I've seen too many problems that came out of the Mississippi situation . . .

When the pattern of growth in Arkansas was when Little Rock and Pine Buff desegregated here, a number of other towns kind of followed suit . . . when the staff developed in Arkansas when I was the director there, we had field staff persons . . . in Eastern Arkansas, and Forrest City and Lee County and Mississippi County. This is the black belt, in Arkansas. Now the last we took in those areas was school desegregation. The largest school boycott we had was in Forrest City. That is St. Francis County. That boycott was around the physical planning of the black school . . . we was raising the question of trying to get better facilities . . . Integration wasn't a big question then . . . SNCC itself had started raising the question about integration so it wasn't a real integration push at that time on our part and we, the national position was to raise questions about the facilities of the black schools but the question of whether or not the students continue to go to black schools or choose a white is that SNCC staff person was not to have none input into what direction that took. So the real hard core leaders of those black boycotts did take the direction of going to the white schools, many of them there. So we didn't have a position against that . . . In the beginning of '67 . . . a number of our staff people were non-Arkansasians but non-Arkansasians expressed the position that they thought the political question that SNCC is now raising, that is the most important issue that SNCC ever raised in the country and because of that everybody felt, everybody said that they wanted to pop political organizing at home . . . People there was from other parts, went back . . .

Cause that is when SNCC broke up and my analysis is that the way SNCC had been organized from the very beginning up to that point, it really fulfilled its function. It had no role beyond that because the decision was that everybody would return home and organize at home. So that's what they did. So I had no problem with that decision . . . I personally was glad to see SNCC not to exist beyond that point as a movement umbrella . . . They learned as a result of experiences that you can't keep on organizing and deciding a thing and organizing it for people. You just have to give them a boost in the direction that they go in.

8.

Arkansas Roots and Consciousness

MICHAEL SIMMONS

After working as a field secretary for SNCC in Arkansas and becoming a founding member of SNCC's Atlanta Project, Michael Simmons served a two-and-a-half-year prison sentence as a conscientious objector during the Vietnam War. Upon his release he continued his activism as a longtime employee of the American Friends Service Committee, ultimately working as the director of Southern African Programs and later as director of European Programs. Today he lives in Budapest, Hungary, where he is co-director of the Raday Salon (http://raday.blogs.com), which provides a forum for discussion of various human rights issues.

The historic oppression of black people was the central domestic issue facing the United States during my youth. The resulting civil rights movement began to capture the attention of all Americans and many people around the world. As a young man I became a part of this movement, which shaped the rest of my life.

Growing up in Philadelphia with parents from South Carolina and Georgia, I was always aware that blacks in the South experienced a more virulent form of racism than their northern brothers and sisters. On family trips to visit relatives in the South, I experienced this reality firsthand.

During my childhood in the fifties my two adult brothers—fifteen and seventeen years older than me—joined the Nation of Islam when Malcolm X was living in Philadelphia.[1] He often visited my home. During my grade school years I can recall many intense discussions among my family and my parents' friends about Islam and Christianity and the plight of African

Americans. The killing of Chicago teenager Emmett Till while he was visiting his family in Mississippi in 1955 was the first time that I began to understand the significance of what was being discussed. I realized that this could have been me.

As a sixteen-year-old high school sophomore, I met Bill Crawford, an African American communist who owned a bookstore in Philadelphia. In the early sixties, finding books on black history was difficult to impossible, and Bill's store was a gold mine. Bill's store had copies of Herbert Aptheker's *History of Negro Slave Revolts* and the first volume of the *Documentary History of the Negro People in the United States*. He gave me a copy of the book *The Negro National Question* by Harry Haywood, which put forward a concept of a black nation that corresponded with the political teachings of Malcolm X.

Subsequently, I got to know Max Stanford, founder of the Revolutionary Action Movement (RAM). Max was working on a national committee to support the struggle of Monroe North Carolina NAACP president Robert Williams, who had advocated armed self-defense for the African American community. Discussions with Max about the Marcus Garvey movement and the writings of the black historian J. A. Rogers introduced me to the ideas of two of the twentieth century's architects of Black Nationalism.

Building on Robert Williams's militant stance, the Philadelphia chapter of the NAACP had elected new leadership in 1963. Challenging the historic middle-class orientation of the NAACP, the new president, Cecil B. Moore, sought to transform the NAACP into a working-class activist organization. The first public activity of this new leadership provided me with the opportunity to participate in my first demonstration, which was against employment discrimination in the building trades. The day before I joined the demonstration, there had been a violent confrontation with the police. For the first time I saw that violence toward civil rights activism was not limited to the South.

By the time of my high school graduation I was filled with many contradictory thoughts about the civil rights movement. On the one hand, the public narrative was in support of integration and the nonviolent philosophy of Martin Luther King. Yet my conversations on issues of Black Nationalism and armed self-defense prevented me from adopting this narrative uncritically. This dilemma was heightened by the brutal behavior of the white community and the police in Birmingham, Alabama, and the assassination of Mississippi NAACP leader, Medger Evers. Closely following these debates, I began to feel that SNCC was the one organization that presented an organized structure that incorporated essential aspects of both trends.

In 1964, my friend Dwight Williams, who later joined SNCC with me, and I went to Atlantic City to support the challenge of the SNCC-organized Mississippi Freedom Democratic Party (MFDP) to the "official" Mississippi delegation. I witnessed the duplicity of the Democratic Party leadership as they tried to force the MFDP delegation to accept a compromise that only allowed the MFDP to take two seats. Significantly, I took note that the "leaders" of the civil rights movement justified this compromise as a "practical" solution.

The attack on black people in Selma, Alabama, known as Bloody Sunday, 7 March 1965, led Dwight and me, along with other students and professors, to organize a march of over three thousand people in Philadelphia in solidarity with the Selma Movement. This was the first time that I played a central role in an act of protest, and it led to the formation of a student group that developed programs for the black community surrounding Temple University.

During spring break in 1965, Dwight and I drove to Atlanta to visit the national SNCC office. During the visit we met Jimmie Travis, a Mississippi SNCC veteran who had been shot in the head in 1963 during an assassination attempt on SNCC leader Bob Moses. Upon finding out that we had planned to go to Mississippi, Jimmie encouraged us to bypass Mississippi and go to Arkansas SNCC. He felt that the '64 Atlantic City defeat had created a malaise in the Mississippi movement. He also said that there had been internal struggles over leadership with many white volunteers challenging the leadership structure of SNCC and demanding more say in the organization. Counter posing Mississippi with Arkansas, he said that Arkansas had an organized leadership structure with a more focused and disciplined project. Being enamored with Jimmie, we followed his advice.

Upon our return to Philadelphia we began the process of applying to join SNCC. This included filling out an application through the Philadelphia Friends of SNCC. One aspect of the process was to be interviewed by a white Temple University sociologist. I was very resentful of the fact that this white woman had the power to reject my application to join a black organization. During the interview I realized that she was trying to determine if I were an "angry black man." From my point of view, then and now, the only black person who should have been rejected from a movement to fight the oppression of black people was one who was *not* angry.

We left Philadelphia on 13 June for a thirty-three-hour bus ride to Little Rock, Arkansas. Upon arrival we met other volunteers—black and white—from various states. We remained in Little Rock for a week for an orientation that focused as much on personal safety as it did on the program. During the orientation week I got into an intense argument with a white woman volunteer. I had made the statement that I did not want to ride in a car alone with a white woman. I went on to say that if I did, I would not sit beside her. The volunteer chose to see the statement as a personal attack on her in particular and all white people in general rather than my concern for my—and her—personal security. It was one of the times that I experienced whites viewing a black point of view in terms of its impact on white people. This also occurred during the summer when, during a mass meeting, a volunteer objected to a person saying "white people" instead of "some white people."

After orientation, the volunteers were dispatched to various projects, with me going to West Helena and Dwight going to Forrest City. The Arkansas state project was co-directed by Arkansan Jim Jones and Bill Hansen, a white SNCC veteran from Ohio. The Helena project was directed by Howard Himmelbaum, a white New Yorker who had joined SNCC earlier in the spring. The project was made up of about ten volunteers with equal racial diversity.

The Helena project included the communities of Marvell and Elaine. The work in these communities was focused on the elections of the Agricultural Stabilization and Conservation Services (ASCS). This body had the power to set prices for crops grown in the respective counties and black farmers were often cheated by the ASCS board members. The main SNCC project activities were voter registration and voter education. The work included going door to door in the rural areas outside West Helena to try to get people to register to vote. This was a difficult process. Registering to vote had always been viewed as an act of defiance by whites and there was a history of violent white attacks on potential and actual black voters.

One of the most dynamic activities during the summer was the Freedom School. It had over one hundred children and young adults as regular attendees. The school had regular academic subjects along with African and African American history. As a northerner, it was shocking to me that after all of the armed federal efforts to integrate schools eight years earlier in Little Rock, children still were forced to attend segregated schools.

During the summer we had very little contact with non-SNCC white people and confined our activities to the West Helena black community. The segregated housing patterns meant that we seldom saw white people and security concerns prevented attempts to interact with whites. On one occasion we took a group of young people to the public swimming pool. The security guard at the gate stopped our group and called an official at the site to talk with us. We informed him of the law and that we were exercising our rights under the 1964 Civil Rights Act. During the exchange we noticed that people were leaving the building. When we finally got inside we realized that they had drained the pool and a few minutes later they told us that they were closed for repairs.

My one foray into Helena proved to be the most eventful experience of my time in Arkansas, which stretched from the summer into the fall. One Saturday, while driving a car usually driven by Bill Hansen, I went into Helena to get a part for a minor mechanical problem on the car. While the man behind the counter was helping me he happened to look outside at the car and said, "Ain't that Hansen's car?" As he spoke he began to reach under the counter. Almost immediately, other male customers began to converge around me. Sensing danger I bolted toward the door and jumped into the car. The counter man came to the door with a gun pointed at me. In a total panic, I leaned over practically lying on the passenger seat while starting the car and drove back to West Helena. After talking with my SNCC colleagues I went to make a report to the sheriff. The man who had pulled the gun had already reported the incident to the sheriff but claimed that I had created a ruckus in his store. I was arrested and charged with disturbing the peace and some other charges that I have since forgotten. I immediately made bail. At my trial I was convicted, given a thirty-day suspended sentence, and told to leave the county. Before I left the courthouse the man who had pulled the gun threatened to kill me.

Like most SNCC workers I had a very cynical view of the FBI. However, my criticism was not that they collaborated against the movement but they did not do all that they could do to address injustice. With that in mind I contacted the Arkansas FBI office to make a report on the incident at the store and at the trial. I arranged to meet with an Agent Smart in Little Rock. During a meeting that lasted over two hours I found him to be respectful and sympathetic to my situation. He told me he would file the report but warned me that I should not get my hopes up and that he doubted if anything would be done. Nevertheless, he felt it was important to have a record of these incidents.

Later that summer another SNCC worker and I were assigned to open up a SNCC office in Marianna, Arkansas, in neighboring Lee County. We did not have any contacts in Marianna when we arrived so one of our first meetings was with the local African American funeral director who was a "gatekeeper" and crisis manager in the community. He helped me secure housing with an older woman.

A few days later the funeral director informed us that the sheriff wanted to meet with us. We arranged to meet him at the funeral parlor. The sheriff proceeded to tell us how peaceful "his" town was and that there was no need for people like us. He went on to say that if some trouble started it would tax his human resources and he would have to deputize men, "off the soda trucks" who were not trained law enforcement officers. Therefore, he could not be responsible for what they might do. This veiled threat was very clear to me.

My month-long work in Marianna, in retrospect, was thoroughly compromised by my inexperience. While I developed good contacts I was never able to actually develop an organization or a viable program. Since the summer was coming to an end and most volunteers were leaving I was reassigned to West Helena.

At the end of the summer the community had a big party for all the volunteers. During the event I made the observation that the community was giving a special deference to the white volunteers. My reaction was not one of jealousy but anger over a sense of extreme gratefulness and sub-servience showed to the "good white folks" who "came to help us." None of the white volunteers seemed to think that there was anything wrong with the accolades that they were receiving and could not understand my anger. However, I viewed it as a continuation of the subservient behavior that I had seen displayed by my southern relatives during my youth. The fact that it was being done voluntarily did not lessen the lack of dignity and self-worth that it displayed.

While I was home for a brief post-summer stay in Philadelphia in September, a full-scale confrontation had developed in Forrest City, Arkansas, over school desegregation. Students were boycotting classes and picketing the school board. Over two hundred young people had been arrested and the SNCC worker Millard "Tex" Lowe was charged with some draconian law that would have kept him in jail into the next decade if he was con-victed. Dwight and I rushed back to Arkansas to support the work.

Prior to the protest Cleve Sellers, program secretary for SNCC, and Julian Bond, communication secretary for SNCC, had visited Arkansas. The local authorities automatically assumed that they were responsible for the Forrest City protest and were looking for them. One night a group of SNCC workers were meeting in the SNCC office in Forrest City. One of the workers was a white woman. Late that night we heard an unmistakable knock on the door announcing the police, and we were told to open up and stand against the wall. Knowing the danger to black men being caught with a white woman, we immediately put the woman in a closet in the office before about ten or more police entered. They did not have their guns drawn but they all had five-cell flashlights and clubs in their hands. As we were lined up against the wall listening to threats on our life, I spot-ted my "friend" FBI agent Smart. Excited, I said, "Agent Smart, I . . ." and he cut me off saying, "Shut up, you black sonofabitch!" I was shocked and stunned. My entire experience with Agent Smart was a lesson I have never forgotten.

During that summer I attended a SNCC Executive Committee Meeting in Atlanta with Hansen. I had also gone to a SNCC conference in Mississippi and a seminar at the Highlander Folk School in Knoxville, Tennessee. All of these experiences made me feel that, though well organized and effective, Arkansas SNCC had minimum impact on the direction of the organization as a whole.

During his stay in Arkansas Cleve Sellers asked me if I wanted to become a campus traveler and organize SNCC chapters on southern college campuses. Although I felt guilty about leaving Arkansas I could not reject the offer. So by late October my nearly five-month effort in Arkansas had come to an end.

My experience in Arkansas SNCC had a lasting impact on my future work in SNCC and the movement in general. The most significant aspect of my post-Arkansas experience in SNCC was my participation in SNCC's Atlanta Project. Founded in February 1966 to support the electoral efforts of Julian Bond, the project is known for its promulgation of the Black Power philosophy associated with Kwame Toure (then Stokely Carmichael).

During this period I discovered *The Wretched of the Earth* by Franz Fanon, which focused on how defensive violence played an essential role in the psychological liberation of the Algerian people. Going beyond the issue of violence, Fanon elaborated on the empowering impact that taking control of their lives had on the Algerian community. Reading Fanon helped me contextualize my experiences. I began to reflect on my recent past. Things like talking to a white sociologist as a prerequisite for joining SNCC, the views of many white 1964 volunteers about taking a leadership role in SNCC, and my experiences in Arkansas under a white project director began to crystallize into a view that black control of the civil rights movement was an act of empowerment and capacitation. I began to realize that the process of liberation was as important as liberation itself. Indeed, if the black community felt that it owed its liberation to white people the fundamental problem of subservience to whites would not be addressed. It would only perpetuate a racist paternalism that was as destructive as the overt racism that we were fighting against.

Black Power changed the direction of SNCC and the entire civil rights movement. However, what became known as the Black Power movement has always been an aspect of the struggle of black people for justice and equality. Nevertheless, the dominant historical narrative about Black Power focuses on its impact on white people. Instead of viewing Black Power as an expression of self-determination of the black community, Black Power is viewed as an act of defiance and disrespect by ungrateful, irrational blacks toward the largess of "good white folks." The failure to organize the white community seldom features in this narrative. The discourse on Black Power suggests that it restricted participation in the civil rights movement and it is not addressed as an attempt to expand the movement to the white community. Whites who took the view that if they could not work in the black community they would leave the movement are never critiqued for this myopic political position. Rather they are projected as victims of an extreme group of black nationalists who "infiltrated" the civil rights movement.

In trying to clarify the Atlanta Project's view of Black Power, we wrote the Atlanta Project's "Black Consciousness Paper." The paper was an attempt to clarify some of the issues raised by Black Power. We explained that rather than being an attempt to "throw white people out of the movement" Black Power was an effort to address the fundamental power imbalances between blacks and whites. In part, my understanding of this imbalance and support for Black Power was an outgrowth of my experiences in Arkansas SNCC.

I have spent my life fighting against the oppression of people. Going beyond civil rights, I became a human rights activist. This led me to refuse to be inducted into the U.S. military, resulting in a two-and-half-year jail sentence. Since my SNCC experience, I have spent my life fighting against the oppression of people. These struggles have taken me to four continents. However, the lessons of building democratic grassroots organizations and providing the space for oppressed people to speak for themselves—lessons learned in SNCC—continue to be the foci of all my efforts.

9.

Maeby Civil Rights

SANDERIA SMITH

As a child, Sanderia Smith attended a SNCC Freedom School in Gould. Her mother, Essie Mae (Dale) Cableton, was a prominent local civil rights leader. Smith holds a degree in accounting from the University of Arkansas at Pine Bluff and an M.F.A. in creative writing from Arizona State University. Currently she lives in Dallas, Texas, where she is at work on a novel inspired by her experiences as a youthful supporter of the civil rights movement.

Indoor plumbing was the last significant change in Maeby, Arkansas, before 1964. Until then most colored folks kept outhouses, pigs, chickens, cows, and whatever else in their backyard. Whites threatened to tear down their restrooms and take ownership of their farm animals for years, but nothing ever happened. Finally, the city council passed ordinances, which allowed only flushable toilets and small pets inside city limits. My family installed a commode in the outhouse, called it a bathroom, and started using store-bought tissue instead of newspaper.

We moved all but a few laying hens out to my uncles' farm, with the promise of labor and a prize pig every season. Some people struggled to meet the city's deadline so we all pitched in and by the time we were about finished even I'd learned a few new skills. Because we'd raised livestock in town all my life, I was taken aback by the quality of the air after they were gone.

Folks started concocting stories about the changes long before we were done and I looked forward to hearing more of them during the ensuing years. Telling stories was as common to us as peeling peaches. We intertwined events from the past, present, and future as if they were all one.

Granny was a master storyteller. The way she weaved details made it hard for me to tell what was true or not or if she'd taken part in it. I believed she may have been sitting in the tree when Eve tempted Adam with the apple.

Instead of years of telling how the animals were moved, a much bigger story was lurking in the horizon, one that left the city's ordinances a faint memory and caused fiery debates whenever anyone broached the subject. Even, years later, when our memories had begun to fail, those events remained the topic of discussion at town reunions and family visits. I profess it started the week I sat on the Mourning Bench, but my grandmother Muhdea said it was the day my mama, Esther, returned home from a three-year hiatus in Chicago. In the interest of settling an argument, since they both happened during the same week, we turned to the one thing my great-grandmother, Granny, and most colored folks agreed, it ramped up the summer Mrs. Carrie Dilworth brought three civil rights workers to our house right along with our welfare rations.

In the middle of July when I was eight, I helped Granny look after the children. I'd rather been in the cotton field with my friends instead of babysitting especially when Esther was around. She talked on and on about nothing I cared to listen to. "Don't pin the diaper like that. It'll come loose and stick the baby. You left crud around the edges of the plate. Wash it again." I wasn't listening. Every year I'd pleaded with Granny from cotton picking all the way through cotton chopping season to let me go to the field but she hadn't given in yet.

That morning Esther walked out on the porch, mouth running. "Is the baby wet? When did you check?"

I got up and went in the house.

"You better start answering me. I aint Granny you know." She told the kids to go play in the backyard so they wouldn't follow her down the road. Lured them back there with two pixy stixs, grape and orange.

"Esther, we ain't finish cleaning yet," Muhdea said as she walked past me. "You need to come on back in here till we get done."

By then, Esther had headed up the road. Muhdea walked out on the porch and hollered at her again. She turned the corner and was gone. I moved to the furthest side of the living room. "Your mama just might drive me crazy one day soon. See if that baby will take a bottle and come help me in the kitchen."

Granny came out the kitchen with the bottle. I laid him next to the other two babies in the quilt-patched baby pen, which used to belong to me. I folded a diaper and propped the bottle on it so the milk would flow into the baby's mouth. While I was still getting the baby situated, Aunt Sally knocked at the door as she let herself in the house.

"Mozelle, you in there?" she said, calling Muhdea.

We were supposed to be good to her cause she knew voodoo. She fixed a potion for Uncle Jab to get him to marry her and has helped other women trap their husbands too. Muhdea told me to stop listening to gossip but don't eat or drink nothing she gave me.

Granny sat on the davenport and Muhdea dragged over to the rocking chair. Aunt Sally kept right on talking. "Carrie Dilworth will be here directly." She was out of breath and sat down next to Granny away from the duct-taped seam with the wire sticking out.

"Whew," she continued. "Carrie was just on my street. I came to warn you. She got them people with her too."

Granny rubbed her hand up and down the duct tape, covering the crack. She caught hold of a string, wrapped it around her finger, and pulled it out.

"Now, what people you talking about?" Muhdea said in a way to calm her down.

"Them folks Reverend Jefferson been warning us about. You know them civil workers."

"You sure that's who it is?"

"Yeah, Mozelle. She got a white gal, riding right up there in the front seat with her. Then to top it off, a white man and a colored boy is riding in the back of the truck with the welfare rations. They can't be up to no good." She patted her chest as if it would lower her heart rate. "I had to rush over here and let you know ahead of time." I'd been anxious to see the people who had Reverend Jefferson so fired up. A few folks in town said they'd seen them but they'd kept to the low end of town. I thought Reverend Jefferson had scared them away from our end of town.

The news didn't seem to rile Muhdea as it had Aunt Sally, but sometimes it was hard to tell with her. She believed in not showing emotions in front of other people.

"Well, Sally," Muhdea said. "We can't let Carrie upset us. Best thing to do is pay her no mind. Listen but don't take it in. Reverend Jefferson told us if she can't get folks stirred up, they'll leave and go someplace where people might want to start a ruckus."

"I know you right, Mozell," she said. "But I can't be as calm as you and I don't think other folks will be either. Like I said, a white girl and a colored boy is with her. Take it like you want to. Don't say I didn't warn you."

I went and got her a glass of water. She swallowed it down in two gulps and asked me for another one.

"She'll be here directly. I'm heading on out to warn the rest of the folks before Carrie make it down this way. It'll be a shame for them to get caught off guard like we did."

"You go on then, Sally. I appreciate you letting us know. We'll be ready for her when she gets here."

I handed her the second glass of water and she waved it away. Muhdea closed the screen door behind her, and watched while Aunt Sally walked out the yard and down the road. "You be careful out there in that heat. They said it supposed to get up to a hundred today."

"You watch out for her now, Mozelle. Don't let them talk you into signing up for nothing. Tell everybody you can before hand."

Muhdea sat next to Granny. "What you think Carrie's up to with them white folks?" Granny stayed silent. "I think most of us at First Baptist won't get mixed up with them. Now, Esther." She scratched her wig. "I almost wish she had stayed up North. Can't ever count on her to do the sensible thing." Muhdea couldn't have wished for her to leave more than me. I daydreamed about her sisters calling and telling her they found the pot of gold at the end of the rainbow and she needed to come back and help them spend it. Maybe she'll sign-up with them civil rights folks and they'll take her with them when they leave town.

Muhdea and Granny sat and talked as if I wasn't listening. I knew better than to get in grown folks' conversation. "Don't trouble yourself over Esther," Granny said. "She ain't even told us why she back here. Whatever brought her here might take her back just as fast."

A couple hours later Mrs. Carrie drove up in front of our house with the community's surplus packed in the bed of her green and beige Chevrolet truck. She delivered it every month and folks walked over from all four streets to pick up their food. Our streets weren't paved or had signs with names written on them like Markham or Carol Lane as they had on the white side of town. Our roads were gravel and we named them ourselves. The main road in-between the church and Sister Tucker's store was Front Street, the one behind our house was Back Street, while ours was called Jones Street cause so many family members lived on it, and East of the church was Side Street. We usually gathered in the road, kids played and grown folks talked while we waited for Mrs. Carrie. Nobody came out of their houses to get their rations of hash meat, pressed ham loaf, rice, government cheese, butter, powdered milk, and eggs that day.

We grew most of our food in the garden like whippoorwill, purple hull, crowder, and black-eyed peas; cabbage, turnip, collard, and mustard greens; pinto and butter beans, watermelons, okra, tomatoes, onions, sweet potatoes, cucumbers, and every other kind of vegetable that survived. We raised chickens and hogs in the country. Whatever we didn't grow or raise, we bartered with each other for it. We traded poultry and pork with Mr. Nichols for beef. Items were included in the church announcements. The welfare commodities helped stretch our food in late summer while we waited to slaughter livestock in the fall.

Mrs. Carrie blew her horn two or three times. She hadn't ever had to blow it before. She looked a lot like Granny, tall, thin, long mingled gray and black hair, and high cheekbones like an Indian and proud like giraffes. They could be mistaken for sisters or at least first cousins.

I stood at the screen door. Muhdea walked past me. She had to take after her daddy cause she didn't look nothing like Granny, short, cold black, short kinky hair and wide hips. He died before I was born and ain't no pictures of him.

"Don't you come out here," she said and gave me the eye.

By now, every household had heard the news and waited to take their lead from Muhdea. Reverend Jefferson had business at the county seat and wasn't in town that day. I wondered if Mrs. Carrie planned it that way. Even Sister Tucker hadn't hobbled across the church ground on her cane as much as she liked a reason to talk. She made too much money to qualify for the rations but she came every month anyhow and we shared with her the items she wanted to taste.

Muhdea acted friendly. "Hey, Carrie," she said. "Who you got out here with you?"

Granny came and stood beside me and we both watched the commotion. Muhdea wasn't being phony. It was our way of being kind to visitors whether we liked them or not. Mrs. Carrie seemed proud to introduce the freedom workers.

"Hi, Mozelle," she said. "These are the SNCC workers I've been telling you about for months. They work for the Student Non-Violent Coordinating Committee that's headquartered in Atlanta, Georgia. This here is Lauren Joiner. She came all the way from New York City."

Muhdea shook Lauren's hand.

"She little, ain't she," Granny said.

"Yeah, but she got on a pretty summer dress," I said. "And I like her long straight reddish brown hair."

I wondered if her hair was the same color as the ladies on TV. We watched a little black and white set at Sister Tucker's store. She bought a cellophane cover and put it over the screen. It turned the black and white pictures to color, which changed all the time. On one station, actors' faces were red and then green when the commercial came on. We never knew the true color of their clothes either, but it was a colored TV all the same.

"What his tee shirt say?" Granny said pointing at the white boy. She was only able to read and write her name and was proud of it.

"Power to the People," I said.

Mrs. Carrie introduced him to Muhdea. "This is Jim Johnson. He's from Maine."

Jim wore glasses, jeans, and a tee shirt. "Hello, Mrs. Jones," he said. "It's a pleasure to be here. Thank you for inviting us."

"The pleasure is all mine," Muhdea said. Granny shook her head.

"Where's everybody?" Mrs. Carrie asked.

"They'll be here directly." Muhdea looked back at us.

Mrs. Carrie put a smile in her voice and made her last introduction. "Bob, come up here, Bob." She reached for his hand. "What are you doing all the way back there?" Bob walked around and greeted Muhdea. Granny nudged me. "This is Bob Carlton," she said. "He's from Georgia."

"Too black, ain't he, Granny?"

Muhdea shook his hand. He kept scratching his beard as if bugs were in it.

"Gal, you hush up talking about folks." She was right. I'd gotten caught up in the activities and forgotten my manners. "He is wrinkled and scrubby," she said.

Jeans and tee shirts seemed to be the uniform for civil rights workers. Mrs. Carrie looked around as if she expected to see the people walking down the road. Then she told the three of them about Muhdea. "Ya'll, this here is Mrs. Mozelle Jones. She practically runs First Baptist Church. She works in the fields during the day and at the Roadside Café in the evening." She looked at the white girl Lauren. "The cafe will be one of the first places we integrate." She went right on back to telling them about Muhdea. "Mozelle is raising her grandchildren because their mothers had to leave town to find jobs to support them. Mrs. Jones is a pillar in the community. She's making sacrifices no white mother would ever be required to make."

Mrs. Carrie talked about Muhdea like somebody I'd never met. I stood up a straighter proud she was my grandmother. Granny smiled too. Nobody told me Esther had left town cause she couldn't get a job here to take care of us.

"Standing in the door there is Mozelle's mother Mrs. Pearl and her granddaughter Sarah." She raised her arm in the air and beckoned me with her hand. "Sarah, come on out here and meet everybody."

I looked for the okay from Granny. She nudged me on out the door but I could tell she wasn't happy about it. Muhdea gave me the eye again as soon as I stood next to her. I'm used to getting it from Granny but I didn't know how to read hers.

"Sarah, this is Bob, Lauren, and Jim." I shook hands with them. We smiled. Muhdea grinned so wide I saw her wisdom teeth. "Sarah and my granddaughter Annette are great friends. She'll be riding up to Little Rock with me to pick her up at the bus station in a few weeks. They are two of our shining stars," Mrs. Carrie said.

Granny promised me and Annette before she left for Chicago that I'd be waiting at the Greyhound bus station for her when she got back. I'd never been no more than nine miles from home. Mrs. Carrie said she'd take me to see the capital and some other sights too. I'd been making plans all summer.

"We're starting a Freedom school," Lauren said. "I'm going to teach Negro history. Do they teach it at your school?"

"We learned about a few people like Frederick Douglass and Sojourner Truth," I said.

"I have many books written by and about Negroes," she said. "Would you like to see them sometime?"

"Yes ma'am." I hoped she'd stop asking me questions and I looked at Muhdea to see if I'd been talking too much.

Lauren opened her mouth to say something else but we saw the neighbors, two to three of them paired together walking toward the truck. Mostly older women and children too young to be in the field like Mrs. Mildred and her son Junior. Sister Ollie clacked along on her cane with Rosy, who was drying her hands on her apron. She'd been washing dishes. Sister Tucker walked with Mr. Bolden. He still had the pruning shears in his hand. Funny how I'd never noticed that everybody looked as if they'd stopped in the middle of work. We were cleaning the house and feeding the babies before Aunt Sally interrupted us. I couldn't recall a time that I'd stopped by anyone's house and they were sitting around doing nothing.

The civil rights workers told us why they were in our town. We were fortunate to have them here. Other cities needed their help. Mrs. Carrie's long history of service throughout the countryside was the reason they chose our town. "I've worked long and tirelessly. Now I feel as if I have an army of support. With God's help, we will get some things done this time," Mrs. Carrie said. "These young people left college and their families to be here.

It sounded like the same old things Mrs. Carrie had been saying every month when she delivered our commodities and nobody heard her. We needed change. We had much less than the white folks. We must demand equal rights. They were going to do whatever it took to help us integrate. The white folks had good schools with proper heating, new books, new athletic uniforms, and state of the art facilities.

"You have worn out-dated books and wood stoves," Jim said. As if we didn't already know it. "I was taken aback when Mrs. Dilworth showed me the high school. There are actually rats living in it. You have to register to vote and integrate the schools. I will be working with you to get it done."

How was he planning to help us if he was afraid of rats? No man around was scared of them. If he couldn't handle rats what would he do when he felt the wrath of Reverend Jefferson?

"President Johnson passed the Civil Rights Act this month. Does anybody know what that means to you?" Bob said. Nobody answered. "We will explain what it means to you and what we are going to do to enforce these rights." He wiped the sweat off his face with his hand. A couple of grasshoppers jumped out of the Johnson grass into the bed of the truck. Where were the mosquitoes when we needed them?

"There shouldn't be any white only and colored only signs to keep us separated," Tim added. I thought they'd sound more like Reverend Jesse Jackson but they talked like every day, not like they were giving a speech.

A few people clapped. "Looks like rain, Carrie," Mrs. Mildred said. Wasn't a cloud in the sky. Any other time Mrs. Carrie would've known that meant give me my food I need to go.

"Ask yourself, why do you live on one side of the tracks and them on the other?" Bob said. I listened. "We're going to organize. We're going to register and vote. First we have to remodel Mrs. Dilworth's two-story house."

"We're going to live upstairs and make a library, freedom school, and meeting hall out of the downstairs rooms," Jim said. If they can make anything out of that old, run-down, falling apart, unpainted house, I was sure they'd be able to get us some new books.

"How would you like to attend the all-white school?" Jim asked me.

"I'm fine at the colored school, sir. We don't mingle," I said. Before he asked me any more questions and I said something Reverend Jefferson wouldn't be proud of I went back inside and stood at the door next to Granny.

"They ain't Moses and we sure ain't the children of Israel," Granny said. "How them young folks think they will lead us? Men and women who ain't married, and white and colored living under the same roof. Carrie opening a big can of bait and they might get out and crawl all over Maeby. She won't never learn."

"Never learn what? What did Mrs. Carrie do? Did she do something to you?" I said.

"Wouldn't be Carrie if she wasn't stirring up something. She means well. It just don't turn out that way."

"What you mean by that?" I asked but she was done talking. I wanted to ask about my trip to Little Rock.

When Esther first left for Chicago she walked up to the Esso station with her brown striped suitcase, waited on the side of the highway and flagged the bus down. There wasn't a bus station in Maeby. The closest was further north in Pine Bluff. Muhdea took us up to the highway so we could wave goodbye. My youngest brother Nod was too young to know what was happening, two months old. Esther was the oldest but the last one of her sisters to leave home. Nod was her fourth child and she was still in her early twenties. "Don't forget me," she said. Before she came home the other day, I'd pretty much forgotten her altogether.

Annette wrote that the greyhound dog doesn't get off the side of the bus and run along beside it like it did on TV. I wanted to see for myself. That was one thing I didn't want to take her word for. It looked so real on TV.

What if Granny wouldn't let me go now that Mrs. Carrie had these folks in town? I pretty much knew I wouldn't be riding all the way to Little Rock with white folks. Why did Mrs. Carrie have to bring them here before we could go get Annette?

"Can't you hear, gal?" Granny said as she pushed me away from the door, jarring me out of my thoughts. "You don't need to be listening to them folks anyhow. You better start your work before Mozelle get back in here."

Granny walked outside and got our rations off the truck while Jim was still talking. She didn't say a word to nobody. Granny took the box with our name on it out the bed of the truck and walked right back in the house without saying a word. Some of the folks turned their whole body around and watched her until she disappeared in the house. All they wanted to do was get their food and go home to their chores. Mrs. Carrie and them civil rights workers were wasting their breath. Reverend Jefferson had told us not to pay them any mind.

Right after Granny got back in the house, Esther walked up. Bob was asking for volunteers to come down to Mrs. Carrie's old house and help them change it from an eyesore to a community center. Nobody raised their hand. Then her voice came out of the crowd similar to that of the people who lived around here but citified.

"What kind of help do ya'll need?" Esther said.

I walked on back to the kitchen. Granny handed me a can of hash meat and I put it on the shelf, wood planks nailed to the wall. We kept canned and dry goods on one side of the wall and dishes, pots, and pans on the other. I put the cheese and eggs in the ice box. "I'm sorry, baby, hand me back that can of hash." She took down a pan to cook it. "Mozelle will be out there all day messing with them people. Carrie acts like she don't know we got things to do and the others is too ignorant to tell her they got to get supper on the table. They families will be hungry when they get home from the field." I handed her a can of hash meat. "The last thing they needed was for your mama to show up asking questions. She wouldn't be studying them if that old straggly beard colored boy wasn't out there."

"Granny, what if the things Mrs. Carrie said made sense to the people. Our stuff is worse than the white folks. Their side of town looks a whole lot better than ours."

"You or Carrie ain't telling me nothing I don't already know. We make do, child. We make do and we'll be fine without Carrie bringing this mess here. You deserve better but I don't want no heap of mess. What Carrie doing might turn families against each other. It may even start a riff between some folks and the church. You see what I'm trying to tell you?"

I didn't but I was sure if Granny said it—it was right. She wouldn't take up time trying to explain it if it wasn't important. Folks in our town got along fine and I'd be all right if I never sat in a cafe. I stacked the rest of the food on the shelves. While we talked it struck me that this might turn Annette and me against each other.

"Granny, what about Annette? Will this only be with grown folks or can children turn on each other, too?"

"It'll be a bad thing if children get caught up in grown folks' mess. You remember what happened to them little girls in Alabama. That's what happen when you bring in folks from the outside who don't know our ways. We'll take each day as it's given to us. Right now she ain't here so no need of worrying about it. We have to wait and see how all this pans out. Ain't no telling what'll happen around here with a white woman and a colored boy under the same roof. The whites won't like that at all." She shook her head as if she was trying to shake something loose in her brain, and continued. "If Carrie wanted to start some trouble with the whites and colored she done went and got herself a whole heap of it now."

I started to ask her if I would still be able to go to the bus station to pick up Annette. I felt it wasn't the right time and kept quiet. I'll do what she said and wait to see how it all panned out.

I'll write Annette and ask her if she had any ideas on getting around this mess. She was good at coming up with ways to stump grown folks. Them civil rights people wouldn't keep me from seeing the Greyhound bus station.

Muhdea came in the kitchen and started peeling white potatoes for supper.

"Carrie still out there?" Granny said.

"Yeah, but she finally gave the folks their packages. They left as soon as she handed it to them. Esther Mae is still out there though."

"Oh Lord," Granny said.

"Oh Lord is right. I opened my mouth to say something to her but had second thoughts before I said anything. I figure I'll tell her to keep her distance later tonight," Muhdea said.

I walked back to the screen door and looked outside. Sure enough, Esther was laughing it up and running her mouth like an open hydrant.

10.

Excerpts from an Interview with Bob Cableton

ROBERT WRIGHT, CIVIL RIGHTS DOCUMENTATION PROJECT

Robert Cableton was born in Arkansas and raised in Mississippi. He worked as a SNCC field secretary in Gould, Arkansas, between 1965 and 1967. While in Arkansas, he married Essie Mae Dale, a local civil rights activist. Later he returned to Indianola, Mississippi, where he died in 2007 at the age of sixty-eight.

WRIGHT. This is Robert Wright, the date is September 24, 1968, and I'm in Indianaola, Mississippi. I'm interviewing Mr. Bob Cableton, who is a former field secretary for the Student Nonviolent Coordinating Committee in Arkansas . . .

CABLETON. I was born in Arkansas and brought up in Mississippi as a farmer . . . December of '64, I believe it was—or '63—I'm not clear on it— some whites infiltrated the state of Mississippi; it is called the Summer Project, I believe . . . I more or less was lured into the movement because of the things in Mississippi that most black Mississippians at that time was afraid of, and that is the white man, what he would think and how he would react to one's being involved in a so-called Civil Rights Movement . . . And I was reluctant, to be very honest. I was very reluctant. At that time, I was working at Ludlow's, owned and operated by white people—

WRIGHT. This is in Indianola?

Source: Civil Rights Documentation Project, Moorland-Spingarn Research Center, Howard University

CABLETON. Right. And more and more, I would see these people walking to and fro in town and in the country areas, trying to get people out to register; talking about MFDP.[1] And so, I felt, being a Mississippian, myself, that I—I felt that I was being walked on, in a sense, by the northerners from Philadelphia, San Francisco, various northern cities, coming to Mississippi to liberate me. That made me feel sort of little, but I never told a person about this. And so, at this particular time, John Harris was here. I think he's from San Francisco—no, I'm sorry, from Alabama—

WRIGHT. Birmingham.

CABLETON. Birmingham, Alabama. John Harris, he was the project director here in Sunflower County. He wasn't really to me an inspiration because to me he didn't have the people heart. To me, John was a glory boy, but maybe at the time I didn't understand John . . . Well, John Harris, as far as he was concerned, it seems that—I don't know, it just might have been an element of jealousy between John and myself—but I tried to get on SNCC staff here, but John always told me it was better to be a part of MFDP, than to be a part of SNCC, as such . . . Well, maybe he could have been right, I don't know, but Ben Goodings from Arkansas—you ever know Ben? Reverend Benjamin Goodings?[2] We met in Knoxville . . .

WRIGHT. When was that?

CABLETON. At the workshops . . . on Federal programs . . . And being I told him about the situation in Mississippi, he asked me was I working for SNCC or what my position was. I said no. I said in Mississippi I can't get a hold, you know, because the brothers, you know. He say, well, I tell you what—say, I believe I can use you—you look like a good organizer. I believe I could use a good guy like you in Arkansas. I said, I don't know, man. Tell you what, he said, here's my address and phone number . . . So I gave Greenwich a ring and told him what was going on.[3] So, the next thing I know, Greenwich pops up to pick me up to take me over to Arkansas. So there in Arkansas, he was the state project director, and our office was in Little Rock on Ninth Street. At that time the staff was integrated; Bill Hansen and other whites was involved in the movement.

WRIGHT. Was Jimmy Jones working there then?

CABLETON. Oh, yes—no, pardon me—at this time Jim Jones was project director, right; because Jim had to stop work and go to school . . . In Arkansas I helped to organize an organization called the Gould Citizens for Progress.

WRIGHT. This was in Gould, Arkansas?

CABLETON. Right, Lincoln County.

WRIGHT. How far is this from Little Rock?

CABLETON. About 76 miles.

WRIGHT. Was that out in the country?

CABLETON. Yeah, it's a cotton town.

WRIGHT. I see. Out in the Delta area bout?

CABLETON. Yes, very flat country. And I had heard so many stories about Arkansas being a liberal state, that things didn't happen in Arkansas like they did in Mississippi, you know, in terms of the black and white man. So I went there by myself—no other person that worked in the area with me doing county work, no transportation, no nothing. And so what happened, we thought of organizing the Gould Citizens for Progress, feeling that this would involve every person within the limits of Gould and the township. Okay, so we did . . . We start to getting counter-actions from the so-called older leadership, like the preachers, the teachers . . .

WRIGHT. How did you organize? You didn't go to these traditional leaders at first, you just—what did you do?

CABLETON. Well, that was one of the traditions of SNCC is to do this, but, as you know, the older people, during those times and even now, are the wrong people to go to for the kind of work that SNCC was engaged in; especially if they was known as local leaders at first. Okay, these people were known as local leaders in their civic clubs and their church and the deacons. They was by shouters, and all, and so you—a young man with a beard could not get through to them, but that was my first attempt . . .

WRIGHT. When did you go over there?

CABLETON. I haven't the date, exactly.

WRIGHT. Was it right after the November thing? Early '65?

CABLETON. Right after early '65 . . . April—something like April—and things, like was beautiful for the Gould Citizens for Progress until the power structure began to deal directly with me as a project director for the Student Nonviolent Coordinating Committee; meaning, if they could stop my maneuver, which was very ugly, then that would kill the Gould Citizens for Progress, you see. Okay, their first attempt was to be liberal, was to be nice; say you people are this, that, and the other, and you're pretty good folk; but when we first waged our first boycott on the white merchants of Gould . . . it was just to exercise black power in terms of the dollar, and to get respect from the white side of the city. I wasn't as militant, then, as I am now . . . And when this thing happened-—I know exactly how it happened-—the Ku Klux Klan. Just like that. And so they waged a complete boycott—spontaneous SNCC didn't have anything . . . to do with. They did it on their own. Now, naturally, SNCC would be accused. We were accused of waging a boycott on the downtown area.

Okay, we boycotted the schools in Gould the session of . . . '65–'66 school year—that brought . . . about turmoil right there and after the boycott. Out of the boycott, one merchant went completely out of business.

Then in Arkansas they would use—the same as Mississippi—the best Tom to stand things still. They would send the best Tom to the mass meetings to bring back the messages to the power structure . . . And one year after the Gould Citizens for Progress was organized a two-story building was burned by the Ku Klux Klan, which was our headquarters. These types of things. About in February '67 I made a mistake. I was arrested with four charges hung on me: drunk, disturbing the peace, attacking an officer, and obscene language—cursing, or whatever you want to call it—which cost me nine months on the county farm and a $500 fine.

WRIGHT. Nine months! Did you stay there the whole time?

CABLETON. No. Attorney George Walker[4] from Little Rock was my lawyer. I got an appeal from that . . . Served 11 days in the penal farm in Phillips County, and I made it out through legal assistance, and the case now is pending in federal courts.

WRIGHT. How did the Arkansas project of the state, as a whole—all the people working on it—how did they relate to the rest of the SNCC organization, as far as its activities in Mississippi and Georgia, places like that was? It seemed like Arkansas never got much publicity; and there weren't that many resources put into it. Did you feel you were being cheated or stuff like that, or did you think the project didn't deserve that much attention, or what?

CABLETON. I know the project deserved that much attention, you see. And not only did the project deserve that much attention—not only in Arkansas but any place that SNCC had set up—the project needs attention. But what did happen is this. You know, in each state where there is a SNCC project [that] was usually headed by a person that was able to muster up enough publicity to make SNCC what it were. But apparently— well, okay, it seemed to me Arkansas, was a state known from 1957, I believe, to be a quote, an "NAACP state" because of the Daisy Bates ordeal, and that's one reason why SNCC didn't get the kind of attention, I believe, that it got in Mississippi. And Arkansas, too, as I said earlier, supposed to have been a liberal southern state, you see, but I would like to say here that Lincoln County, I believe, is the poorest county in the world. I believe you'll find more rednecks in Lincoln County than you would find in the whole state of Mississippi . . .

WRIGHT. And you say that they have the same kind of terrorism as in Mississippi?

CABLETON. Same kind. Same kind or worse . . .

WRIGHT. Are there people still in Arkansas working for SNCC? Just when did they leave and what do you think the impact was of SNCC people working in Arkansas? Was anything at all accomplished?

CABLETON. Yes, something was accomplished. I'll have to say this for

SNCC. Anywhere the SNCCer worked for over a period of three months, she did something good for somebody. I'm not saying that everybody in SNCC was—how you say it, were Moseses or what have you, but you had some real good people and some hard-nosed people in SNCC. And now, I think what you could do is go to Gould, Arkansas, or any other area where I worked in Arkansas, and I think SNCC's banner has been carried high. I think so because, actually, in Gould, the people didn't know anything about, apparently, a movement until SNCC was there. Okay, NAACP was there but they only met in a small church and drank coffee and went back home. And the big shots were the only people who attended the meeting; the little people though they had to pay to go in. So this is the type of thing that you had in Gould . . .

The first thing we talked about was their dues for our meeting. Is the local project directors able to go back to the various project areas and self-subsistent, be supported by your community? My answer was yes, but the question is, what people want to know, in rural areas, and anywhere that they're connected with a national organization is, is the national organization concerned about them, in this particular locality, as they are concerned about the national organization. You see what I'm saying? So, I think the Gould Citizens for Progress found out that SNCC didn't see them, they didn't recognize them, you see; and I tried to keep this covered up because people would ask me, well, you never get a call from the national office? What's happening in Atlanta? So it put me in a position to have to lie for Atlanta, until I got tired of lying for Atlanta. And I think it's us, we are the Gould Citizens for Progress. And I've had people in the Gould Citizens for Progress go further and to suggest, when . . . they found out that SNCC was broke . . . let's organize here to take up money and send in to the national office to keep SNCC alive . . . I had to tell people not to send their money to the national office is because the national office did not respond positive to the Gould Citizens for Progress . . .

WRIGHT. So you think it was different in other states? I mean, SNCC's relationship to the communities in the project.

CABLETON. Right, and the project director, as such, projecting programs—

WRIGHT. Oh, I see. So you're saying that the project director in Arkansas, maybe if you had a different project director it would have been different? Or one with a name?

CABLETON. Right. Ones that were willing to project programs; the kind of programs that were going to the people, you see, instead of being caught up in state programs—

WRIGHT. Like state elections and stuff?

CABLETON. Things like that and fumbling around, getting to catch these dollars that these politicians are throwing out . . . That happened to SNCC in Arkansas. The next thing is what happened to SNCC in Arkansas is Bill Hansen. No black person from no northern city in this country could get along with white Bill Hansen, and he had black constituency within the leadership of the Student Nonviolent Coordinating Committee in Arkansas to keep him in a power position, which may, in a real sense, force the black people out of Arkansas. But this is what happened in Arkansas . . .

WRIGHT. What was Jimmy Jones' relationship to Hansen?

CABLETON. Jimmy Jones was a puppet . . . as far as I am concerned. And after me spending hours at night thinking what is wrong with the Arkansas project and coming up with this. What is wrong with the Arkansas project? Mississippi is just across the river; we could even form a coalition, I said to myself. You dig it? And be just a dash of SNCC . . . If our tactics are so wrong in Arkansas, why can't we cross the river and find out what's happening in Mississippi, our sister state? Things are beginning to die, die, die, die. As a matter of fact, I feel that some of the project directors, or the so-called leadership personnel in SNCC, actually wanted SNCC to die at that time it died; to put them in power positions in the state.

WRIGHT. Do you know if they were black or white, or both?

CABLETON. Black. SNCC project directors were black. You know how we worked . . . maybe I'm the project director, just say, for the Third Congressional District. Look what you have in the Third Congressional District. You have sheriffs of each county . . . Maybe out of eight counties—well then, you have eight sheriffs there. Maybe these eight sheriffs have a meeting and say [give] him $6000 to hush his mouth, or offer him a job . . . You see what I'm saying? These things happen in Arkansas . . .

Bill Hansen could not accept the fact of working under the auspices of a black, a black leadership.

WRIGHT. He was project director for a long time?

CABLETON. He was, right—for a while—and he was able to maneuver in such a way that he could . . . fold or twist the minds. Jim Jones has a very strong mind, and I questioned how Bill could do him that way . . .

WRIGHT. Did you bring all this up in meetings or something?

CABLETON. Oh, no. I wouldn't have lasted long enough to organize the Gould Citizens for Progress. If you brought things up like that, you wouldn't last long . . .

11.

Lessons from SNCC—Arkansas 1965

NANCY (SHAW) STOLLER

Nancy (Shaw) Stoller graduated from Wellesley College in 1963. After suspending her studies to work with SNCC, she earned a Ph.D. in sociology from Brandeis University in 1972. Today she is a research professor of community studies and sociology at the University of California, Santa Cruz. In 1982, she was denied tenure due to her activist scholarship. However, in a 1987 land-mark settlement, Stoller was awarded tenure, back pay, and damages. Her research and activism concern issues of racial equality, healthcare, prison conditions, and equal rights for sexual minorities.

It was early February 1960. I was a first-year student at Wellesley College, an elite women's school in a suburb of Boston. I had accepted an offer to enroll because I thought it would challenge me academically and provide a welcome change from the segregated environment of my childhood in Hampton and Newport News, Virginia.

Wellesley turned out to be virtually all white, with quotas set for both Black and Jewish students, but with significantly more Jews than Blacks, I could see the Black quota, but it was not until years later that I realized I was part of a Jewish quota. My Wellesley cohort was filled with debutantes and private school graduates. Those who had any politics at all seemed to be conservative Republicans. I wondered how I would survive socially even if I passed all my courses.

Four months after my arrival, in early February, the *Boston Globe* reported the beginning of a "sit-in" movement at the lunch counter of the Greensboro, North Carolina, Woolworth five and dime store. Television news showed the sit-ins as well as the beginning of a support movement in the North that was characterized by sympathy pickets of Woolworth's. I gathered three other staff members from our college newspaper; we made some signs and crossed through the college gate to the local Woolworth store. Thus our sympathy picket and my direct-action career began in February 1960. At seventeen, I had become a local activist and leader.

That summer while living with my parents near Washington, D.C., I got involved with the D.C. area Non-violent Action Group (DC NAG) by joining their picket line at the segregated Glen Echo Amusement Park. DC NAG was a founding member of SNCC, with several of its members traveling to the organizing meetings held in spring and summer of 1960 under the tutelage of Ella Baker. As a NAG member, I participated in sit-ins throughout eastern Maryland, worked on food and clothing drives for Black southern families deprived of jobs and homes due to voter registration attempts or other activism, and did other support work for southern organizing. I spent all my college vacations whenever I wasn't working— summer, winter, Thanksgiving—with my DC NAG community. Stokely Carmichael, Courtland Cox, Cleve Sellers, and Mike Thelwell were all DC NAG activists. Stokely was an especially good friend, and we continued to be in touch long after the demise of SNCC in the late sixties.

When the opportunity arose to work in Prince Edward County, Virginia, in the summer of 1962, I went there via the Northern Student Movement and the Prince Edward County Christian Association. There were maybe ten to twelve of us from the Boston area who worked in Freedom Centers, which were set up to teach reading and writing to elementary schoolchildren who had been out of school for the past three years, because the whites in the county preferred to have no public schools if the alternative would be integrated schools. Prince Edward County was one of the original counties in the *Brown v. Board of Education* lawsuit. And here it was eight years later . . .

I graduated from Wellesley in 1963 and started graduate school right away. A year later in December, I dropped out and went to work full time for SNCC. SNCC had grown enormously from its origins in 1960, evolving from a loose collection of direct-action organizations to a central office in Atlanta with field workers coordinating large projects throughout the South. Although the Mississippi Freedom Summer brought massive attention to SNCC, it also strained the leadership of the organization, especially as some volunteers refused to go home after the summer, insisting that no one could tell them what to do. SNCC leadership felt that there were "too many" hangover (white) volunteers from the 1964 Freedom Summer project, but I was brought on in a staff position anyway because I had a long history with the organization and was thought to be a responsible organizer. And most importantly, Stokely, a core member of SNCC's leadership team, vouched for me.

Arkansas was in the hinterlands of SNCC publicity and consciousness, in some ways a good thing for the members of the Arkansas Project. I'd heard the project itself was much calmer than others. On the other hand the state was not thought of as a Deep South place, even though its eastern half was dominated by the Mississippi Delta and race politics of plantations, segregation, and poverty. So I was going to a project and a state that were marginalized in both the national consciousness and in SNCC.

By January I was in Little Rock beginning my duties. The first day I got my photo taken, "just in case you disappear and we need to use it." My salary started: $10/week. I moved in to a one-bedroom shared SNCC apartment in an all-Black housing complex across the street from Philander Smith College, also mostly Black. My roommate was Arlene Wilgoren, another white woman from Boston. We often had others sleeping on the living room floor.

Other members of the project during that time were Bill and Ruthie Hansen, Jim Jones, Ben Grinage, and various volunteers from around the U.S. During the latter part of my time there, we were joined by my boyfriend, later to be my husband, Donald (Kwame) Shaw, an African American artist, printmaker, and civil rights activist from Boston. Don was assigned to the West Helena and Forrest City office of SNCC because we were afraid that if he and I were in the same city, we might forget to stay far apart and the consequences could be dangerous for him, for us, and for SNCC's work.

Most of the time I worked out of the Little Rock office. My primary job, assigned by the SNCC office in Atlanta, was coordinating the Freedom Centers within the state. This meant getting supplies distributed and dealing with details like phones, transportation, and other communication challenges. The United Auto Workers (UAW) in Detroit donated four or five Dodge sedans—chosen because they were the fastest cars of their type. We had a lot of driving to do around the state and we wanted to have a good chance to outrun either the KKK or, if necessary, the police. They also sent us a bright yellow 3/4-ton truck so we could deliver supplies. Because of my job, I got first rights on driving the truck, which was a big thrill.

One of the great things about SNCC was that when a person could do something, SNCC philosophy made it clear that no one could say, well he isn't educated, or she is just a woman. So women in SNCC asserted their skills and got respect. Most of the people I worked with in SNCC from 1960 to 1965 were just too busy trying to get things done and valuing each

body in the struggle to hold on to traditional roles. In fact, from the start, it was traditional roles—of racial subservience—that were being challenged by SNCC. As the required roles of race lost value in the civil rights movement, people seemed to see that the expectations of subservience by young people and women were also inappropriate. At the same time, I felt I often got more respect from African American coworkers (male and female) than from white men in our project. I think that there was a deeper respect in the Black community for the strengths of women than in the white world.

Our office also put out the *Arkansas Voice,* a monthly newspaper, modeled on the *Student Voice,* which was published by SNCC's Atlanta office. We started our state paper because someone donated a press. Atlanta sent us a volunteer who figured out how to make it work; the next thing I knew I was writing articles on our various projects around the state.

In late February, we heard that the cafeteria in the state capitol was still segregated. No blacks allowed. Given that the public accommodations act had been passed—years ago, that the sit-in movement was five years old, and this was after all, a *state capitol.* We knew we had to do something. We would have a sit-in.

We developed a plan, discussed our options—what if we were arrested? What if we were served?—and selected a day to have our sit-in.

On March 11, 1965, a group of us, both SNCC workers and local supporters, arrived at the cafeteria. First we confirmed the segregationist policy: I selected an item and paid for it; then a Black member of our group entered the line, selected an item and was refused when he tried to pay. The rest of our group joined us at the start of the cafeteria line. The line came to a complete halt. Now, no one was being served, Black or white. I don't remember how long we stood there, but I do remember well that suddenly the hallway behind us was filled with state troopers telling us to leave. No one moved. We were sure we'd be arrested. But no. Instead they started hitting us with billy clubs and driving us up the stairs. Eventually we found ourselves outside the now-blocked doors of the capitol on its broad patio and stairs leading down to the street.

We walked back to the SNCC office to plan again. Twice more we went to the cafeteria, each time recruiting new people willing to be beaten by the police. The third time, an unknown person threw some kind of gas bomb and the hallway stairs up to the air was filled with droplets that stung the eyes and made breathing difficult. It wasn't tear gas, but something worse. Soon we were not only hit and bruised but also gasping and vomiting.

Soon a lawsuit filed by the NAACP came before a judge in Little Rock. I testified about being able to buy lunch, as a white person, while the Black SNCC worker gave his testimony about being denied service. Within a few days, the decision came back: The cafeteria must be open to all or stay closed. The following Monday it reopened, now for everyone.

While most memoirs of life in SNCC center on the bravery, creativity, and hard work of SNCC staff and volunteers, there was also a painful side. There were many internal conflicts—arguments about priorities, race, sexism, tolerating the whims and personalities both of the volunteers and of the staff. There was competition for publicity and leadership.

I attended the SNCC Waveland conference in Mississippi soon after I began my new affiliation with the Arkansas project. This conference was characterized by intense emotions (including a lot of drinking every night). There were daily—and nightly—discussions about democracy versus education and privilege as sources of power, white-black dynamics, grassroots leadership challenges, the stresses of growth, and the relationship between the Atlanta office and the field projects. Several projects had recently experienced violent attacks. Stress was high, and some people were at the breaking point emotionally.

At Waveland, aside from the lengthy processing and arguments about the shape of SNCC membership and leadership, many got drunk, and a fire was started in one of the rooms—I remember seeing the trash and the ashes. At least one woman reported being raped. We all knew that these things were a result of the enormous stress that the staff had been under during the preceding summer and into the fall. (It was only a few months since Freedom Summer and the deaths of Chaney, Goodman, and Schwerner.) But no matter how difficult things were within the organization, we couldn't afford negative publicity. Even violence within the organization had to be kept hidden. I had to face this personally as a victim of violence in Arkansas.

One night in Little Rock someone organized a party. It was mostly students from Philander Smith and those of us who lived in the apartments across the street were invited. I remember going with my roommate Arlene. Someone, a guy from the college who had been to some of our actions and occasionally hung out at our main office, walked me back to our apartment. I'll call him Y. As I stepped inside the door to the empty living room, Y leaned in and kissed me. I wasn't interested and quickly stepped back. He stepped in and pulled the door shut behind him. I tried to say goodnight and open the door to get him out, but Y guarded it with his back and started pushing me toward the apartment's bedroom. I struggled and told him to leave. This struggle went on for what seemed like ten to fifteen minutes and included my going to our living room balcony to call out for help. No one responded. I remember being shocked that although there were lights on around the apartment complex, no one came to a window or called out: "Are you OK?"

Everyone in the complex knew which was the SNCC apartment and that two white women lived there. We were the only whites in the entire apartment complex at that time. I felt a sinking sensation: no one wanted to get involved. No one cared that I was calling for help. Or maybe they cared but didn't have the courage, or the foolishness, to act.

Eventually, Y did rape me, on one of our mattresses. Then he got up, said goodbye, as if it were something normal, and left. It was as if my "No's" were just a usual part of the process. I felt so defeated. Not only did he seem to feel imperviously casual about this, I knew that my options to respond were severely limited.

I couldn't call the police. He was Black and I was white. It would be a disaster all around: for him as a black man accused of assaulting a white woman; for me as a white female member of a civil rights organization and therefore considered a "nigger lover" anyway; and for our local SNCC project and the Little Rock Black community, because it would take attention away from the movement and put it on this sordid mess.

I talked with my roommate, who listened sympathetically. By the next day, I knew what I wanted and I got it.

I wanted SNCC to ban him from the office and from any activity that SNCC was involved with. He could not come to any rally, march, demonstration, or sit-in. And he would be told why: that they knew what he had done, that SNCC did not tolerate that kind of behavior, and that therefore he was exiled permanently. I spoke with the two Black staff members I trusted most in our project. Another SNCC member offered to beat Y up, but I was opposed. We were supposed to be a nonviolent group and I for one, did not want to be part of using violence, even on someone who had already been violent. Although I was not a complete nonviolent Ghandian, since I thought it was OK to defend yourself when someone tried to kill you, I did not—and still don't—believe in choosing violence when your life is not immediately under threat. And I strongly believed in the nonviolent strategy for the movement. Someone agreed to tell Y what we had decided.

As far as I know, our male SNCC members did not beat up Y. But he never showed up at another SNCC event during the next eight months that I was in Arkansas. When my partner Don arrived two months later, he also wanted to confront my attacker, but I dissuaded him. I wanted it to be in the past with no further attention wasted on Y. And so it was, as far as I know.

This experience within Arkansas SNCC, of creating a community response to personal violence, has stuck with me throughout my life and reinforced my belief that turning to the law must always be a later response and that the first strategy should always be to think about the victim, the community, and the healing process and then to strategize a nonviolent way ahead. While I gradually felt personally safe and did change my behavior around men I didn't know, I didn't speak publicly for several years about the incident or our response to it. I did not want my story to feed into racist perceptions of Black male–white female relationships, so I thought long and carefully about how to share the complexity of my experiences during that spring in 1965.

I returned to graduate school in the fall and continued to work on issues of racism, primarily with the Boston Action Group on access to jobs and with People Against Racism, an organization focused on working to build a movement in the white community. For the last thirty years, I have been involved in various social change movements. From my experience in SNCC, I learned democracy, compassion, anti-elitism, how to listen, and how to laugh at myself. I also discovered the incredible power of everyday people when they put their minds to a task.

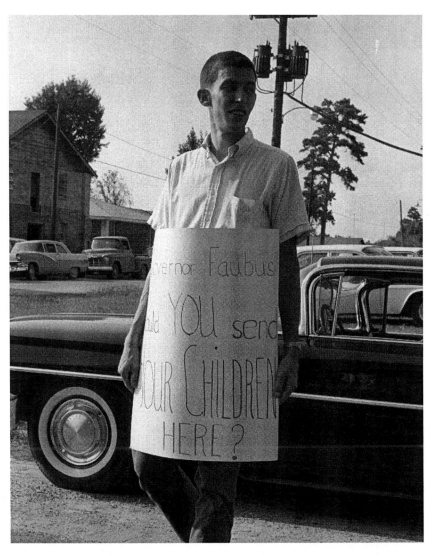

Bill Hansen demonstrating in Pine Bluff, 1963. Photo from the Orval Faubus Papers (MS F271–301) box 907, item 22. Special Collections, University of Arkansas Libraries, Fayetteville.

SNCC inspired demonstration in Pine Bluff, 1963. Photo from the Orval Faubus Papers (MS-F271–301), box 907, item 14. Special Collections, University of Arkansas Libraries, Fayetteville.

Gould Freedom School students, 1965. Laura Foner is seated on the far right. Photo by Tim Janke.

SNCC supporter Marion Cox, SNCC field secretary Bob Cableton, and SNCC Freedom School student Annette Cox showing the school's curriculum. Photo by Tim Janke.

SNCC field secretary Bob Cableton, Essie Mae Dale, SNCC volunteer Tim Janke, Annette Cox, unidentified child, and Glenda Cox. Photo courtesy of Tim Janke.

Residents of Gould, Arkansas, who supported SNCC, identified as Dolly Dale, Kenneth Harris, Beulah, Robert Hall, Troy, and Sam King. Photo by Tim Janke.

The Gould Freedom House, nicknamed "the Hall," was owned by SNCC supporter Carrie Dilworth. Photo by Tim Janke.

A meeting of the Gould Citizens for Progress, a local civil rights organization founded by SNCC supporters. Photo courtesy of Laura Foner.

A meeting of Gould Citizens for Progress. Photo courtesy of Laura Foner.

SNCC staff member Laura Foner conducting a class at the Gould Freedom School. Photo by Tim Janke.

1965 meeting at the Gould Freedom House, the three figures on the left are members of the Bynum family who were strong SNCC supporters in Gould, on the right is Laura Foner. Photo by Tim Janke.

The woman in the light-colored dress in the center is Carrie Dilworth, one of the strongest SNCC supporters in Gould, Arkansas, and a former organizer for the legendary Southern Tenant Farmers' Union. Photo by Tim Janke.

Freedom School Picnic. *On the left* (with the long braid) Sanderia Smith, *center* SNCC field secretary Laura Foner, *far right* SNCC supporter and former Southern Tenant Farmers' Union member Carrie Dilworth. Photo by Tim Janke.

Rev. Benjamin Grinage, the third director of the Arkansas Project, giving instructions to protesters in Pine Bluff. Photo by Vincent J. O'Connor.

SNCC supporters distributing flyers in Pine Bluff, circa 1965. Photo by Vincent J. O'Connor.

Local Arkansan youth staging a spontaneous counter protest to SNCC demonstrators in Pine Bluff. Photo by Vincent J. O'Connor.

SNCC members Dwight Williams, Vernon Crutchfield, and Linda Moore conversing at a picnic. Photo by Vincent J. O'Connor.

Field secretary Howard Himmelbaum. Photo by Vincent J. O'Connor.

Statewide SNCC staff meeting in 1965. Photo by Vincent J. O'Connor.

SNCC staff member Nancy Stoller. Photo by Vincent J. O'Connor.

SNCC members Nancy Stoller, Laura Foner, and Myrtle Glascoe. Photo by Vincent J. O'Connor.

Nancy Stoller, John Allerdice, and Linda Brown at a 1965 picnic for the summer project volunteers and SNCC staff. Photo by Vincent J. O'Connor.

Millard "Tex" Lowe and Pat Gladman converse in the foreground. Photo by Vincent J. O'Connor.

Jim Jones, the second director of the SNCC Arkansas Project, leading a prayer. Photo by Tim Janke.

Pine Bluff youthful supporters of SNCC. Photo by Vincent J. O'Connor.

The SNCC Freedom Singers performing in Pine Bluff. Photo by Vincent J. O'Connor.

Photo of the Freedom House in Mitchellville, Arkansas, circa 1965. Photo by Dwight Williams. Wisconsin Historical Society. Image ID 23666.

Demonstration at Greyhound bus station in Stuttgart, Arkansas, in 1965. Photo by Dwight Williams. Wisconsin Historical Society. Image ID 23660.

SNCC supporters attending a 1965 court hearing in Little Rock concerning the Forrest City student protest that year. Ben Grinage is in the center wearing a white shirt and dark tie. Photo by Dwight Williams. Wisconsin Historical Society. Image ID 23663.

Arkansas SNCC veterans Laura Foner, Mitchell Zimmerman, Nancy (Shaw) Stoller, Bill Hansen, and Arlene (Wilgoren) Dunn at the SNCC Fiftieth Anniversary Conference at Shaw University in April 2010. Photo by Rita Reynolds.

Arkansas SNCC veterans Michael Simmons, Dwight Williams, and Mitchell Zimmerman at the SNCC Fiftieth Anniversary Conference at Shaw University in April 2010. Photo by Rita Reynolds.

12.

An E-mail Interview with Tim Janke

JENNIFER JENSEN WALLACH

Tim Janke was a summer volunteer in Gould, Arkansas, in 1965. He graduated from Reed College in 1968. That same eventful year, he worked as a volunteer for the Eugene McCarthy campaign in Oregon and refused induction into the armed forces. Janke worked for several years restoring antique furniture before beginning a career as a purchasing agent for a hospital. Now retired, he lives in Deer Island, Oregon, where he was active in the local campaign to elect Barack Obama. His interview was conducted on July 12, 2009.

WALLACH. What were you doing before you joined the Arkansas Project?

JANKE. I had just finished my sophomore year at Reed College in Portland, Oregon, in May 1965.

WALLACH. Why did you choose to go to Arkansas?

JANKE. A college friend of mine had just been accepted to work with SNCC in Macon, Georgia, and shared his excitement about it. He gave me the information necessary to apply to SNCC, and I was accepted for an opening in Arkansas.

WALLACH. How long where you there? What SNCC activities did you participate in?

JANKE. I hitchhiked to Little Rock, Arkansas, in June of 1965 and left after that summer in time to begin my junior year in college in the fall. I participated in orientation in Little Rock and then moved to Gould, Arkansas, staying initially at the house of Carrie Dilworth with another volunteer. Bob Cableton of the SNCC staff arrived shortly thereafter and we began organizing meetings in a vacant house, owned by Ms. Dilworth, that became the SNCC Freedom Center in Gould. Throughout that summer we went house to house in an ongoing voter registration drive. About midway in the summer we successfully integrated a local restaurant that had previously required black customers to take out food from the back of the building and not be seated inside. Additional volunteers arrived and summer classes in black history and other subjects were taught in the Freedom Center.

WALLACH. Where did you live? What were your living conditions like?

JANKE. At first in Gould I stayed with another SNCC volunteer with Carrie Dilworth in her house. Later the volunteers stayed in rooms in the upstairs of the Freedom House. The living conditions were comfortable. The house was furnished simply but very adequately.

WALLACH. What was your relationship like with other members of the project?

JANKE. The relationships were easy and comfortable from the very beginning. I had spent high school in a Canadian boarding school, so living and working on a round-the-clock manner came easily to me, and I enjoyed it.

WALLACH. In your estimation, what were the project's greatest successes? Failures?

JANKE. I think the greatest successes were both the successful restaurant integration with its subsequent celebrations and feelings of accomplishment within the community, and the voter registration drive that provided a focus for community organizing.

WALLACH. Were you ever arrested?

JANKE. I was arrested, or at least arraigned, by local authorities following an incident in which I was beaten leaving a convenience store. The local sheriff, Harold Pearson, led a search for my attacker. When the attacker was eventually found and the matter was taken to the local judge, the attacker counter-charged me with attacking him, and charges against both of us were dropped.

WALLACH. What was your emotional state like while you were a member of SNCC?

JANKE. I was twenty-one years old during this summer, and had a fearlessness and feeling of indestructibility that has long since diminished. I had previously spent a year in Harlem with the pilot program of what became the Domestic Peace Corps and VISTA (Volunteers in Service to America). This I think gave the experience a feeling of continuity for me, a natural step forward in my life. I think this provided a calm and balance I would perhaps not otherwise have had.

WALLACH. How did local Arkansans—both black and white—respond to the arrival of SNCC in Arkansas?

JANKE. The prior work and ongoing presence of Carrie Dilworth was very evident early on. I had very little contact with local white citizens except for the sheriff and judge, as mentioned above. I felt the response by local black citizens was generally warm and interested, which I attribute to our operating under the aegis of Ms. Dilworth and the extraordinary leadership of Bob Cableton.

WALLACH. What was your relationship like (and the relationship of the larger project) with members of SNCC who operated elsewhere? Did you feel connected to the larger organization? Isolated?

JANKE. We had contact with other SNCC workers in nearby Pine Bluff and Dumas, both in Arkansas. Jim Jones of the Little Rock headquarters, and, later, Benjamin Grinage also paid visits to Gould. I felt sufficiently connected in that way.

WALLACH. What were race relations like in the project? Within the state? If applicable, what was your response to the shift of the organization towards "Black Power?"

JANKE. I wasn't aware of the shift of SNCC towards "Black Power," which I think occurred after I left SNCC. In Gould and in my experiences in SNCC outside Gould I felt part of a team, regardless of differences in race. The town of Gould was physically divided into white and black by the highway and by railroad tracks. I felt safe and welcomed among black locals in Gould. I stayed out of the white part of the town, uncertain what the white response would be to an "outside agitator," as the sheriff referred to me.

WALLACH. Why did you leave Arkansas?

JANKE. I left to return to college in my junior year.

WALLACH. How has your understanding of the movement and your role in it changed over the decades since you were involved with SNCC?

JANKE. I read the 1968 Kerner commission report on the state of American race relations and agreed with its conclusion that the U.S. was moving in the direction of separate black and white societies. Intellectually I supported the thrust of Black Power with its emphasis on turning inward and strengthening the black community, but emotionally I missed the easier feeling of give and take.

13.

An Interview with Millard "Tex" Lowe

JENNIFER JENSEN WALLACH

*The Texas native Millard "Tex" Lowe interrupted his studies
at Texas Southern University to work for the SNCC Arkansas
Project. After leaving Arkansas, Lowe continued his activism in
Texas and completed his college degree. For thirteen years he
taught at both the secondary and college levels in Jamaica,
earning a postgraduate diploma in education from the University
of the West Indies. Lowe has resided in Los Angeles since 1984,
teaching science at several local schools. Today he is a member
of the faculty of the New Designs Charter School in the Watts
neighborhood. His interview was conducted on September 24,
2009.*

WALLACH. When and where you were born?

LOWE. I was born in Texas, and I went to Texas Southern University. I
left in my senior year after this black history conference. We had a lot of
folk who came down, namely John Lewis, Stokely [Carmichael], Ron
Karenga, Amiri Baraka, James Farmer, Martin Luther King, Jesse [Jackson]
. . . This was back in 1964, the latter part of 1963. After that I made a
decision. I was going to go South and join the movement. So I withdrew
from school and went down to . . . recruitment at Tuskegee.

I caught a Greyhound bus to Tuskegee, Alabama, to go to work for
SNCC as a field secretary. It was in that meeting when I introduced myself
as "Millard Lowe." Stokely himself, Kwame Ture, said, "No, no, no I'm
not calling anybody 'Millard.' It sounds like 'my lord.' From now on you're
going to be 'Tex.'" That stuck. I became "Tex Lowe." And then I was sent
off to work in Arkansas . . .

It was 1964 when I first got to Arkansas. I was there with Jim Jones with the Arkansas Project. We met in Pine Bluff, but I was eventually sent to Forrest City, Arkansas, to work with . . . the local people there on voter registration, and we got into school desegregation.

WALLACH. What did your parents think about this? Were they supportive?

LOWE. My father was dead. He died when I was one year and six months old. I was raised by an aunt and an uncle in Texas. They were a bit upset . . . I went to Freeport, Texas, and told my aunt I was leaving, I was joining the movement. She got very teary eyed and got concerned about my safety. I just said, "This is something I need to do." And so I took off. They were okay. When I got arrested, my sisters Joyce Goods and Sula called making inquiries about my arrest. My aunt cursed out a few people.

I got arrested actually in Forrest City about five or six times. At one point, we got arrested and went to Forrest City jail. Then about ten o'clock that night . . . a dog catcher's truck backed up to the jail and took myself and four other students . . . who had been arrested along with us for demonstrating and transported us in the middle of the night to the Mississippi County Penal Farm. And no one knew where we were for about four or five days or a week . . .

WALLACH. Do you remember what prompted the arrest exactly?

LOWE. Oh we were demonstrating to desegregate the schools in Forrest City . . . and marching for voter registration as well. I was arrested for being an outside agitator, a communist contributing to the delinquency of a minor, and all kinds of trumped-up charges. I was arrested as "Tex Lowe," so my family had trouble finding me.

WALLACH. How did you get out of jail?

LOWE. Eventually the SNCC legal department got us out of jail after a week or so. Ironically, the person who came to get us was my dear, dear friend Bill Hansen . . . Of all people to send down was Bill Hansen. You send a white guy. I thought "Oh, God, they're gonna kill us now." They sent Hansen, who always thought he was black. "Why did they send you down? We'll never get out of here now."

WALLACH. When you volunteered for SNCC how did you get assigned to Arkansas?

LOWE. Well decisions were made, decisions as to where they thought I was needed . . . We also were running a Freedom School, and I was about to graduate from college, and I could be of use there . . . doing what we called Freedom School teaching, teaching folk about economics, about voters' rights, about the Constitution, et cetera . . . That was fine with me. Wherever there was a need I was willing to go . . .

The person we stayed with was Mrs. Clay, who was the owner of Clay's Funeral Home there. Her husband was dead, but she and her brother ran the funeral home. We stayed in the old funeral home where we had our Freedom School. She housed us, and the police kind of gave her a rough time, but she was an established black person in the community because often the white funeral home had to bring some of their bodies to the black funeral home person because he was the expert on reconstruction, reconstructing faces and things like that for people who had been burned in car accidents, et cetera. Anyway, there is another story about hiding in coffins when the police came for you. I remember several times hiding in coffins.

WALLACH. When you say "we," who exactly are you talking about?

LOWE. At that time there were a lot of students working with us and other SNCC workers. I am sure you talked to Mike Simmons, who is Europe now . . . he came down to Arkansas for a while . . . The police came by, and we were hiding in those coffins. That's a very weird feeling.

I remember the FBI agent who followed us around every day. Would you believe that his name was "Inspector Smart?" I told Smart, "You know what if something happens to me you're a dead man too because the brothers are going to come and get you. Your job is to protect me . . ." I got to talk to Smart all the time, give him a rough time.

WALLACH. Did you feel like he would protect you? Did you have any confidence in him at all?

LOWE. No. He worked for the FBI. He did what he was told to do. You know at that time I didn't have much trust in people on the other side who weren't members in the movement working. So I figured anybody could kill you at any time. You know I've been chased off the road sometimes in Arkansas by the Ku Klux Klansmen who shot at the old funeral home where we were. Smart was doing his job. He was a federal agent, and some federal agents were probably members of the Ku Klux Klan as well. So I just kept reminding him that your job is to protect me and all of these civil rights workers, and if anything happens to us your ass is grass too. Excuse my French.

WALLACH. When things happened to you like the shootings or being run off the road did you consider leaving Arkansas to protect yourself?

LOWE. No, I believed the same as Dr. King believed. If you have nothing to die for, what do you have to live for?

WALLACH. So in your mind you thought you could die as a result of these activities?

LOWE. Oh, yeah, I prayed several times like when they came and picked us up in that dog catcher's truck . . . There were about five of us, about six of us . . . and it's the middle of the night, early morning and some of the kids started crying so I sort of gave them an elder pep talk, which ended up with "Shut the 'f' up. If we're going to die, we're going to die like men and women. There won't be no crying in here." So I figured where we were going was probably the last place we were ever going to be, because I figured they were going to take us out and shoot us or hang us or whatever. We had no idea we were going to the Mississippi County Penal Farm, but that was the longest drive. I don't know how long it was, but it seemed like it should have been twenty or thirty hours before we got there. I was ready to die then because I assumed we were dead anyway. So I just prayed on that. You know, you prayed. Okay if it's time to go then you better make it right with the big person upstairs.

It was interesting when we got there . . . I had a huge head of hair and a beard which they shaved off and stood me in front of these guys and said, "This is the nigger that is causing all of the agitation in Forrest City." Pointing to the white prisoners and the black prisoners, "You should kick his ass. " So they're not going to put me with the white prisoners; they're going to put me with the black prisoners. So I have to convince these brothers that kicking my ass is not going to get you out of here. You're just kicking your own ass if you do that. So I was able to do that, convince the brothers not to beat me up.

It started raining, but they said we had to go pick cotton. They . . . said we had to go pick cotton or we'd be thrown in the hole. I refused to pick cotton so I'm thrown in the hole . . . So it rained the rest of the time we were there, so we couldn't go out and do anything, except we did some ditch digging one day. I thought we'd probably end up in this ditch, which we didn't. Like I say after a week or so, I don't know how long it was, Bill Hansen finally came with the release papers . . .

WALLACH. You said that Mrs. Clay let you stay with her and was very supportive of the movement.

LOWE. Yes, she was very supportive. She's the person who gave us housing.

WALLACH. Would you say that she was exceptional?

LOWE. The people in Forrest City were very supportive. Another family, a very important family there, was the Bradley family . . . We even ran Mrs. Bradley for school board. She lost, but we actually ran her for school board. The Bradley family . . . had their own farm there so they were able to take care of themselves and didn't have to worry about losing their job. . . . And Forrest City had a lot of people who were very supportive, who took a lot of risk. You have to also consider that you're putting people at risk as well, and I know some people suffered.

Oh I remember once we went . . . to this diner to desegregate this diner. That's another long story, how desegregation got confused with integration.

That's another pet peeve of mine. So anyway we went to this diner. They were going to serve us to keep from getting in trouble, so what they did was they gave us dirty water, and they gave us food loaded with salt. So our point was, okay we're going to eat this food and drink this water because we're not leaving. And we stayed there. And one of these cracker-type persons went to the . . . jukebox and punched up of all people Nat King Cole, but the song was "Bye, Bye Blackbird."

WALLACH. When you were in Arkansas as a young man did you feel connected to freedom struggles around the world or did it just seem like a local problem?

LOWE. Oh, yes. This was a world struggle you know. We taught a lot about Africa. One of the courses I taught was an African course in the Freedom School, and we felt the link with Africa. My heroes were people like . . . Kwame Nkrumah [and] Jomo Kenyatta. So we kept that bond and tie with the African continent and with the Caribbean, with Stokely from Trinidad and a lot of others from all parts of the world . . . We were all in this whole thing together, this worldwide struggle

WALLACH. Do you think that the local people in Forrest City had that same sense of interconnectedness?

LOWE. I think they did from what we were teaching young people, they could see the connection. Older people could realize the struggle, but yet we had to deal with what was happening in their own struggle. It is hard to talk about what's happening to somebody else thousands of miles away when you're suffering from basically the same thing. What was interesting was I took a picture from a magazine and hung it up on the wall and asked the young people where they thought it was. They thought it was in Mississippi, Arkansas, Alabama, or in Louisiana somewhere, but I said, "No, actually this is Africa. This is in South Africa where it says 'whites only' by the water fountains as well." So you see that what was going on in the continent was also going on here. There wasn't much difference in terms of the impact of what was going on in South Africa and what was going on in America at the particular time.

WALLACH. When you look back at what you did in Forrest City, what do you think were your most successful moments?

LOWE. I think giving people a sense of being somebody and being some-one who had a right to all of the amenities that everyone else had. . . . I know that Forrest City is a completely different place than it was thirty, forty years ago, and the greatest thing was to see young people developing that sense of pride . . . I think the voter registration and getting people reg-istered to go and vote despite the risk they were taking was to me the great-est sense of accomplishment. And to see people willing to march in the street willing to put their own lives on the line along with you . . . I think Forrest City owes its advancement to the people of Forrest City, the black folk who took the movement seriously and threw themselves into it despite many friends who were actually afraid. They were afraid too, but they did it because they were afraid. Sometimes fear is the greatest motivator of bravery.

14.

Arkansas SNCC Memories

LAURA FONER

Laura Foner was born into a family of politically active leftists in New York City. She earned a degree from Brandeis University and did graduate work at Rutgers and Columbia Universities. Foner spent almost a year working for SNCC in Gould, Arkansas. She then continued her activism by joining Students for a Democratic Society, becoming involved in the 1968 student strike at Columbia. She later was involved in the women's and labor movements. Today she is a children's librarian and an active member of City Life / Vida Urbana, a radical community organization dedicated to promoting social justice and affordable housing.

Forty-four years have passed since I worked in Arkansas SNCC. I carry the experience with me daily, but trying to put myself back into what it was really like has been both difficult and very rewarding. I have tried to be as truthful as my selective, faulty sixty-five-year-old memory will allow.

Background

Growing up in a left-wing family during the height of the Cold War, I learned a version of U.S history never taught in school. At home I learned a story of U.S. slavery, which stressed the history of the slave revolts and the work of abolitionists such as Frederick Douglass. Feeling isolated from American "mainstream" culture and politics, I longed to be part of a movement for fundamental change.

During high school, some of my friends and I joined the NAACP youth group in a neighboring town. And we spent our Saturdays picketing the local Woolworths, in support of the boycott that followed the first southern sit-ins. Something was stirring in this country, something really important and inspiring. I wanted to be part of it.

I first learned about SNCC in my sophomore year of college when one of the early leaders spent several weeks at Brandeis. He organized a group to travel to Georgia during spring break of 1963. Fearful, but excited, I signed up. I was disappointed (and relieved) when the trip was canceled at the last minute; someone had decided it was too dangerous.

The following fall, I left for a year of study in Paris. Just before my departure, I attended the 1963 D.C. Civil Rights March. I felt the power of hundreds of thousands of black and white people, from unions, churches, and schools, all marching together. I was in France when the three civil rights workers were murdered in Mississippi. I knew people who were there. I both feared for their lives and envied their participation in Mississippi Freedom Summer. I vowed to "go South" when I finished college the next year.

The Friends of SNCC chapter in Cambridge, Massachusetts, had contacts in Arkansas SNCC. A Brandeis graduate, Arlene Wilgoren, was already in Arkansas. Arkansas SNCC had decided to sponsor a Summer Project targeted to the communities in eastern Arkansas. Hopefully, bringing in some northern college students, black and white, would bring national attention to these organizing efforts and help the local people feel part of a national movement and less frightened about joining in. As I set off on my journey, my parents said goodbye with very mixed emotions; they were proud, nervous for my safety, and very disappointed (especially my father)[1] that I had turned down a scholarship for graduate studies at Harvard to work with Arkansas SNCC.

Arkansas

I landed in Arkansas after a week of training in Washington, D.C. SNCC veterans taught us nonviolent tactics: how to protect ourselves and each other if we were being beaten, and how to nonviolently resist arrest. We role-played being taunted and spat on and watched them demonstrate how to convince an elderly southern black person to get up off the porch and come to a meeting. And then we were put on a bus.

My first two weeks in Arkansas were spent in Pine Bluff. Ben Grinage asked if I would be willing to move to Gould, Arkansas. Ben, who later became the Arkansas SNCC project director, was the AME church minister of Gould and knew the community well. Local activists, including experienced organizers like Mrs. Carrie Dilworth and Mr. Bynum, had invited SNCC to Gould. Both had organized with the Southern Tenant Farmers' Union in the 1930s and the NAACP in the 1950s and early 1960s. They were impressed with SNCC's youthful energy and willingness to take risks.

The project was staffed by twenty-six-year-old Bob Cableton, an African American from Indianola, Mississippi, and two white college student summer volunteers. There had been much debate about whether to include a white woman. The fear was that my presence would inflame the white population and escalate an already tense situation. Despite the risks, we decided I should go. I had some awareness of the complications of being a white woman. I had read about the post-Reconstruction period and the history of lynching. During my time in Arkansas, gender and women's issues were always right under the surface. Many of the strongest local leaders were women, and black and white women were on staff. Yet these issues were never overtly discussed.

My coworkers had been very busy "working in the field," mostly doing voter registration, traveling the countryside trying to convince people to exercise their right to vote. It was decided that this was much too risky for me, and I was confined to town. I was not to travel very far and never walk alone at night. I was given the job of helping to set up a "freedom school," library, and community center in a large, run-down wood-framed two-story house owned by Mrs. Dilworth. The house had served in the past as a food co-op during the STFU days and a funeral home. Over the summer, we turned one room into a classroom, another into a library, and the largest room into a meeting hall. Our library was stocked with donated books including W. E. B. Du Bois's *Souls of Black Folks* and Richard Wright's *Black Boy*. Local children, who had never before seen a book written by a black author, were surprised and delighted. We held regular classes in black history, government, and French. We also sang and played lots of children's games. The girls taught me jump rope rhymes and dances. The boys played basketball and mumblety-peg.

The adults formed their own local organization, the Gould Citizens for Progress, which held regular evening meetings at the Freedom Center. Each meeting started and ended with the lively singing of Freedom Songs: "Ain't Gonna Let Hal Pearson [local sheriff] Turn Me Around," "Woke Up this Morning with my Mind Stayed on Freedom," and "We Shall Overcome." While voter registration continued, the project desegregated two local restaurants. The group also mounted a boycott of the only store on the black side of town, owned by Hal Pearson, to protest his constant racist harassment.

Despite KKK threats, firings, and intimidation, many local black residents became active and several emerged as strong leaders. The most moving and inspiring moments of my time in SNCC came from participating in this process. I saw grown men who had always walked with their heads bowed down on the white side of town straighten up and look white people in the eye, heads held high. We spent a lot of time going door to door, sitting for hours on the porches of whoever would invite us to join them.

As far as we knew, all the whites in Gould were hostile. Many in the black community were, too. They saw us as outside troublemakers and wished we would go away. Family members were divided, which was tough in a small town. We went to every church and asked to address the congregation. (As a Jew, raised in a nonreligious home, going to southern black churches was a very new experience. More than one person told me I was the first Jew they ever met, and one said she was surprised I did not have horns.)

During my eleven months (July '65–June '66) in Gould, I was lucky to live with Mrs. Carrie Dilworth. She lived in a comfortable house, and I had my own room. She was my mentor, protector, and friend. Towards the end, I learned that she slept with a loaded gun. When the summer ended and the other white volunteers left, life changed. Bob and I remained as the SNCC folks. Bob slept at the Freedom Hall but often shared meals with me at Mrs. Dilworth's. We were a strange pair, but in some ways we made a great team. Bob was an effective organizer; he had a sly sense of humor and could talk easily with people as he shared a similar background. He loved music and dancing; he would throw his head back and belt out a freedom song. I was a young, ardent, college-educated white girl, full of outrage at the injustices people there faced and a sense of hope, possibilities, and connection to the wider world. We would spend hours talking strategy. We talked about the growing war in Vietnam, conflicts in the Movement, the urban rebellions in Watts and Harlem. Sitting at Mrs. Dilworth's kitchen table, we read Malcolm X's speeches and analyzed them line by line. Bob was filled with rage and hatred towards whites. It seethed under the surface and, despite mutual respect, his feelings towards me had a love/hate quality (which reached a peak when I finally decided to leave). And my feelings were probably love/fear. But the work we did together was powerful. Just as Arkansas SNCC operated very independently from Central Headquarters, Bob and I operated very much on our own. We were in regular contact with Ben Grinage and went to some statewide meetings, but the local leadership determined most of the work. Their strength, wisdom, and experience, despite the lack of certain skills and resources, are largely responsible for the successes of the Gould SNCC project.

After the summer, our major campaign was defying the local plan to begin court-ordered school desegregation with "controlled choice": a way to stall integration. Although black children had signed up for every grade, their parents were told at the end of the summer that only children in two grades would be admitted to the white elementary school. We had spent a lot of time during the summer talking with children and parents about their right to go to any school they wanted. This was unacceptable.

As a result of extensive community discussion about what a *fair* integration plan would look like, Gould Citizens for Progress came up with a plan: demolish the substandard black high school and require ALL the elementary students, black and white, to go to the now "black" elementary school and ALL high school students, black and white, to go to the now "white" high school. The "white" elementary school could become a junior high school for everybody. Each school would have an integrated staff of black and white teachers. The plan, we argued, was the only fair way to achieve true integration in Gould. Obviously, no white families were going to "choose" to send their children to the black schools and the few black children "choosing" to attend the white schools faced the unfair burden to being a small minority in a sea of hostility. We mounted a full-scale campaign during the fall, including a legal suit against the Gould School Board that went all the way to the U.S. Supreme Court.[2] Meanwhile, when school opened in the fall, a large group of black families (and Bob and I) marched up to the white elementary school demanding that all the black students who had registered be allowed to attend. The students were dressed up and carrying their school supplies. Only the students in the two grades were allowed in the door. The rest of us picketed the school, singing and chanting loudly. There were cops, news reporters, and many threats. (Sheriff Pearson ordered me into his car and threatened to "chop off my head and throw it in the river.") But nobody was arrested, and we eventually dispersed.

The fight about education continued, including running a candidate for the local school board, but the experiences of the few black children in the white school that year were very sobering and caused some of us to begin to look critically at the goal of integration. These students would come to the Freedom Center and tell their stories of spending every day with hostile students and more hostile teachers. They were proud of themselves for standing up for what was right and conducted themselves with great dignity and bravery. But they missed their friends and teachers who knew and understood them. They did not want to always have to act like model students.

These questions paralleled the debate going on in SNCC about moving from "integration" (do we really want to "integrate" into this racist society?) to "black power" (which could mean everything from building black political power through elections to seeing black people as a colonized nation and advocating "revolutionary nationalism" and everything in between). Two of the black Arkansas SNCC members, Dwight Williams and Mike Simmons, both from Philadelphia, left to found the Atlanta

SNCC project, as part of moving SNCC towards urban organizing and more radical politics. They, and others, led one of the first black protests against the Vietnam War at an induction center in Atlanta, declaring that blacks would not go fight a white man's war against other poor people of color.

One indication of the thinking in Arkansas SNCC about these issues comes from my letter dated March 30, 1966, written to a Colorado woman whose Friends of SNCC group was sending me $10/month (I became an official SNCC staff member in the fall, but don't think I got paid): "You also asked about the validity of certain rumors that SNCC is going 'black nationalist.' I can only tell you what little I know. There are some people in SNCC who have that orientation—there have almost always been some. Certain people are trying to raise the issue again, but it seems that most of the people in SNCC do not agree; it is probably a small group. At any rate, Arkansas SNCC is unanimously opposed to such an orientation (all the staff—black and white) and that's what's most important. I would very much like to know where you heard this from—who or what source?"

I was clearly not prepared for the vigorous debate I witnessed at the May national SNCC meeting. The debate was largely between black SNCC members; there were few whites remaining in SNCC. I was fascinated by the discussion and excited by what Stokely Carmichael and his supporters argued. They said the time was past for blacks to be asking for acceptance within white society or to expect the Democratic Party to grant real equality. They saw urban blacks and anticolonial struggles in the third world as allies in the freedom movement. As someone who grew up believing in the need for revolutionary change, I welcomed this thinking and did not feel like it was "anti-white" or personally threatening. I felt conflicted, however, when I listened to the passionate words of John Lewis and other old-time SNCC members who argued that the power of the Movement came from a belief in love, community, nonviolence, a better way of being with each other. Our political strategy needed to reflect our values and our vision or we were lost. I was too new to SNCC and knew too little about the earlier years to really appreciate what this debate meant to longtime SNCC members and how painful some of the subsequent decisions would be.

Leaving Gould

Bob and I returned to Gould, not knowing what SNCC's new direction would mean. Arkansas SNCC was opposed to any decision to move to an all-black organization. But I had already been questioning how long I would stay in Gould. I knew I was not planning to live there long term, unlike Bob, who married a local leader and stayed for many years. And I was increasingly thinking that the job of white people should be to work with other whites to understand how racism poisoned life for all of us. But leaving was really hard. I felt guilty and very sad leaving the people I had come to care about so much and who had welcomed me into their lives. I thought about staying in Arkansas and organizing with southern whites. Very conflicted, I finally left Gould in late June and moved to Madison, Wisconsin, to work with the National Coordinating Committee to End the War in Vietnam.

Working in SNCC was one of the highlights of my life. I feel privileged to have been a small part of a glorious, flawed, complicated effort to bring about badly needed change. The experience of witnessing the power of a social movement to effect collective and personal transformation has stayed with me as a source of hope all my life.

15.

An Interview with Gertrude Jackson

JENNIFER JENSEN WALLACH

An Illinois native, Gertrude Jackson moved to Arkansas when she was seven years old. She and her husband, Earlis Jackson, were farm owners, leaders of the local civil rights movement, and staunch supporters of SNCC. In 1978 Jackson became a founding member of the Boys, Girls, Adults Community Development Center in Marvell. She continues to work for the BGACDC, seeking ways to combat the impact of poverty on the residents of her community. Her interview was conducted on March 6, 2009.

WALLACH. How did you get involved with the civil rights movement?

JACKSON. I guess the first thing I was going to tell you about was the Turner school boycott . . . My husband was the one who started the boycott, and we all worked together with that . . . There was a school in each community, which were twelve communities. So they decided to bring about five of those schools together and build a school in the center . . . The school was beautiful. It was great. We had organized our PTA and were doing great things, but all at once the system started backing up and water would run . . . out the bathroom down the halls and things. So the children used to come home and say, "Ooh, the bathroom flooded today." Well, we didn't pay too much attention. "Ooh, mama, that water getting bad. We can't drink this water." So this went on a long time, and so one day my husband decided to go and look for himself and he found it very horrible . . . And SNCC was there. [SNCC members] Mr. Howard Himmelbaum and Myrtle Glascoe and all. [Himmelbaum] talked to us about going to the school board and kind of advised us, directed us on how to go to the school board. Well, they would say the bathrooms are all right. The only thing is the children just don't know how to use the bathroom, and this went on for a few years. It went worse after it went on.

WALLACH. But it was a new school?

JACKSON. It was a new school.

WALLACH. But it just wasn't built well?

JACKSON. Now when my husband was in World War II when he came back he went to school and he took up plumbing. He went to . . . board meetings. He'd say the grading is going uphill, and that's why it's backing up. You know they laughed at him . . .

We would go to board meetings and . . . they made fun of us and said we didn't know what we were doing. On our way home my husband says, "You know if I could get people to take their children out of school I bet they'd fix it." This was on a Thursday night. He got up that Friday morning. We had a country store where people kind of congregated. He went and talked to the people, the men who sat around, and they all went down and took a look at the school . . . When they looked at it they decided they would take the children out. Then the men got in groups, some went one way, some went another, knocking on doors, asking people to keep the children at home until they fixed the bathroom. I know SNCC was there because Howard, Mr. Himmelbaum, he put it in the paper. So that's what happened, we stayed out of school. The press that was there, said that Monday out of three hundred children wasn't but thirty there . . .

So finally we called the . . . Phillips County Health Department. The fellow who came down and checked the bathrooms . . . looked and said, "Well, there's nothing wrong with the way it's put down." So then SNCC, Howard, knew how to call the state. So he got in touch with the state, and the state came down and checked it. And it was put up just like my husband said; it was put up wrong. And they made them dig it up and do it all over. So that got the water back in shape and the school started back. So that's kind of the end of the Turner school boycott.

WALLACH. Were you fearful about doing this boycott?

JACKSON. I sure wasn't. There were a few men that lived in our little town that said they needed to come over there to whip my husband. But we got through that real good, but it became fearful further up the road when school integration came up. That's when it got rough.

WALLACH. But as long as you were not protesting segregation you felt that your lives weren't in danger, that you wouldn't be harmed?

JACKSON. Yes, that's right . . . I'll tell you like this, when your mind's made up, your mind's made up, and nothing deters you. When you have a made up mind, you go through struggles. Now we made it through the

Turner school boycott without any situations, but where we hit it in the sixties was when we were ordered to integrate . . .

Marvell the school district decided to obey the rules and go on and integrate so this is what they did. When I look back I see that this was a poor way of integration. They had to integrate by "choice forms." They would send these choice forms to black schools and have the parents come in and sign up where do you want your child to go, to the black school or to the white school . . . Now the first year . . . this is the way they decide to do it. They're going to take three years to integrate. The first year they would do up to the fourth grade. Then the next year they would go up to the eighth grade. So they went on and did it the first year. I think they had maybe about ten or twelve black children that signed that their parents let them go over there. Then the next year it went up to the eighth grade. That's when they refused; they said they would not do it. They would not send the choice forms, they wouldn't do any of this stuff . . . I read the choice forms and it says you don't go to school at all even if you intend to go to the same school unless you sign this choice form . . . This form says don't go to school at all. So at this meeting we decided that we'd just boycott. We wouldn't let anyone go to school.

What we had to do then was to drive around through the community again and say, "Keep your children at home. Keep your children at home and we'll have a meeting on Sunday . . ." It worked real great . . . We had the church packed, cars all around, so we decided that day we would not march. We would just stay out of school . . . I decided and another lady says we're going to go to school . . . and see how the boycott is coming. So we went up to the school and just sat and watched the buses. The buses came in. Some had one child. Some had none. Some had three or four. They'd just make their rounds. So while we were sitting there a lady came by and said, "They heard you all was going to march. And they're over there; they've got the school wrapped up with trucks and guns all around the school." And the lady with me said let's go see, and it was just like they said. They had that place surrounded, and it was like they intended to do away with us that day . . .

Then Mr. Howard Himmelbaum, the SNCC worker, suggested . . . about filing a suit against the school. Everybody was for that, but the school would have to have a name of somebody to do it. So everybody was a little reluctant to do it, so my husband said, "I'll do it. Use my name." So it comes out, Earlis Jackson has filed suit against Marvell High School . . . We went all the way to St. Louis to court.[1]

To make a long story short, Judge Harris ordered the school to go on and integrate, and instead of going through the eighth grade like we had planned, we're going to pull in the twelfth grade, too . . . They pulled the twelfth grade children in, and I had two, three children over there without any incident. They did fine. They would do little things like they sure were told not to mix . . . and the teachers would do things like not give them their grades and some of those things . . . You know they tried to make it hard for them.

WALLACH. Did you ask your children if they wanted to go? Was it their decision or yours?

JACKSON. I think it was mostly all of ours together because they were all going to the meetings with us and all. We all did it together.

WALLACH. Were you scared to send your kids into that hostile environment?

JACKSON. You know, we went through some tough times, but we made it.

WALLACH. Did people threaten . . . you and try to intimidate you?

JACKSON. We had some damage done. Now one night, my little girl, they had a ball in the house and you know how children get to arguing about a ball. Now my husband said put that ball on the porch. She opened the door to put the ball out there, and she said, "The shop's on fire!" The shop is where we kept the farm equipment, you know, your tractors and trucks and things . . . When she said the shop's on fire, he was in the bed, but he hit the floor so quick [and went] out there in his pajamas . . . What they had done was they had taken this big truck that you haul your workers in, people who chop cotton and pick cotton . . . they had taken the cap off the truck and stuffed a rag or something down in it and set it on fire. That was burning. So what my husband did, he went to the neighbors, got a chain, hooked it to the truck, hooked it to his tractor, and pulled it across the field. Now all this time the children were screaming and hollering, "Daddy come back, come back." But he pulled that truck out from under that shed to keep it from destroying everything. The truck sat in the field and burned up . . .

Another thing they did to us I never will forget. [The children] walked out one morning to go to school and a cross had been burned in the yard . . . I always thought when I heard them say "burn a cross" that they built a cross and stood it up, but what they do is make a cross out of gasoline and light it on the ground. Anyway, like I say, when your mind's made up.

WALLACH. What did you think about the SNCC volunteers? Were you happy when they came to town?

JACKSON. I sure was. It was like a deliverer had come. We were very happy.

WALLACH. But even before they came it sounds like you were already starting to protest. They didn't start it.

JACKSON. They didn't start it . . . Say for instance the Turner school boycott . . . my husband made up his mind himself.

WALLACH. But it was nice to have people supporting you?

JACKSON. They knew more about how to call the newspapers . . . They assisted in things like that. We leaned on them. It was just like a deliverer had come to the state, come to our city . . . They just got to be like family.

WALLACH. Do you remember when they left? What made them leave the community?

JACKSON. I guess we had gotten everything settled and we had gotten everything put together. They went on to other places.

WALLACH. Did most black people support SNCC and support your activities?

JACKSON. We had enough to support it to do what we needed to do, but some was fearful. They sure were . . . Some thought we just didn't need to make that step to go to the white schools. A lot of them was afraid . . . but there was a lot who wasn't afraid.

WALLACH. Do you think that those who were the most fearful were those who were economically vulnerable; they were worried about losing their jobs?

JACKSON. Right . . . because a young lady came to me and said, "Ms. Jackson, you all live on your own land, can't nobody make you all move." Most of them lived on people's places . . .

We had a good banker. When it was all over and everything was kind of settled, the banker talked to my brother-in-law and said, "Jim everything is about settled now, so you all just kind of hole up because people have been trying to tell me not to give you loans." And if we couldn't get loans we couldn't survive . . . He said now school's all shaped up and everything is in place, you all kind of hole up, because you have made a lot of enemies. And all your enemies ain't white . . .

WALLACH. After this whole struggle, after things were integrated, how did you feel?

JACKSON. I felt great. People still kind of look at you strange. "There's that woman."

16.

My Arkansas Journey

ARLENE (WILGOREN) DUNN

A Boston native, Arlene (Wilgoren) Dunn studied mathematics at Brandeis University and later earned an M.B.A. from Northwestern University's Kellogg School of Management. Dunn spent more than a year working in the Pine Bluff and Little Rock offices of the SNCC Arkansas Project. Since then she continued her activism as a member of a variety of organizations, including People Against Racism (PAR) and the Race Relations Council of Northern Indiana. She also enjoyed a successful career in the airline industry, ultimately working as director of financial analysis at Midway Airlines.

This is a story of how the experience of working in the civil rights movement of the 1960s completely transformed the life of a Jewish girl from Boston.

I worked for SNCC in Arkansas for fifteen months in 1964 and 1965. Although this was a short period of time, its impact was profound and is still with me, nearly forty-five years later. This journey actually began seven years earlier, fittingly enough, with a triggering event that occurred in Little Rock, Arkansas. In the fall of 1957 I was a high school sophomore in Boston, attending a city-wide college preparatory school. Although I lived in a very homogenous Jewish community, I attended school with a more diverse student body. When the Little Rock Nine students attempted to integrate Central High School I was shocked to see TV news footage of angry white mobs and the Arkansas National Guard preventing them from entering the building. Here I was receiving an excellent education in a safe environment, while there were teenagers, like me in all ways except my skin color, being refused what I took for granted. Later in life, when I came to understand more about white privilege, I read a quote from Robert Terry, author of several books on race, including *On Being White* and *For Whites Only* that could describe me: "Being white in America is not having to think about it."

In February of 1960 I participated in my first civil rights action when I was a freshman at Brandeis University. A group of students demonstrated at the Woolworth's in Harvard Square in support of the lunch counter student sit-ins in the South. After graduating from Brandeis, I moved to New York City and became quite active with the New York SNCC office, which was primarily involved in fundraising to support the organizing and action campaigns in the South. Early in 1964 plans were solidified for the 1964 Freedom Summer, which was to bring one thousand (mostly Caucasian) students from the North to participate in voter registration drives in Mississippi. As I was no longer a student, it did not occur to me to join this effort. I was content to provide support through volunteer work in the New York office. We were a dedicated group—young folks willing to do just about anything, from menial tasks such as stuffing envelopes to calling people asking for financial support.

Excitement about the summer project built over the spring months, and we raised a lot of money. There were times when I was tempted to join up, as the excitement was very contagious. But I had held my job only eight or nine months, so taking a few months off seemed out of the question. Then the fateful day in June occurred when news of the disappearance of three civil rights workers—James Chaney, a black youth from Mississippi, and two white northern volunteers, Andy Goodman and Mike Schwerner —came to light. The New York SNCC office placed a full-page ad in the *New York Times* and donations began pouring in. Hate mail also arrived. One evening I opened a letter containing extremely vile statements and a specimen of feces. That did it for me. I decided then and there that I was not going to stay away out of fear or hate. I spoke with Julie Prettyman, the director of the New York office, about the possibility of my going despite the fact that I had not participated in the volunteer training, which included important exercises in methods of nonviolent demonstrations. She reported back that I could go to the Atlanta office, SNCC national headquarters, and request an assignment, but that there was no guarantee that I would indeed be placed. Within a week I had quit my job, walked out on my apartment lease, got rid of most of my stuff, and was on a bus headed to Atlanta.

I stayed there for a week, helping out in whatever way I could. I was soon on another bus headed for Pine Bluff, Arkansas, where I would work for SNCC as a field secretary, the title given to everyone. My salary was subsistence level (about $20 a week), but housing was provided. The next fifteen months would be one of the most memorable times of my life, in personal as well as political ways.

Some of my memories were introductions to a new culture. I was offered many new foods—greens and other vegetables cooked with fatback, which I tolerated but did not really like, sweet potato pie, which I love to this day, and chitterlings, which I tried only once. I was offered pig's feet, which I never tried. We mingled with the community socially, and I especially enjoyed evenings at the Elks Club where there was often a live band, sometimes quite famous blues performers such as Bobby Blue Bland and even B. B. King. They did not have a liquor license but you were allowed to bring your own liquor and buy "setups"—mixers, lemon, lime, or whatever else you liked to mix with liquor. We ate, drank, and danced until the wee hours.

My SNCC responsibilities were primarily in managing the office. Occasionally I joined in a group canvassing in the community to encourage people to register to vote. I remember a small house we visited where the family was clearly struggling with poverty. The furnishings were simple and well worn, yet the house was clean and had a dignified presence. There were pictures of Martin Luther King and Jack Kennedy on the wall. The family welcomed us into their home and listened to us with respect. My time in Arkansas was my first real hands-on experience of the level of poverty so many people in this country endure. Those images have stayed with me and help to inform my political and social thinking to this day.

I got to know a group of students at Arkansas AM&N, the historically black college now known as the University of Arkansas at Pine Bluff. I dated one of the students for a while, fearlessly appearing in public with him and riding on the back of his motorcycle. Some of my SNCC colleagues expressed concern that I might be endangering the project as well as my own life (and his), but we were determined to live freely and openly express our belief in racial equality.

The director of the Arkansas Project was Bill Hansen. Bill was tall and lanky with a strong, square jaw. With his very long legs, he often strode with such determination it was difficult to keep up. He had little tolerance for the requests of some of the women in the project (myself included) that men and women should be regarded as equals with regard to job assignments and leadership roles. And it wasn't just about men and women. Bill ran the entire project in a domineering way. He was very focused on the goals for SNCC. We had long discussions about policy or proposed activities, but in the end, Bill seemed to always prevail, whether because everyone eventually agreed with him or he simply decided enough was enough and "dictated" the policy. Bill was very strong willed, as am I. So we were frequently in conflict.

And yet, I learned a great deal from Bill and have always valued his substantial intellect and his willingness to share his understanding of history and politics. He had a keen understanding of the role of racism in every aspect of American society and was always willing to take the time to share this knowledge.

Arkansas SNCC was small and not in the media spotlight as much as the Mississippi Freedom Project in 1964 or the Selma to Montgomery March in 1965. But we took ourselves very seriously and worked on the same issues, such as voter registration, freedom schools, and desegregation of public facilities. We had many political discussions to help motivate us and provide context for our work, but what sticks in my memory are the intense, often all-night, discussions at national SNCC meetings. When I attended those meetings, I truly felt part of making history. I began to relearn American history, a process that continues to this day. I learned about thinking strategically and about the connections between domestic racism and American foreign policy. And I began a process of coming to grips with white privilege and how that affects my life as well as the lives of people of color.

My most memorable experience during my time with the Arkansas SNCC project came shortly after the passage of the 1964 Civil Rights Act, which outlawed discrimination in public accommodations. A common practice for many public restaurants and similar establishments in the South was to declare themselves as "private clubs" to avoid having to serve blacks. Governor Faubus (the same governor who had called out the National Guard in 1957 to prevent the Little Rock Nine from entering Central High School) had the nerve to declare the cafeteria in the basement of the capitol building a private club. When we heard about this, we quickly put a plan in motion.

Another white SNCC worker in the office, Nancy Stoller, and I went to eat at the cafeteria two or three times. Sure enough, there was a guard of sorts at the door. He did not ask us anything, certainly not if we were "members." We engaged him in conversation, making sure he would remember us, and giving him an opportunity to request a membership card. A few days later, just before the lunch hour, we returned with about twenty of our closest friends, most of whom were black. Among the group were adults, college students, and a few high school students.

As soon as we arrived, the guard stood up and said, "I'm sorry, this is a private club." Nancy and I protested, reminding him that we had eaten lunch there several times before and he never mentioned anything about a private club. He hemmed and hawed and stammered and would not let us proceed. Shortly, someone from inside the cafeteria closed the doors. Then the manager came out and tried to reason with us. He returned to the restaurant when we refused to leave. Soon, people started showing up for lunch, waving their wallets, showing a driver's license, social security card, business card—anything to feign a "membership" card. Some were allowed in early in the confrontation, but soon, no one was being admitted.

The layout of the basement and the entrance to the cafeteria was interesting. As in many capitol buildings, there are large, expansive hallways. There was a set of stone stairs at each end. The cafeteria was at the end of a rather narrow hallway off this expansive hallway, about ten to twenty feet wide by fifteen to twenty feet long. The twenty of us were crammed into this small hallway, waiting and wondering what would happen next. Soon we saw what looked like an imposing display of Arkansas state troopers inside the cafeteria facing out. I don't really know how many there actually were, but it sure looked like a lot and they were all very tall and very big.

We were again warned to leave and when we did not, the troopers stormed out and began beating us with billy clubs and fists, chasing us down the hall to the stone steps leading out of the basement. We scrambled our way out of there with the troopers on our tail making sure we left the building. We suffered a few minor injuries—a few knots on heads, bruises and scratches, but nothing serious. We regrouped at the SNCC office to discuss what to do next. It was a raucous discussion, a free-for-all with many people describing what had happened to those who did not go. We decided to go back the next day and attempt to enter the cafeteria again.

The same events happened the next day, even worse, as the people in power could not believe we would actually return after being beaten up. When we returned a third day, the troopers threw down canisters of some kind of tear gas that felt like hot mustard in our nostrils, eyes, and throats. We demonstrated a total of four days and Governor Faubus closed the cafeteria rather than serve blacks. The cafeteria remained closed for several months, until a suit brought by the NAACP Legal Defense and Education Fund forced them to reopen and serve anyone. At the trial, both Nancy and I testified about how we entered the cafeteria unchallenged. The defense attorney tried to discredit us by saying we were "outside agitators" from the North, but Nancy pointed out in a sweet southern accent that she was from Hampton Roads, Virginia.

In the summer of 1965 there began to be stirrings within SNCC about "Black Power" and the role of whites in the *black* civil rights movement.

At one meeting something occurred that has stayed with me all these years. A young local southern black woman stood at the front and said that she wanted to work in the movement. She wanted to type the newsletters and print the leaflets and it shouldn't matter that she could not type as fast as the white girls from the north.

After many discussions filled with emotion and tears, I began to understand that my presence was a deterrent to the success of the movement. I left Arkansas and within a year or so became involved in an organization called People Against Racism which worked in the white community to help educate people about how racism and white privilege damages all segments of society.

As I write this in 2009, the United States has an African American president and certainly some progress has been made since 1965, but, alas, racism is alive and well in America and the fight continues.

17.

The Civil Rights Movement in Pine Bluff

VIVIAN CARROLL JONES

*Vivian Carroll Jones is an Arkansas native who became involved
with SNCC in Pine Bluff as a high school student. After high
school, she married and had three children. In 1973, she became
the first African American to be hired by the city attorney's
office. This was a bittersweet victory, however, and she quickly
filed a complaint with the Equal Employment Opportunity
Commission due to discrimination at the workplace. This experience led her "to pursue higher education and entrepreneurship,"
and she earned a degree in social studies from the University
of Arkansas at Pine Bluff, a health sciences degree from the
University of Arkansas at Little Rock, and a degree from the
Agape School of World Evangelism. For over twenty-five years
she worked as a nurse and health educator at South Central
Career College, Aspen's Career One, Jefferson Hospital, and
at the University of Arkansas for Medical Sciences. Her
unpublished memoir, "Arkansas's Pine Bluff Civil Rights
Movement," is excerpted here.*

SNCC was born out of a student cry from a people who demanded that
freedom and inequality was long overdue and out of a need to challenge
man's inhumanity towards his fellow man . . . Late in the summer of 1962,
two young field representatives from SNCC's headquarters came to our
town . . . The representatives were a young black man by the name of Jim
Jones and William (Bill) Hansen, who was white. Robert (Bob) Whitfield
came also and would become the spokesperson for SNCC and the Pine

Bluff Movement. Whitfield and Jones were students at what was then AM&N College. Reverend Benjamin Grinage was also a field representative for SNCC.

These men became key figures in orchestrating and organizing the Movement in Pine Bluff. There were many . . . who gave their time, love, prayers, finances, and their physical involvement. There were many whites who were instrumental and involved in areas that were not known by the media . . . Let us not forget the courageous high school and college students, many of whose parents lost their jobs because of their children's involvement in the Movement . . .

I felt a sense of mission, a sense of assignment, a sense of calling, a sense of being set aside for a purpose, for an hour of history at hand . . . The time had come for the nation to look at itself and turn from the practices of injustice and segregation. When we look back on human history, we see that God has always used a people that he would set aside to bring His will on earth. The Movement in Pine Bluff and throughout the South, I believe, was God using people, who happened to be students, both black and white, to bring about His purpose and change the earth . . .

At sixty-one years of age, I look back through the years past and I see teenagers out until 10:00 P.M. knocking on doors, selling two-dollar poll taxes to individuals who had never voted. I see myself and other teenagers walking in picket lines for hours, sitting-in at lunch counters, libraries, movie theaters, being attacked by police dogs, along with many other injustices and indignities . . .

In August of 1963, Arkansas governor Faubus would come to Arkansas AM&N College to dedicate the new Vocational Arts Building. Governor Faubus would be met by student protesters from the college and the Pine Bluff Movement, which included protesters from the four high schools . . . The feelings of the protesters were that the governor had not been supportive of educational improvements at the college level.

During Governor Faubus's dedication and speech, we peacefully marched in single file carrying signs that read, "Governor, would you send your children here?" and "Beautiful buildings do not represent quality education." The police and state troopers stood by as we quietly and orderly carried the protest signs. There were no arrests that day. During the governor's speech, flyers were passed out to the crowd, which announced upcoming mass meetings, where issues and concerns of the community would be discussed. The president of AM&N College, Dr. Lawrence Davis Sr., was not in agreement with our protesting the governor's presence on campus and would later dismiss those students who were part of the protest and the Pine Bluff Movement.

President Davis was an excellent educator and leader who pursued the highest quality of education for his people and AM&N College. Yet there were harsh consequences for being known as a freedom fighter, demonstrator, protester, SNCC participant, freedom riders, and agitator. That is just a few of the many names that we were called for our involvement in pursuit of civil rights. What we would experience in the early days of the Movement was that we would not be held in high regard by everyone, even in our own community. I and other high school students would also be dismissed from school because of our being involved in the struggle for equality.

Good, solid education was our paramount concern for our people. Our demands and concerns were not to integrate with white people. We had good black teachers who were excellent educators, who were committed to and who loved teaching their students, who taught morals and values, and were committed to excellence . . . Therefore, our issues of protest were not for better educators or to mingle with whites. The issues were: allow me to have choices, the freedom to choose, and to exercise all of my God-given rights. . . . I do not believe that integration was the driving force behind the civil rights movement. As I look back over the Movement's history in the South, I see that integration was the end result of breaking down barriers and walls that prohibited people of African descent from experiencing all the rights and privileges of a free people . . .

Students were aware of the consequences of joining the Movement . . . We had to make a decision to protest for civil rights or go to school. The high school students were able to return to school. Many of those who were suspended from college classes were not able to return that semester . . . Many of the college students were living in campus housing, therefore when suspended they would have to find housing. Lack of housing accommodations for these suspended students would lead to the birth of the Freedom House, which became home for these suspended students. Students were joining the movement daily. The numbers had increased to almost two hundred. During the mass meetings, strategies and plans were decided about how to protest and how to march at several locations at the same time. Our numbers were such that we could split into different groups and demonstrate at two or three locations at the same time. This strategic move would always confuse the police about where our next targets of protest would occur. This method of protest and demonstration proved to be effective in making sure we were not all jailed at the same time. The objective for using this method was to always have protesters available to protest, march, or picket whenever some members were being jailed . . .

I recall on one afternoon, the group that I was demonstrating with was picketing Cohn's Department Store on Main Street in downtown Pine Bluff. We marched in single file in front of the department store carrying signs of protest against their unfair hiring policy . . . As twenty-five members of our group protested the hiring policy of this business, another group of protesters was marching at the public library. Still another group of twenty-five protesters was demonstrating at Oakland Park.

This plan of protest had many advantages and proved to be very effective. When the group was arrested at Oakland Park, the groups at the other two locations were able to continue demonstrating and replace those at Oakland Park who were arrested . . .

The student movement could always count on black businessmen to put up bail for us when we were arrested . . . Mr. Lewis Yancey and H. O. Gray would be among the first to arrive at jail when we were arrested . . . My sister Vernett and I were arrested and jailed during five different protest marches. Our concern was to be released from jail as soon as possible. On one rare occasion, we had to remain in jail seven days . . .

Those were the times when the support of the community was vital. The racial atmosphere was of such anger and hostility that the policemen would shove us and make threats. Therefore, it was crucial that the community responded to us. Coming to the jail as soon as we were arrested and making daily contact with us kept us encouraged. It also made the police accountable for our safety . . .

The day before each protest march, we would gather at the mass meetings for prayer and songs. Praying and singing was like being baptized before going out into battle. Many times the meetings would continue on to midnight. I read where Harriet Tubman would always go down to the river and baptize herself before each rescue operation. I am sure she must have felt that power from God was needed for her to be successful in the rescue of slaves from bondage. We also knew the importance of being spiritually renewed before each protest march. Our lives were always in danger and the protection of God was needed . . .

We were beginning to realize the cost of freedom. The nation would become stunned when three civil rights workers were killed in Mississippi. A young black freedom fighter named James Chaney and his two white companions, Michael Schwerner and Andrew Goodman, had disappeared and would later be found buried after they were slain.

When news of their disappearance and murder reached us, the Pine Bluff SNCC headquarters called a special mass meeting for prayer and discussion of our safety. We now realized that there were those who were willing to halt integration and equal rights by killing . . . Our parents had now begun to worry about our safety. My own mother would consider now forbidding my sister Vernett's and my continued involvement in the Movement . . .

Peaceful nonviolent confrontation and resistance was a method that Dr. King felt would be the best weapon in bring about change in America. I also felt this method was the appropriate method for bringing about change in America. Many more lives would have been lost if violence had been used . . .

Nonviolence would be the victor in desegregating McDonald's restaurant in Pine Bluff, Arkansas, and in desegregating other public facilities. During the summer of 1964, the Pine Bluff Student Movement would openly challenge segregation at McDonald's restaurant . . . The night before the big demonstration, a mass meeting was called to plan the strategy for peaceful, nonviolent demonstrations. We were apprehensive and yet not frightened . . .

The previous night of prayers, songs, tears, and final instructions had prepared us for the moment of history. Robert Whitfield, chairman of the Pine Bluff Movement, Bill Hansen, a white field representative, and Reverend Benjamin Grinage were now ready to lead us in the protest against McDonald's restaurant. Jim Jones, another field representative for SNCC, would accompany us on that summer afternoon. As we entered the restaurant in a single file, we orderly made several attempts to place our orders. We were repeatedly ignored by the waiters. White customers continued to come in and place their orders. The orders were served over our heads to white customers while we stood in line for service . . .

As the white customers came inside the restaurant, some would shove us or use profanity directed at us. While we were inside McDonald's, attempting to place our orders, a mob of about two hundred white youth were gathering outside . . . Some of the youth were carrying bats, bottles, and bricks. This was one of the rare occasions that we hoped the police would show up . . . As the mob continued to gather outside, we began to plan our next move. Then, without warning, the air conditioner was turned off at the entrance to the restaurant. The front doors of the restaurant were locked at the same time. We were now crowded into the small entrance of the restaurant. We were unable to exit and no one could enter . . . Due to the lack of air inside the enclosure, we began to experience feelings of suffocation . . . Some of us began to panic. I recall wondering if I would make it out alive . . .

When the police arrived to arrest us, the doors were unlocked. We knew that we would be arrested but we were glad to be able to breathe . . . We were charged with failure to leave a place of business and we were told that we were under arrest . . . As we exited the restaurant, the mob outside began to attack us with bottles and clubs. One of the students was shoved through the glass window of the restaurant but was not seriously injured. We had been taught in workshops how to protect our heads and faces. It was now time to use the methods we had learned. Some of us would sustain injuries before the police could arrest us. As we braced ourselves against the mob's attacks, the police were also unleashing the police dogs on us. There were screams, and we all had a fear of being bitten by the police dogs. We were then hustled into what they called the paddy wagons and we escaped the mob and the dogs. But one student was bitten and was later treated.

We were hurried off to jail . . . This would be the first arrest for some us. We did not quite know what to expect . . . We were not handcuffed nor were we beaten . . . After being fingerprinted, each of us was photographed. We would now have a criminal record and we would join the other protesters who were in jail. Twenty-four students were already in jail who had been arrested at the Pine Bluff Library . . .

As young students, we were eager to be called freedom fighters. But we had not experienced going to jail and actually being locked up behind bars. The moment of reality was before us . . . Many students were beaten in jail in other parts of the South. I was not aware of any protesters being beaten while in jail in Pine Bluff. We were crammed into small cells and were served three meals a day. We would encourage ourselves by singing freedom songs . . . These were the songs that kept our spirits soaring over the many months of demonstrations. I pondered over the idea of having a police record. Then suddenly it did not matter. I felt a sense of honor during those days of incarceration. I would feel a sense of assurance that I was going to jail for the civil rights of all people . . .

The summer of 1964 would be one of remembrance and hard work . . . Destruction of racism in America would not be an easy task . . . The old ways of living would not easily give way to a new season . . . From my earliest childhood, I can remember an unspoken friction between the races. Much of the racism we experienced as children was during our trips to town or walking home from school. This was before demonstrations began in our city. Our downtown trips exposed us to another form of racism. We were aware of separate water fountains in Kress and Woolworth's. As children, we could not understand the difference of separate water fountains. But we were unable to sit at the lunch counters for a coke or lunch. This was quite a contrast from our own neighborhood.

We grew up in a neighborhood where black and white families lived together. During my earliest years growing up in Dakota Street and Ohio in Pine Bluff, I do not recall conflicts with our white neighbors. We were all poor families. We lived together and played together. Our neighbors on either side of us were white families. When my mother braided our hair, she braided the little white girl's hair next door. There was a sense of family in our neighborhood. The exchange of food was very common. There was lots of fun and laughter within our neighborhood. We did not attend the same schools or the same church, but there was a sense of respect for each other. The local grocery store would always allow my parents credit. Johnnie Turchi, who was the owner of Turchi's Grocery, always treated us with respect and dignity. We often played with their children. Years later after becoming adults, we would discuss the old neighborhood with the whites who lived there. We agreed that both races shared a unique richness, and we learned valuable lessons from each other.

Those early years of living and growing together in an integrated neighborhood would provide me with valuable race relation skills even as a child, while teaching me acceptance and love for people of another race. We were not taught to hate or to make a difference because of color . . .

Dr. King and the leaders of the civil rights movement had now turned their attention to the poor in America, because the poor in America was not limited to blacks. At that time, there were more poor whites in America than any other group in America . . . Decent housing, health care, quality education, and employment were some of the issues that poor whites faced just as blacks had always faced . . .

Pine Bluff was slowly becoming desegregated. Public schools had been desegregated . . . Pine Bluff High School was among the schools that had been forced to comply with demands of student protest and enforcement of desegregation laws . . . Things were even changing concerning family life. Two SNCC fieldworkers were married out of state. One white and one black. However, at that time, Arkansas law prohibited interracial marriages, but there would be no legal action taken against the couple. In the area of government, D. W. L. Molette, a local black dentist, would run as an independent candidate for Fourth Ward alderman against a white incumbent . . . The incumbent won the alderman seat. However, a new black was emerging in Pine Bluff and was eagerly meeting new challenges and opportunities . . . Biracial committees and SNCC leaders had met for many months discussing and negotiating plans of desegregating the city without more violence. Both sides were willing to talk and find a means of peaceful settlement . . . The city was beginning to find ways to live together and the spirit of brotherhood was beginning to be demonstrated in the city . . .

[By the late 1960s], the civil rights movement in Pine Bluff had come to a close. Passage of the Civil Rights Act and Voting Rights Act had ushered in the beginning of an era of people in America realizing that Americans of all races would begin building and growing together for the betterment of America and all of its citizens . . . The civil rights movement had made its mark in history and left a legacy that would long be remembered in Pine Bluff . . . The days of demonstrating and marching seemed so far behind us but not so far in memory. Segregation and Jim Crow laws had been lifted. Integration was being tested through the city. All was not well, but the city and its black and white citizens were working together and moving toward equality and brotherhood. Jim Crow signs were removed from public places. Public facilities were now integrated . . . Employment opportunities were opened up to blacks. And yet the racial problems were not totally resolved in Pine Bluff nor in America . . .

We must believe that the future offers hope and new beginnings. We maintain the power to rebuild and shape our lives, our nation, and our world. We still have time to make choices of life, love, and peace. The past has much to reveal to us about the future. We have made great strides in race relations as we continue to work together towards brotherhood . . .

III.

Historical Documents

18.

"Up Against the Obstacles" (1960)

Inspired by the lunch counter sit-in in Greensboro, North Carolina, on February 1, 1960, fifty students from Little Rock's historically black Philander Smith College staged a similar protest at the downtown Little Rock Woolworth's on March 10, 1960. However, participants in this and other sit-ins that same year received harsh fines and jail sentences. The protracted legal battles that followed encouraged them to abandon temporarily their efforts. In the following document draft, Philander Smith student Frank James describes the motivations of the students involved in the initial protest.

"UP AGAINST THE OBSTACLES"

Little Rock, Arkansas

The spirit reached the boiling point at 11:00 a.m., March 10, 1960. It was on this day that the students of Philander Smith College cast their lots into the New Student Movement. The initial movement was impulsive in nature; however, organization began shortly there after.

The students shared the opinion that our action was not taken merely as Philander Smith College students following a trend, or as persons acting under the influence of others, but rather we felt it our moral obligation as American citizens who so happen to be born Negroes. And by this fact of which we have had no control, we are discriminated. We felt that as Americans we were deprived of privileges shared by other American citizens. A citizen of the United States of America regardless of race, creed, or color . . .

With the obtaining of more education the question "why discriminate me" has become a constant nightmare in the lives of every man who

Source: Reel 4, *Student Nonviolent Coordinating Papers, 1959–1972* (Sanford, NC: Microfilm Corporation of America, 1982)

has been discriminated. It is then felt that someone has to move. The older heads with idlesome ideas are thinning out, consequently with each new generation will come more and greater accomplishments. So it is our duty to make it possible for those of the future, who are discriminated because of skin pigmentation, to have better roads to travel than are present for us . . .

We the students of Philander Smith College like other students across this wonderful America have sacrificed and pledged ourselves to use intelligent and peaceful means to right the wrongs imposed upon us. We will use peaceful means to protest against those enterprises and establishments who because of race, creed, or color, discriminate its patrons.

The action here in this unique of all Southern states, Arkansas, has been up against many obstacles . . . The students mingled among themselves discussing the possibility of staging a protest in downtown Little Rock . . . Although the students had little knowledge of non-violence, [they] were able to avoid any incidents . . . Those students who felt that they should participate were invited to join in and those who feared the consequences that might be a result were urged not to partake in this fight for human dignity . . .

by Frank James
Senior, P.S.C.

19.

"The Student Nonviolent Coordinating Committee"

Nat Griswold was the first director of the Arkansas Council on Human Relations, which was founded in 1954. The organization had ties to the Southern Regional Council and supported efforts to desegregate public schools and accommodations in Arkansas. The national SNCC office sent organizer Bill Hansen to Arkansas in 1962 at the behest of the ACHR. In this excerpt from his unpublished autobiography, Griswold recalls Hansen's arrival in Arkansas and gives his brief assessment of the group's activities in the state.

The Student Non-Violent Coordinating Committee

The Arkansas Project of SNCC was not firmly established until October, 1962. As early as March, 1960, students at Philander Smith College, stimulated by the news of the sit-ins and encouraged by the NAACP, sat in at lunch counters on Main Street. Sit-ins were resumed in November of the same year, led by dedicated and courageous students. Officially, Little Rock gave them rough treatment—quick arrests, stiffest court penalties possible under Arkansas laws, delays in final court adjudication . . . Nevertheless, these students were harbingers of things to come. They aroused firm support from most adult Negroes and understanding sympathy from liberal white groups. Facetiously these students called themselves, "Arsnick."

In October of 1962, Bill Hansen came from the regional office of SNCC to organize the Arkansas Project. Bill and the project functioned

Source: From Nat Griswold, "The Second Reconstruction in Little Rock," 1968; Book II, Chapter VI, "The Role of Negro Arkansas," and Book III, Chapter I, "Arkansas SNCC and Carmichael's Black Power"

characteristically through 1965. The "Black Power" policies instituted by Stokely Carmichael ended the Arkansas Project in 1966.

The role of SNCC in Arkansas was similar to that played elsewhere. Direct action on the main streets was the fuse that started stalling business leaders to make changes. This brash confrontation with the obvious points of injustice opened the way for helpful action by the liberal organizations of Negroes and whites. White liberals in the larger towns and at universities gave moral support and enlightened public interpretations. Small groups of college and church young people sponsored SNCC speakers and quietly participated in a few projects, most of which were out of the state . . .

Bill Hansen . . . reached Little Rock from the Atlanta Office of SNCC on October 24, 1962. Tall, lean, with a nervous bounce in his walk, Bill consumed fabulous quantities of food and sleep on the infrequent occasions either was available. He came to the South from Xavier University, Cincinnati, on a "freedom ride" in 1961. Previously, non-violence became an article of his faith through observations and personal experiences with organized labor. He stayed in the South and endured the punishment reserved by racists for "white Negroes," including a broken jaw in prison.

With Hansen's guidance and that of his successors, Arkansas SNCC experienced significant achievements and frustrating failures. In Little Rock, students of Philander Smith College, organized by Hansen and Worth Long, a student, began sit-ins at lunch counters downtown on November 7, 1962. Organized businessmen who had done their homework in advance asked for terms from the students on November 9. A "Negotiating Committee" was agreed upon. It functioned as the agency for change for many months. Downtown restaurants, hotels, theaters, and restrooms were opened to all. Most first-rate cafes, cafeterias, and laundromats throughout the city were desegregated. The committee remained largely anonymous.

Meantime, Pine Bluff became the center for activities of SNCC. With assists from business and human relations leaders of Little Rock an interracial negotiation committee was formed there. College and high school students, rather solidly supported by Negro adults, repeated the success of Little Rock. With rallies at Allen Temple Methodist Church, street marches and sit-ins unchecked by violence and mass arrests, and songs in jail loud enough to attract Dick Gregory to the scene, the students operated from "Freedom House," through which flowed the usual procession of Negro and white volunteers. From Pine Bluff as a center, Snickers touched down at many points in east and south Arkansas with varying degrees of tribulations and achievements . . .

SNCC came to the South and Arkansas with a refreshingly simple creed, "Freedom, freedom, freedom, now." To these students "freedom" was a clear, concise concept: free participation in all aspects of the common life. They were not hard to understand. Their message carried across the nation and aroused the moral sense of thousands. Their achievements, direct and indirect, are monumental. Integrity was their chief weapon. In Arkansas, the early veterans of SNCC separated from it when Carmichael came into power, separated because of dedication to its original principles, because of their integrity.[1]

The immediate objections of these Arkansas veterans of SNCC since have been endorsed and supported by older Negro leaders of the nation, who have exposed in detail the fatal defects in Carmichael's Black Power, its direction, its strategy, and methods.

20.

"Field Report, Pine Bluff, Arkansas" (1963)

In November 1962, community leaders in Little Rock agreed to desegregate most downtown public facilities. This success prompted SNCC member Bill Hansen to begin organizing other communities in the state. Together with Ben Grinage, who became the second staff member of SNCC's Arkansas Project, Hansen set up an office in Pine Bluff in late 1962. Their earliest and most eager recruits were students at the historically black Arkansas Agricultural, Mechanical & Normal College (AM&N) who protested segregation under the banner of the newly created Pine Bluff Movement. The following field report and press releases detail some of the early difficulties and triumphs of the Pine Bluff activists.

FIELD REPORT

(Pine Bluff, Arkansas)

TO: THE STUDENT NONVIOLENT COORDINATING COMMITTEE
FROM: WILLAM W. HANSEN, FIELD SECRETARY
SATURDAY, MARCH 23, 1963 through FRIDAY, APRIL 5, 1963

Saturday the effectiveness of the boycott became readily apparent. We had many people downtown picketing and handing out flyers asking the people not to buy downtown or at the Jefferson Square Shopping . . . Many people made comments concerning the obvious lack of Negro customers and shoppers downtown. The good white folks are starting to hurt.

There are rumors that negotiations are being set up and that someone wants to talk to the Pine Bluff Movement. At this point, though, we don't know anything definite.

Sunday we had our mass meeting at St. Peter's Rock Baptist Church
. . . We had the biggest turnout yet. Their were about six-hundred people
there. What is also heartening is that we are really getting the street folks
who will make this a movement. Up until this time the mass meetings
have been largely comprising these members of the church where we are
meeting, college people, and professional people with the poor folks only
making up maybe half the audience. Now the mass meeting is ninety percent those kind of people. A great number of high school students are
also coming to the mass meetings . . .

I called the Hotel Pines for reservations for a Mr. L.S. Nash and
party of six. I got the reservations. When Leon Nash, Mildred Neal,
Shirley Baker, James Jones, Ruthie Buffington, and Spurgel Hicks went to
the hotel that night they weren't given a room. As a result they sat down
on the couches in the lobby. After sitting there for about four hours they
reclined on the couches and prepared to go to sleep. At this point they
were arrested and charged with "failure to leave the premises at the
request of the proprietor" and "loitering." They were taken to the city
jail. The bond was set at $1800.00. One of the six, Spurgel Hicks,
wanted out but the rest all agreed to stay . . .

Tuesday night we sat-in at the Saenger Theater but when the group
was threatened with arrest Bob decided to leave because most of the
people there had not contemplated going to jail.

The next night, Wednesday, the plan was to go to jail if they forced
the issue. That night twenty-seven people, including Bob Whitfield and
Ben Grinage went to the show. They were allowed to stand there for
about forty-five minutes before they were told to leave. When they didn't
leave they were arrested and charged with "creating a disturbance in a
public place of business." The bond was set at $1500.00. Most of the
people arrested were students at Merrill and Southeast High Schools
here. When I went to visit the kids in jail the next morning they had
transformed the place. The cops really looked like they had had a tough
night. I could here the singing from six blocks away. I understand that
they kept up the singing all night long. None of the kids wanted out.

I got phone calles all day long from everyone in town it seemed.
Mothers were especially troublesome but I managed to talk my way out
of every bad situation. All the mothers but one eventually aggreed to
allow their sons and daughters to stay in jail if they wished. The big
problem in people coming out of jail was with parents who wanted them
to come out rather than the inmates themselves. One little fourteen year
old girl actually got angry with me when I said that I was going to post

her bond because her mother wanted her out. She told me to have her mother come to the jail so she could talk to her, I did this and and I'll be damned if she didn't talk her mother into letting her stay.

Thursday night sixteen more people went to the Saenger. They were all arrested and charged with the same thing . . .

Rev. Robinson has been causing trouble all week. Saturday morning we got word that he had gone to the jail and told everyone their that HE was going to get everyone out. It also seems that he was having a meeting at his church. Ben, Rev. Roberts, and myself, went to the meeting. We asked him what he had planned. He said that he had been arranging for bail with some people that he knew. We said that we already had the bail arranged for when we needed it. He promised that he wouldn't do anything on his own and that he would come to the executive committee meeting that afternoon. At two o'clock I got a call at the house saying that everyone was out of jail and that they were over at Robinson's church. When I got to the church he was in the process of defaming both Bob and myself. Finally Bob had had enough and told all the kids that he was leaving and going over to Freedom House. Every single one got up and followed Bob out. That was a real blow to the good Rev. and his ego . . .

Monday night we got word from our Attorney, George Howard, that he wanted to see us. In our conversation he said that it is obvious that a power struggle is going on inside the organization between Robinson and ourselves. He went on to say that he had talked to a city official with a big mouth earlier in the day and that the official told him that Rev. Robinson had made a deal with the chief to the effect that if the chief would let him everyone out of jail he (Robinson) would see to it that there were no more demonstrations and arrests. The chief readily aggreed. When we found this out we finally decided that Robinson had to go . . .

Tuesday night we had a special executive committee meeting at which a motion was passed asking for Robinson's resignation. It passed 12–2. Then he refused to resign so a motion was passed expelling him as chairman of the boycott committee and as a member of the negotiating committee. We didn't expel him from the executive committee itself because then he would really be able to say that we threw him out. When he saw that we weren't going to expel him from the executive committee he resigned. We accepted his resignation readily . . .

Our negotiating committee met the white folks on Wednesday night. We are calling a moratorium on demonstrations. A date has been set for the first phase of desegregation which no one is at liberty to divulge. The big problem is going to be trying to hold off the Negro community which is ready for battle and letting them know that we aren't pulling out. There is a rumor around that we have accepted money to hold off. Naturally when we stop demonstrations people are going to wonder what happened and we aren't able to tell them . . .

21.

Press Releases: "Students Attacked with Ammonia in Pine Bluff" (1963) and "Pine Bluff Movies, Schools, Park Open to All" (1963)

These two press releases describe both some of the difficulties and some of the successes of the Pine Bluff activists.

FOR IMMEDIATE RELEASE
JULY, 1963

NEWS RELEASE
STUDENT NONVIOLENT COORDINATING COMMITTEE
6 Raymond Street, N.W.
Atlanta 14, Georgia
Tel: 688-0331

STUDENTS ATTACKED WITH AMMONIA, ACID, IN PINE BLUFF SIT-IN

PINE BLUFF, ARKANSAS, JULY 29—Three students and a field secretary for the Student Nonviolent Coordinating Committee required medical attention here yesterday after they were attacked by whites throwing ammonia and bottles at them. The students, members of the Pine Bluff Movement, had been staging a sit-in at McDonald's restaurant, a drive-in hamburger stand, when the violence occurred.

Sources: Box 3, "Jefferson County Field Reports," William Hansen Papers, Martin Luther King, Jr. Center for Nonviolent Social Change, Inc., Atlanta; Box 48, "Arkansas Pine Bluff," *Student Nonviolent Coordinating Papers, 1959–1972* (Sanford, NC: Microfilm Corporation of America, 1982)

Bill Hansen, director of SNCC's Arkansas project, said that 25 Negro students sat-in at the restaurant yesterday in the fourth successive day of anti-segregation demonstrations. They brought blankets and books and sat in the glass-walled inside cubicle for four hours.

About 60 whites gathered at the door of the restaurant, Hansen said, and began throwing ammonia inside. The restaurant's manager, a Mr. Knight, threw cokes, ice and water on the students also. As police watched from across the street, whites continued to throw ammonia and acid. One Arkansas A&M student said his handkerchief was "eaten up" after he wiped a substance from his face.

When the students left the restaurant and were walking to the parking lot, Hansen said, the "whites moved in. James Jones, a SNCC field secretary, was knocked out by a flying bottle. Helen Rogens, 15, had a knife thrown at her. A beer can hit Carolyn Hall, 14, on her foot." Hansen said he was knocked down and inadvertently fell on Beatrice Burns, 16. All four required medical attention.

Hansen said the whites were "egged on" by L.D. Poynter, head of the Pine Bluff branch of the White Citizens Council. He said he would protest the lack of police protection to the F.B.I., local police authorities, and the Justice Department.

FOR IMMEDIATE RELEASE
JULY, 1963

NEWS RELEASE
STUDENT NONVIOLENT COORDINATING COMMITTEE
6 Raymond Street, N.W.
Atlanta 14, Georgia
Tel: 688-0331

PINE BLUFF MOVIES, SCHOOLS, PARK OPEN TO ALL

PINE BLUFF, ARKANSAS, JULY 29—Members of the Pine Bluff Movement announced that five movie theatres here have agreed to accept customers without regard to race.

Bill Hansen, a field secretary for the Student Nonviolent Coordinating Committee (SNCC), said the Saenger, Pines Drive-in, Zebra Drive-in, Malco and Community theatres all had integrated by today, July 29.

Hansen said 43 people were arrested at the Saenger Theatre in late May, then members of the Pine Bluff Movement staged stand-in demonstrations there.

The SNCC worker also said Pine Bluff's formerly white-only park opened to Negroes a month ago, and the city's white-only swimming pool will accept Negroes next spring.

Members of the Pine Bluff Movement have "sold" 925 poll taxes to Negroes in six weeks. Arkansas registration applicants have to purchase a poll tax to get their names on registration lists.

Hansen also said members of the Pine Bluff Movement had negotiated integration of city schools here, beginning in September. Grades one and two will integrate this year, and two grades a year after that until all school levels are integrated.

SNCC worker Hansen began work here with students from Arkansas A & M University. When anti-segregation protests began, 15 were suspended from the state-run Negro school. Eight of those expelled remained and formed the core of the Pine Bluff Movement, which grew out of attacks against segregated lunch counters.

22.

Letter to Ruthie Hansen from Bill Hansen (1964)

In the following letter, Bill Hansen informs his absent wife, Ruthie Buffington, about events in SNCC's Arkansas Project. Buffington, an African American Arkansan, married Hansen in October 1963. Because interracial marriage was illegal in Arkansas, the couple wed in Cincinnati, Hansen's hometown. When they initially met, Buffington was a student at AM&N College in Pine Bluff. Soon, however, Chancellor Lawrence Davis suspended fifteen students for participating in civil rights demonstrations. Buffington and several others were permanently expelled. At the time of this letter, Buffington is living in Cincinnati and completing her college education there.

Arkansas Project
Student Nonviolent Coordinating Committee

Main Office:	Arkansas Office:
6 Raymond Street, N.W.	420 ½ North Cedar Street
Atlanta 14, Georgia	Pine Bluff, Arkansas
688-0331	Jefferson 5-4436

Friday—2-28-1963[1]

Dear Ruthie,

   I loved hearing your sexy voice last night. At least I can go to bed remembering what your voice sounds like. When your not here and I don't see you for awhile it gets to the point that I don't even remember

Source: Box 3, "William Hansen Personal Papers," William Hansen Papers, Martin Luther King, Jr. Center for Nonviolent Social Change, Inc.

what you look like except, of course, that it looked good. I guess that's why I can't wait to see you again whenever I'm away for some time. I just can't wait to see that good looking woman.

I miss you so damn much, baby.

I just called Dr. Henry this morning in Clarksdale. He will coming over Sunday night to speak at the mass meeting at Allen Temple.[2]

I think that we are going to have some trouble getting the executive committee to agree to break the injunction. The meeting is going to be tonight at the office. Ben and Odail are in favor of breaking the damn thing. I just hope that Roberts isn't too much against it. If he is he can sometimes throw a good sized monkey-wrench into the works. Odail thinks that it is going to be possible to get the students this time to go. Also we have Julius and Bruce here and they work very well with the high school kids, especially Julius. If you'll remember Julius was in the army when we demonstrated last summer and Bruce was in Atlanta and just last week when Gregory and I were arrested the two of them were in Dorchester.[3]

The truck stop opened last night with a big bunch of thugs waiting outside for us to come. When we do go out there it is damn sure going to one helluva scene. Those cats out there are vicious and they aren't about to let us go to far without raising all kinds of hell. I just hope that people don't get hurt too seriously because I'm sure that some violence is going to occur. The price of freedom . . . .

Julius and Bruce are out now trying to steal some mimeograph ink from somebody. We finally got the machine fixed last week. It had to be reconditioned. WD Wells charged $28.74 to do it.

We need some money down here so damn bad we can't see straight. The Plymouth isn't running at all and the Rambler is just barely operating. Both of the cars need new tires. The Rambler has been on the highway for the last time until it gets some new tires. Those things are as bad as the ones that Bruce used to drive on his black Ford.

Pine Bluff made the front page of the Student Voice this week. It also had a picture of Jim on the front along with some of the high school kids. Gregory and my picture were on the inside.

I've got some other things to do so I'll close. I'll try to write you again tomorrow. It's time you write me a letter.

                                        Love, Bill

23.

"Field Report, Phillips, Monroe, Arkansas and Lee Counties"

James O. Jones, one of the students expelled from AM&N for participating in civil rights activities, became a field secretary for SNCC after his college plans were temporarily derailed. After participating in a variety of protest activities in Pine Bluff, Jones and other SNCC supporters began exploring the possibility of organizing in other counties. The following document is a field report that describes efforts to organize in Phillips County, one of the most notoriously racist areas in the state. When Jones arrived, African Americans there still maintained a strong, collective memory of the Elaine Massacre of 1919 when more than one hundred black Arkansans were killed after trying to form a union for agricultural workers.

FIELD REPORT

26 Senatorial District (Phillips, Monroe, Arkansas and Lee Counties)

To: The Student Nonviolent Coordinating Committee
From: James O. Jones, Joseph Wright, Larry Segel and Thomas Allen
RE: work in Phillips County from July 18 through July 21st.

One of the big problems that we have had in Helena is securing a place for a mass meeting. We decided to have a small meeting at some of the bars. Friday night July 18, we held a small meeting at the (Hut) American Legion Building. The manager at the Hut turned off the vender machine and we had about an hour and a half meeting.

Source: Box 10, folder 17, "Arkansas Projects, Jan. 27–May 8, 1964," Student Nonviolent Coordinating Committee Papers, 1959–1972, Martin Luther King, Jr. Center for Nonviolent Social Change, Inc., Atlanta

The meeting was on Voter Registration. We also related some statistics on Philip County. The Civil Rights Bill was outline and explain. There were interesting questions raised concerning the civil rights bill. Seemingly the most common questions raised was does the civil rights bill means we can go to white places without being arrested and has full protection of the law.[1] It seems that this was the first time people really realized our purpose for being in Helena.

The SNCC staff discuss the reaction of the people toward the leflet with freedom written on them. The discussion was thought of because of the limit amount of knowledge that exist among the people in Helena. People feel that when the word freedom is used you mean integration and without a question integration is not what they want.

We printed 2 thousand leflets on register and vote with some additional information. The door to door campaign was used. We received tremendous response. We received a number of phone calls people wanting to know what we plan to do in terms of candidates running and that they will tell their friends to register.

There is an existing organization in Helena call the Voter League. The Voter League consists of people that Negroes don't trust. We have had some dealing with these people. Voter League often endorses people like Lester Graves a candidate for prosecuting Attorney, who is almost a racist. We have been attending the League meeting and raising several questions on getting candidates to speak before Negro ordiance and give to the press their exact platform. These candidates will not do that neither will the league ask them to do so. This way they cannot give the Negroes one platform and white another.

This voter League also gives invitations to ministers and very many middle class people where as we attend we carry working people young people and college students. One terrible attitude that existed here in Helena was the prolaterian did not believe they could do nothing and there was a complete absent of self confidence. These are the people we spent a great deal of time with in convincing them they can do something and that they are not an out cast lost and cannot do nothing.

Another thing you have in Helena is a large numbers of young people that have one year in college but they just drift around the pool hall and other places. To them some body such as the SNCC workers, are what they needed to help them along.

The places where the civil rights demonstrations took places last year were tested after the civil rights bill was past. The only people that will go to these places are these people I just finish describing in the above paragraph.

Yesterday in Helena they were drifters today they became pioneers, the first Negroes to eat at the previous all white places, the first Negroes to go door to door canvassing and a few other thing that are similar in doing.

July 21, 1964, 8 Negroes went to Henry's Drug store and the store closed. The day or two before the staff went to eat and was serve the issue was made that the only people interested in integration were the outsiders the SNCC staff. Monday and Tuesday all Helena had spread the new. Tuesday as people left Henry's Drug store in route home the policeman block their cars in and would not allow them to move for about two hours.

24.

"Annual Report" (1964)

The following document describes both the Arkansas Project's initial civil rights campaigns in Little Rock and Pine Bluff as well as further initiatives in Lincoln, Phillips, and St. Francis Counties. By 1964, SNCC had established a high degree of visibility in Arkansas and had wrested enough concessions from local business leaders and authorities to make it a widely acknowledged force to be reckoned with among those who wished to maintain the mechanisms of white supremacy in Arkansas.

ANNUAL REPORT

1964

To: THE STUDENT NONVIOLENT COORDINATING COMMITTEE
FROM: THE ARKANSAS PROJECT
402 ½ N. CEDAR STREET
PINE BLUFF, ARKANSAS

ARKANSAS PROJECT STAFF:
JAMES JONES
BRUCE JORDAN
CLIFFORD VAUGHS
MILDRED NEAL
IRIS GREENBERG
WILLIAM HANSEN, PROJECT DIRECTOR

Source: Box 10, folder 17, "Arkansas Projects, Jan. 27–May 8, 1964," Student Nonviolent Coordinating Committee Papers, 1959–1972, Martin Luther King, Jr. Center for Nonviolent Social Change, Inc., Atlanta

ANNUAL REPORT

Arkansas has a total population of almost 1.8 million people of which around 420,000 are nonwhite. The nonwhites account for about twenty-five percent of the state's total population. The largest city and the capital is Little Rock with a population of 140,000. Arkansas ranks 49th, ahead of only Mississippi, in all aspects of life that point to a good standard of living.

Arkansas has four seats in the United States House of Representatives. The four are: E.C. Gathings (1st District), Wilbur Mills (2nd District), James Trimble (3rd District), and Oren Harris (4th District). The Arkansas delegation of six (four Senators and two representatives) has often been characterized, man for man, as the most powerful in the entire Congress. Mills is the Chairman of the House Ways and Means Committee and Harris is the Chairman of the House Commerce Committee. Fulbright is the Chairman of the Senate Foreign Relations Committee and McClellan is the Chairman of the Senate Investigations Committee. Gathings is very influential in the House Agriculture Committee and probably the most important man in Congress concerning cotton legislation.

The Student Nonviolent Coordinating Committee first came to Arkansas in September of 1962 at the request of the Arkansas Council on Human Relations. The Council was interested in having something done about the lunch counters in downtown Little Rock that still refused to serve Negroes. There had been an abortive attempt at this in 1960 but the sit-ins were stopped for a number of reasons. As a result in early November of 1962 students from Philander Smith College in Little Rock began sitting-in at the Woolworth and Walgreen lunch counter. Arrests only occurred on one occasion and then only two people, Worth Long and Bill Hansen were arrested. After the two were in jail for three days and PSC students sponsored several mass marches through the city they were released and the white community agreed to open the counters. This was done with minimum of difficulty on the 2nd of January in 1963. The negotiating committee that had been set up continued to negotiate and since then all of Little Rock's theaters and all of its hotels have opened to Negroes. Besides the hotels, lunch counters, and theaters, many restaurants in downtown Little Rock have been opened and also the department stores have hired Negro sales people and have agreed to hire more.

During the first week in 1963, Bill Hansen and Ben Grinage, a new addition to the staff, went to Pine Bluff to begin developing a comprehensive and voter registration in East Arkansas. Pine Bluff is forty-five miles southeast of Little Rock. East Arkansas is the western end of the infamous "black belt" that stretches across the south. It is in the Mississippi River Delta on the West side of the river. It is characterized by a rural economy; its income being derived mainly from the raising of cotton, soybeans, and rice. Arkansas is the fourth largest cotton producing state (following Texas, California, and Mississippi) in the United States. It is also the largest rice producing state in the union. The delta counties range from 40% to 61% nonwhite.

Pine Bluff was chosen as the point of initial activity in the delta for a number of reasons. It is located geographically in the center of the Arkansas part of the delta. The delta's northern point is around West Memphis, Arkansas and it stretches south to the Louisiana State line. Pine Bluff is located about 120 miles north of the Louisiana line and about 150 miles south of West Memphis. It is the fourth largest city in the state and the only city of any size in the entire delta area. Pine Bluff has a population of 53,000 people of whom 43% are nonwhite. The city is the location of the Arkansas AM&N College which is the only state school for Negroes. Prior to the advent of SNCC there was little civil rights activity in East Arkansas with the exception of the school desegregation suit in Pine Bluff. SNCC's plan was to build a movement in Pine Bluff that would not only stimulate the local community but also serve to motivate those rural areas surrounding Pine Bluff that are influenced by the city.

Hansen and Grinage arrived in Pine Bluff on January 6th. As they were leaving the campus of Arkansas AM&N College on the 10th of January they were arrested by the Pine Bluff City Police and charged with vagrancy and suspicion of passing bad checks. The next morning, they were brought out of their cells and warned by the Chief of Police, Norman Young, that if they stayed in town and tried to agitate they would be killed. Later that day the bad check charge was dropped and they were released on $500.00 bond on the vagrancy charge.

The first action centered around public accommodations specifically the Woolworth and Walgreen lunch counters. On February 1, 1963 students from AM&N College and some of the local high school students sat-in at the lunch counters. Immediately more high school and college students joined them. At this time we also started having our weekly mass meetings that have continued with a few exceptions until now. On the 10th of February the President of the College stated that any student that continued to sit-in at the counter would be summarily suspended from school. At this point many of the college students stopped sitting-in because of fear of suspension. Fifteen continued to sit along with the high school students and were suspended.

After a month of constant demonstrations, the lunch counters closed down completely. During this time their food trade had dropped to absolutely nothing because whites who wanted to eat couldn't get near the counters and Negroes who had been buying in other parts of the stores had stopped shopping there.

A boycott of the entire downtown area was instituted. The stores on Main Street were picketed daily. The boycott was judged to be between 80% and 90% effective. The boycott was even observed by Negroes who had come many miles to do their weekend shopping in Pine Bluff. Shortly thereafter mass arrests occurred at the theaters when demonstrations started there.

The combination of the closed lunch counters, a very effective boy-cott, and demonstrations and jailings at the theaters caused to negotia-tions to suddenly bring results. Both the disputed lunch counters were desegregated, and a short time later four of the five theaters opened on an integrated basis. The first theater closed down completely for business and has not opened to this date.

Out of these demonstrations was formed the Pine Bluff Movement. The organization is a cross section of the community. On its executive committee are two ministers (one of whom is the President of the Ministerial alliance), college students, high school students, the president of the Pine Bluff NAACP, several Negro business and professional people, and a few working people. It is hoped that the Pine Bluff Movement can become representative of the entire Negro community and effectively rep-resent it.

As the demonstrations were going on we started on a voter registra-tion drive in the city. In Arkansas a person wishing to vote had to pay a poll tax of one dollar. Approximately 27% of the Negroes in Jefferson County were registered to vote and when we started the voter registration drive. High school and college students canvassed door to door for months trying to get Negroes to pay their poll tax. One thing that became obvious during this time that that was a big reason for Negroes not registering to vote was that even if they did there was nothing for them to vote for in the way of candidates that represented their interests. By the time the registration books closed on the first of October we had registered 1,876 Negro voters. This was an increase of over 1200 voters.

During the summer demonstrations were started at the public park, the public library, and a drive-in restaurant. The park was desegregated after several severe beatings at the hands of white thugs while the police sat in their cars and watched. Twenty-five people were arrested at the Library before it closed for three days. When it reopened it was on an integrated basis. After mass arrests, beatings, & the throwing of acid at McDonald's Drive-in an injunction was handed down at Chancery Court that prohibited any more demonstrations at the drive-in. Months later, in February of 1964, McDonald's desegregated.

During the middle of July SNCC Field Secretaries, James Jones and Jimmy Travis started a voter registration drive in neighboring Lincoln County. The reason that Lincoln County was chosen for the initial expansion of the project was that, along with Jefferson County, it comprised the 20th Arkansas State Senatorial District and sent two senators to the state legislature.

Lincoln County has a total population of a bit over 14,000. 50% of this is nonwhite. Only about 22% of the Negroes were registered to vote. The county is a totally rural one with a farm economy. The largest and only incorporated town in the county is the county seat, Star City, Arkansas.

Star City has a population of 1500. In the 2 ½ months that Jones and Travis worked in Lincoln County before the books closed in October, 428 Negroes paid their poll tax and registered. While in Lincoln County, the SNCC staff worked with the Lincoln County Civics League. The Civics League is composed almost totally of small Negro farmers. Most of the Negroes in Lincoln County live on white owned plantations. This makes it extremely difficult to talk to these people because SNCC people are chased off as soon as they come on the "Man's" property.

In August of 1963, we formed the Citizens Committee for Molette to run a "Freedom Candidate" for city council. Dr. Molette is a local Pine Bluff Dentist who had been involved with the Pine Bluff Movement. Dr. Molette filed as an independent by getting the prescribed number of names on a petition to place his name on the ballot. The committee was headed by a local high school principal, Elijah Coleman, who for some unexplained reason didn't lose his job as a result.

The November 5th election brought out the largest off year vote in the history of the city. Dr. Molette was defeated 4400 votes to 2900 votes. This was the largest number of Negro voters within memory to vote. The contest involving Molette was the only contested issue on the ballot. The only other races were three other uncontested city council positions. In the 1960 Presidential election the total vote was 9000 and in the 1963 the off year vote was 7300. This can be attributed totally to the fact that Negroes had decided to take part in the democratic process.

The campaign produced two very good results. The first was that it finally gave the Negro community a candidate that would serve their interests and therefore have a reason for exercising their franchise and secondly it demonstrated to the white community the latent potential of the Negro vote.

In late October two SNCC staff members, John Bradford and Noah Washington, started working in Helena, Arkansas. Helena is the seat of Phillips County which had a population that is 59% nonwhite. Only about 28% of the Negroes over the age of 21 are registered to vote. Phillips county is the 10th largest county in the state with a population of 43,000. Phillips county is the poorest county in the entire state.

It has the reputation of being the most corrupt and the most brutal for Negroes. According to the 1960 United States census report only three per cent of the nonwhites in Phillips County have completed twelve years of school and 65% of the nonwhite population has not completed six years of school. The median amount of years in school is 5.4. Seventeen percent of the nonwhite workforce is unemployed and of the nonwhites that are employed 72% make less than $1000 per year. In 1919, a severe race riot occurred in Elaine, Arkansas which is in Phillips County a few miles from Helena. In the riot many Negroes and a few whites were killed. The riot stemmed out of an abortive attempt to organize the Negro farm workers. Whites in Phillips County have been using the riots for many years to intimidate Negroes.

In November there was an attempt to sit-in at a local drug store. The police immediately surrounded Cherry Street (the town's main street) with shotguns and other weapons. The sit-inners were arrested. The three SNCC staff members who were in town at the time, John Bradford, Bruce Jordan and Bill Hansen, were immediately picked up whereever the police could find them. Bradford was arrested as he was getting into the SNCC car and charged initially with car theft. The charge was later changed to inciting a riot. Hansen was arrested as he sat in a Negro restaurant talking on the phone with the SNCC office in Atlanta. Jordan managed to hide from the police for four more days by staying in a church basement and not coming out during the day. The police finally caught him in a Negro barber shop. He and Hansen were also charged with inciting a riot. When James Jones, a SNCC field secretary, tried to arrange bond for the three in jail he was told to get out of the county and that if any more SNCC people came into the county they would be arrested as soon as they crossed the county line.

While in jail Hansen and Bradford witnessed a joyful celebration by the Helena Police when they heard that President Kennedy had been killed.

On December 6, 1963, [when] Bradford and Jordan returned to Helena to again try and organize a voter registration drive they were arrested. They had been in town only three hours and were parked in the driveway of the Catholic Church when the police apprehended them. They were charged with "conspiracy to create a disturbance." The appearance bonds were $750.00 a piece the first time and 1,500,00 a piece In early January SNCC workers, James Jones and Bruce Jordan again went into Helena to organize. At this point they haven't been arrested but the intimidation has been very effective. Negroes in Helena are afraid to talk to the SNCC people. When they tried to rent an office space or living quarters they are turned down because Negroes don't want to have anything to do with them.

SNCC people have also worked briefly in Forrest City, the county seat of St. Francis County. We had to pull the people out of there and send them to Phillips County because there aren't enough on the Arkansas staff to cover the existing projects. St. Francis County is very much like Phillips County with a population that is 50% nonwhite. Forrest City with a population of 12,000 is the largest in the county. The median amount of years in school completed is 5.8. Over 61% of the nonwhites have not completed six years of school. 10% of the nonwhite work force is unemployed and of those Negroes employed 72% make less than $1000 per year. In February 1964 Dick Gregory came to Pine Bluff to speak at a mass meeting. Later that night he and Hansen were arrested for trying to get service at a truck stop on the outskirts of town. As a result of the arrests the Pine Bluff Movement started concerted demonstrations at the truck stop. Many people were arrested. The Jefferson County Chancery Court then granted the owner an injunction against the demonstrations at the truck stop which, at this point, hasn't been broken.

In January, 15 merchants agreed to hire one or more Negroes in sales positions in downtown Pine Bluff. One of the stores, Cohen's Department Store, reneged and is now being boycotted by the Movement.

In February, we formed the 20th District Voters League. This organization is bringing together the people of Lincoln and Jefferson Counties to plan action that effects both of them on a district wide basis. The Voters League plans to run Freedom Candidates in the November elections. Both of the state senatorial seats from the district are up for election and all five of the seats in the state house of representatives are up for election. Some or all of these candidates will be opposed by the Voters League.

Eventually similar organizations will be formed in other parts of the delta. These organizations will be tied together to get all the Negroes in all the delta in a highly organized and effective political organization that will run candidates and hopefully reform all of East Arkansas.

25.

"Hansen Resigns SNCC Post; Says Negroes Should Lead But He'll Stay as Adviser" (1964)

Like other white civil rights workers throughout the South, Bill Hansen found that he was under a great deal of scrutiny, both from hostile whites who viewed him as a race traitor and from liberal whites who applauded him for making personal sacrifices for the cause of civil rights for African Americans. As a result, he was the subject of a great deal of media coverage. By 1964, Hansen began to worry that his local celebrity status was becoming a distraction and was giving the misleading impression that white, rather than black, activists were at the vanguard of the movement. The following newspaper article announces Hansen's decision to step down as director of the Arkansas Project in favor of black leadership.

Hansen Resigns SNCC Post; Says Negroes Should Lead But
He'll Stay as Adviser

By ANNE REEVES

PINE BLUFF—William W. Hansen Jr. announced his resignation Tuesday as director of the Arkansas project of the Student Nonviolent Co-ordinating Committee because he believes the group should be led by Negroes.

Hansen, 25, a white man, said that James Jones, 21, a Negro and native of Willisville (Nevada County), had been named acting project director. Jones is expected to be appointed as Hansen's successor by the executive committee of SNCC, which has national headquarters at Atlanta. Hansen said he would remain with SNCC as a field secretary and work out of the Pine Bluff office, SNCC headquarters for the state.

Source: *Arkansas Gazette*, August 26, 1964, A10

Hansen is formerly of Cincinnati. He married a Pine Bluff Negro, the former Ruthie Buffington, October 12, 1963, at Cincinnati.

He announced his resignation at a news conference.

"I felt that I should resign because at this point it [SNCC] is essentially, mainly a Negro movement." Hansen said, ". . . I feel that the situation calls for Negro leadership. The times now demand Negro leadership."

He said, however, that until more white persons allied with Negroes, the civil rights movement would not be complete. "But it is now essentially a movement of Negroes and should be led by them," he said.

"I have always been opposed to white leadership [in civil rights movement] in too many places over the country. White people feel the decisions should be made by them. But it is my personal opinion that [although] no doubt white people play a significant part it is the Negro's place to take the leading responsibility."

More 'Projected'

Hansen said that Negroes were becoming more and more "projected into society."

"Responsible Negro leadership has always existed," he said, "but it has only become apparent through this projection. When Negroes exhibited their leadership the civil rights movement really came to the forefront."

He said that his wife would continue her job as a SNCC field secretary.

Hansen said 11 persons were on SNCC's Arkansas staff. Three of them, including himself, are whites. The other two are Arlene Wilgoren of Boston, a field secretary at Pine Bluff, and Larry Siegel of New York City, a field secretary at Helena who recently went to Atlantic City.

Jailed in Mississippi

Hansen left Xavier University in 1961 to join a freedom ride to Mississippi, where he was jailed. When he got out, he decided to stay in the civil rights movement and went to Maryland, joined SNCC and helped organize demonstrations at Cambridge. He was sent to Little Rock in 1962 as SNCC's first representative in Arkansas. He helped organize some sit-ins at Little Rock and then moved to Pine Bluff in January of 1963.

He said he submitted his resignation two weeks ago.

Jones, who was suspended from Arkansas AM and N college here in 1963 for participating in sit-in demonstrations, has been with SNCC for about two years. Until recently he was director of SNCC's Negro voter registration drive in the Twenty-Sixth Senatorial District with headquarters at Helena.

Jones said that SNCC planned to organize in Lincoln, Phillips, Lee, Monroe, and St. Francis Counties primarily to register Negro voters. He said that less than 50 per cent of the eligible Negroes in those counties held poll taxes but that many more than 50 per cent would be registered before the November election.

Bagsby Attends

James Bagsby, a Negro of Pine Bluff and chairman of the Pine Bluff Movement, also attended the news conference. He said that the executive board of the Movement, an affiliate of SNCC, included representatives of 24 organizations. He said that "several" of the members were white persons, but declined to identify them or say how many there were.

He said that organizations represented on the board included the NAACP, ministerial alliances, fraternities and sororities, women's groups, civic groups and voter leagues.

Bagsby was asked if he knew if there were any members of the Black Muslims, a militant Negro organization, in Pine Bluff. He said he understood there were, although he did not know who they were. He said that he had seen some Muslim literature in Pine Bluff. No Muslim is affiliated with the Movement, however, he said.

Hansen said he understood that the Muslims had a temple at Little Rock.

26.

An Open Letter from Representatives of the Forrest City (Arkansas) Movement (1965)

Between 1965 and 1969 the Forrest City public school system responded to mandates to desegregate by offering a "freedom of choice" plan. In theory, black students would now have the right to attend previously all-white schools. However, in towns throughout eastern Arkansas local authorities used cumbersome and confusing bureaucratic procedures, intimidation, and other tactics to render the "freedom of choice" integration scheme ineffective. Forrest City did not implement a meaningful plan for school desegregation until the 1970–1971 school year. In this document, written in 1965, African American students from the local black high school describe their efforts to achieve a better educational environment at the black high school as well as the immediate implementation of a plan for school integration. SNCC members Millard "Tex" Lowe, Jerry Casey, and Pat Gladman offered these student activists advice and support.

AN OPEN LETTER FROM REPRESENTATIVES OF THE
FORREST CITY (ARKANSAS) MOVEMENT

Approximately two weeks before school was to start a group of Lincoln High students assembled at Forrest City Freedom Center to discuss the development of a group to represent students and seek change in the school. Out of this first meeting came the Students for Action Committee (S.A.C.). Officers were elected and the group was set up to function in a democratic way. Many S.A.C. members had previously been involved in the civil rights demonstrations of summer 1965 in Forrest City.

Source: Box 48, "St. Francis, Co.," Student Nonviolent Coordinating Committee Papers, 1959–1972, Martin Luther King, Jr. Center for Nonviolent Social Change, Inc., Atlanta

In the days immediately following this first meeting the idea grew among the students to develop a petition listing our specific suggestions for the improvement of school conditions. The petition was to be circulated among the whole student body for their approval and signatures and then presented to the school principal for his consideration. Over 1000 students supported the petition and signed it on the first two days it was circulated. In addition, a number of parents took it upon themselves to develop an informal parents committee to support the students. These parents went out into the community and gathered signatures of about 500 parents on the petition. On Tuesday, September 1st, the second official day of classes, we the S.A.C. students, presented our petition to Mr. C. T. Cobb, the Negro principal of Lincoln High, and spent the remainder of the day discussing our suggestions with him. Mr. Cobb admitted that many of the students' suggestions were fair and require serious consideration.

The petition has sixteen demands and is reproduced below:

1. No male instructor for girls' physical education classes.
2. Teachers at Lincoln High School show a complete lack of concern for students who are slow at grasping the material than others. We want to initiate a program in which students will advance according to their comprehension.
3. Put an end to students working in the counselor's office. Students should not have access to the records of other students. If the counselor needs help, someone should be hired to help.
4. More cooperation out of the counselor. Students tell the present counselor their problems and complaints. The present counselor then breaks this confidence by telling teachers what the students say. This is a breach of professional ethics. We demand the placement of a new counselor who has been trained in counseling students.
5. Put an end to teachers using profanity to students. If teachers continue this practice, we demand their dismissal.
6. Elimination of unnecessary fund drives. We demand to have an accounting of all fees that are gotten from the students, and also what happens to the money that is collected from the students.
7. An organized library program. The school board must immediately send for a representative of the accrediting association to tell the school what it needs to add to have an adequate library.
8. Elimination of unnecessary activities during class hours.
9. Immediate accreditation by the North Central Association.
10. A drama instructor.

11. A school nurse who will be qualified to give dental, eye, and ear exams (some students do not even have small pox vaccinations).
12. Busses to carry students to school who live on the outskirts of town.
13. The school board and the Lincoln School administration should meet monthly with representatives of the Student Action Council.
14. Free textbooks for all students.
15. Free lunches for all students who aren't able to pay.
16. Complete integration of the student body, faculties, and school busses of all schools in the Forrest City school system. We demand the institution of the Princeton Plan to facilitate school integration.[1] If this is immediately possible, we demand that registration be opened for the Freedom of Choice plan for this present term.

The next day S.A.C. officers and students again talked with Mr. Cobb. His attitude was markedly different from the day before . . . He flatly refused to consider any of our suggestions. He forbid the circulation of any material pertaining to the petition on campus . . .

[T]he majority of the students realize[d] that they could get no action from the authorities by using formal channels. The parents also resented the harsh and inconsiderate treatment that they had received when they petitioned the school authorities . . . S.A.C. students felt compelled to continue their campaign for improved conditions, we had only the alternative of a school boycott. This boycott would be a frank testimonial to the inadequacies of the education we received at Lincoln School.

On Thursday, September 16, we initiated our school boycott by staging a sit-in in the corridor of the Negro Lincoln High School at 8 a.m. Twenty students were involved. We were approached by Mr. Cobb, the Negro school principal, who tried to get us to go to our classes. However, we refused to do so. About fifteen minutes later, Mr. Irving, the white school superintendent, arrived, accompanied by Mr. James DeRossit, of the school board, Mr. DeWitt Smith, assistant superintendent of schools, and seven local policemen. We were told by the police that we would have to leave the corridor . . .

We then went outside of the school and began marching around the school singing freedom songs. As we walked around the school, our group began to grow—pretty soon we had 150 students marching with us. We were later approached by school officials once again and told that we would have to leave the school campus. We then marched over to a road at the back of the campus, grouped together, and continued singing. Once again, we were approached by school officials and police who tried to make us stop singing. But we would not stop . . .

The white school officials kept saying that people should go back to school and that they would do what they could to meet the demands but that the students had to realize that this "takes time." We then returned to the freedom center to discuss further action in order that our demands would be met.

On Friday morning September 17, we returned to Lincoln High School and picketed. Around 200 students were involved. After an hour of picketing we decided to march down to the white high school to discuss our demands with Mr. Irving. When we arrived at Forrest City High School Mr. Irving came outside and told us to leave. We told him we wanted to discuss our demands. He became rather furious and once again told us to leave because we were disturbing classes. About ten minutes later a fleet of about thirty state patrol cars pulled up. Mr. Irving threatened us with arrest if we did not leave. We refused to leave. He motioned to the police and said, "ok, get them." We were then arrested and taken by school busses to the St. Francis County jail. A number of Negro bystanders were arrested with us. Some of us were packed 40–50 deep in county jail cells—cells which usually hold 30 people. Others of us were sent to the condemned city jail.

Meanwhile, five policemen went to the SNCC Freedom Center and arrested SNCC worker Tex Lowe. That same afternoon trials began for the 198 students and 8 adults. S.A.C. members had not had time to get lawyers; therefore most of the students were charged with "disturbing the peace on public school property." They were found guilty, sentenced to 30 days in jail, and fined $250.00. Those who the police considered "leaders" were sentenced to 60 days in jail and fined $300–$500. Tex Lowe was charged with "disturbing the peace on school property" (even though he was not at the demonstration) and "contributing to the delinquency of a minor." His sentence was six months for the "disturbing the peace" charge and one year for the "contributing" charge. He was tried even though he asked for a continuance until he could get a lawyer.

Some of us were returned to the jail cells after the trial; others were sent to the white swimming pool and the white civic center which served as temporary jail quarters.

About 6pm that same day (September 17) Jerry Casey, SNCC project director, and Pat Gladman, a volunteer from Canada, were arrested and charged with "contributing to the delinquency of minors."

Saturday, September 18, a new group of students marched to the jail to protest the arrests of their schoolmates. No arrests were made. Also on Saturday, Tex Lowe and nine other students were taken to the Mississippi County Penal Farm.

By late Saturday afternoon all those previously arrested, except the ten at the Penal Farm, had been released on bond. On Sunday, those at the Penal Farm were released.

On Sunday night, September 19, Dr. Evans, a Negro representative from Gov. Faubus office in Little Rock, came to meet with the students. He listened to the students' demands and said he would arrange a meeting with the school officials . . .

They looked over the petition which now included a demand that all charges be dropped against those arrested. Some of our demands, they said, would receive immediate attention; others could not be rectified until they received their money under the new Elementary and Secondary Education Act. But they avoided discussion of our two most important points—that the charges be dropped and that the school system be fully desegregated immediately. They said that they could not drop the charges but that the courts would have to do this. They also argued that since their school desegregation plan had been accepted by the Office of Education, they could not open registration or change the way desegregation had been going. But we knew that they had not carried out the plan in good faith. They had re-routed the school busses so that Negro students in the rural areas transferring to white schools would have to [walk] extra miles to catch the school bus. They had also held the registration period before the Office of Education accepted the plan. In May, forms were passed out in school which parents had to bring back in 48 hours if they wanted to transfer their children to white schools.

In addition, the Negro principal had openly discouraged students from transferring: he told seniors that they might not graduate if they changed to the white school. He told other students that if they were expelled from or left the white school for any reason that they wouldn't be able to get back in the Negro school. There was only a little publicity about the fact that the white schools would be desegregated.

After explaining what demands they would act upon, the school officials pulled out a previously prepared typewritten page listing those things they would accept . . .

At a community mass meeting that night (Tuesday), the people and students rejected the school board's proposal because the two most important demands had not been met . . .

We are here in Washington to present our petition to the Office of Education and the Justice Department.[2] We are asking that these government officials take all actions possible to remedy the situation . . .

FORREST CITY, ARKANSAS 1965

27.

Ozell Sutton v. Capitol Club, Inc. (1965)

*In order to circumvent the Civil Rights Act of 1964, which man-
dated the desegregation of public facilities, the cafeteria inside
the Arkansas state capitol reorganized as a private club and
refused to serve black citizens. SNCC members attempted to
integrate the facility on several occasions but were turned back
by state troopers using tear gas and billy clubs. Civil rights
activist Ozell Sutton, then working as assistant director of the
Arkansas Council on Human Relations, successfully sued the
managers of the cafeteria for operating on a segregated basis.
The document below is the United States District Court's ruling.*

Ozell SUTTON v. CAPITOL CLUB, INC.

United States District Court, Eastern District, Arkansas, Western
Division, No. LR-64-C-124, April 12, 1965, F——Supp.——-

HENLEY, District Judge

MEMORANDUM OPINION

Ozell Sutton, a Negro citizen of Arkansas, has brought this suit in equity
to put an end to alleged racial discrimination in the cafeteria facilities
located in the basement of the Arkansas State Capitol. The defendant,
Capitol Club, Inc., an Arkansas non-profit corporation, holds a lease on
the facilities executed in July 1964 by the so-called Capitol Building
Commission . . .

The case has been tried to the Court, and this memorandum opinion
incorporates the Court's Findings of Fact and Conclusions of Law.

Prior to the organization of the defendant corporation on July 21,
1964, the cafeteria in the Capitol had been operated for a number of
years by Mrs. S. E. Tyer under lease from the Commission. The Court
finds from a preponderance of the evidence that while the cafeteria may

have been patronized primarily by State employees it was in fact a public eating accommodation. The Court further finds from a preponderance of the evidence that Negroes were not served in the cafeteria, and that their exclusion therefrom was on account of their race.

The Civil Rights Act of 1964 became effective on July 2 of that year. On July 15 plaintiff was at the Capitol on business and about lunch time he entered the cafeteria seeking service. He was advised by Mrs. Tyer that notwithstanding the passage of the Act, the cafeteria did not propose to serve Negroes until the Act had been tested in and construed by the courts.

On July 21, 1964, Clarence R. Thornbrough, the Executive Secretary to the Governor, and six other State employees, proceeding under Act 176 of 1963, brought about the incorporation of the defendant as a private club. On the same day Mrs. Tyer surrendered her lease to the cafeteria, and a new lease, which seems to be identical in terms to Mrs. Tyer's lease, was executed by the Commission in favor of the defendant corporation. Mrs. Tyer remained in the management of the cafeteria. She was not compensated for her lease, and she continued to use in the operation of the cafeteria her own utensils and equipment just as she had before the surrender of her lease.

The operation of the cafeteria continued from July 21, 1964 until later in March of the current year when it was closed following racial demonstrations which produced some violence.

It is the theory of the plaintiff that defendant corporation is not a bona fide private club: that both before and after defendant's incorporation the cafeteria was operated as a public accommodation; that racial segregation was practiced in the cafeteria prior to the defendant's incorporation and has been continued since; and that the alleged discriminatory operation of the facility is violative both of the Fourteenth Amendment to the Constitution of the United States and of the public accommodations provisions of the 1964 Civil Rights Act.

In defending the case the defendant asserts that it is a bona fide private club; that it is operating the cafeteria as such; that its operation is not State action within the purview of the Fourteenth Amendment; that its operation is in fact racially non-discriminatory; and that in any event it is as a private club exempt from the relevant provisions of the Act . . .

The Court does not believe that a detailed discussion of the facts or of the evidence is necessary or that such a discussion would be particularly helpful. While Capitol Club, Inc. was organized for the ostensible purpose of promoting the convenience of State employees in obtaining meals in the cafeteria more expeditiously than would be possible in a facility open to the general public, the Court finds from the record as a whole that following the defendant's incorporation and take-over of the cafeteria, the operation of that facility continued essentially as it had before. That is to say, before Capitol Club, Inc. was organized the cafeteria was a public eating place in a public building from which facilities Negroes were excluded on account of their race, and the Court is convinced that after the organization of the Club the cafeteria continued to be a public eating place with its patrons not in fact limited to Club members and their guests, and that the cafeteria under Club management continued to exclude Negroes on account of their race just as had been done when Mrs. Tyer was operating the cafeteria on her own account.

Prior to the passage of the Civil Rights Act of 1964 it had become established that the Equal Protection Clause of the Fourteenth Amendment prohibited a State or municipality from operating on State or municipally owned property a public restaurant, cafe, or cafeteria from which would-be patrons were excluded on account of their race or in which patrons were segregated on the basis of race; and that prohibition extended to the operation of such a facility by a private individual or corporation . . .

The Court's conclusion that the defendant's operation of a public cafeteria from which Negroes were excluded on account of their race constituted a violation of the Fourteenth Amendment renders it unnecessary to determine whether that operation was also a violation of the Public Accommodations Sections of the Civil Rights Act.

A decree will be entered enjoining the defendant from any resumption of the activities which the Court has found to be unconstitutional.

Dated this 12th day of April, 1965.

28.

Letter to Arkansas Summer Project Applicant (1965)

In 1965 members of the Arkansas Project decided to invite short-term volunteers from throughout the country to spend the summer in Arkansas. The program was modeled on the far larger 1964 Mississippi Summer Project, when more than 750 volunteers, most of them white and from the North, volunteered to spend their summers working in Mississippi. This large influx of outsiders who were new to the region and unfamiliar with the culture of SNCC ignited racial and class tensions within the organization in Mississippi. Learning from their example, the much smaller Arkansas Project was determined not to undergo the same kind of rapid demographic shift. Organizers in Arkansas invited an interracial group (half black, half white) of approximately fifty people to come to Arkansas for three-month stays beginning in June 1965. The following three documents describe the goals of the project and detail some of the instructions given to the volunteers.

Arkansas Summer Project
Student Nonviolent Coordinating Committee
700 West 9th Street
Little Rock, Arkansas 72201

Dear Applicant,

The Arkansas Project of the Student Nonviolent Coordinating Committee will be sponsoring a Summer Project in Arkansas this year. The main purpose of the project is to develop local leadership and community organizations throughout the black belt areas of Arkansas. To accomplish this end we are asking students from across the country to assist the Arkansas staff from June 1 to September 1. Despite continued harassment, occasional beatings, and numerous arrests during the two years that SNCC has been in Arkansas, much productive work has been accomplished, especially in the area of political activity.

During the summer, we will be working out of Freedom Centers in the eastern and southern parts of Arkansas. The Freedom Centers will be used for classes in voter registration, political education, Negro History, literacy, and various skills. Community meetings and recreational activities will also be held at the Centers. If you work for the summer project you will be expected to participate in any activity that needs your help. This means that you will not be just a teacher; you will also attend meetings, canvass, and work on voter registration.

By the end of the summer the people with whom you work should be able to do the jobs that you have been doing. Your main purpose will be to develop their abilities and confidence, so that the local community can carry on the functions of the Center on its own. No volunteer will be expected to stay beyond the first part of September. This places a heavy responsibility on everyone.

In order to work on the Summer Project you should do the following things:

1. Fill out the Attached application and send it to:
   Summer Project
   SNCC
   700 West 9th Street
   Little Rock, Arkansas 72201 (Phone (501) FR 59081)
2. Raise $165 to pay for all your food and extras during your 11-week stay in Arkansas. We will provide you with a place to live. If you think that $15 a week will not be enough, simply bring more. You must have this money when you arrive in Arkansas. It will be deposited in a special account here and given to you on bi-weekly basis. If you do not think you can raise the money on your own, talk to your local SNCC or Friends of SNCC office about ways to raise it.
3. Arrange for one or more persons to be able to go *at least $500* in bond for you in case you are arrested.
4. You must be interviewed by a staff member of Arkansas SNCC before you can be accepted for the summer project. Staff members will be in Washington, D.C., Boston and New York during the week of April 18 to 24. If you have any questions about Arkansas or the Summer Project, or if you would like to be interviewed, contact the SNCC office in the city nearest you. In some cases,

special arrangements for interviews will be made. Keep in touch with your local SNCC office. After you are interviewed, you will be notified by mail if you have been conditionally accepted. During May, members of the Arkansas SNCC staff will be in contact with you about the specific kind of work you will be doing to help you prepare for your job. When you arrive in Arkansas, there will be a week's orientation session. After this orientation, the final decision about whether or not you will spend the summer on the project will be made.

If you have any other questions, please write or call the SNCC office in Little Rock.

29.

Letter to Collin Minert from James O. Jones (1965)

This is a letter from Jim Jones inviting volunteer Collin Minert to participate in the 1965 summer project.

700 West 9th Street
Little Rock, Arkansas 72201
(501) Franklin 5-9081

May 17, 1965

Mr. Collin Minert
3808 N. Prospect St.
Milwaukee, Wisconsin

Dear Collin,

We are pleased to inform you that our staff has approved your application and would like you to work with us this summer in Arkansas.

As you know, the summer program will run roughly from June 5 to September 1. If you can come earlier, please let us know and we will be glad to have you.

We have not yet decided where you will be working. When you get to Arkansas, please come directly to the Little Rock office. Please let us know at once the date you expect to arrive in Little Rock.

It is our understanding that you do not have money to support yourself over the summer. If you can raise the money, please let us know as soon as you can. Otherwise we will find a group of people to support you at the rate of $15 per week. We will need to know, however, how long you will be here so that we can inform the support group and our Atlanta office.

The enclosed list should help you with your packing.

We all look forward to hearing from you and working with you in Arkansas.

> Yours for Freedom,
> James O. Jones
> State Project Director

30.

"What to Bring with You" and "Orientation Schedule" (1965)

The following instructions and schedule were given to SNCC summer volunteers before their arrival in Arkansas.

WHAT TO BRING WITH YOU

Bring an absolute minimum amount of clothing. The weather in Arkansas all summer is very hot and humid (temperature ranges between 85 and 100 in most places and the evenings don't get much cooler). You may want to bring a hat. Bring casual clothes. Bring at least one or two outfits you can wear to church or to meetings held in church. Girls—you should expect to wear skirts most of the time.

Bring your own linen and towels.

If you have any portable equipment, such as cameras, tape recorders, or musical instruments, we would like you to bring them. Please understand, however, that we can in *no* way guarantee that they will be in the same condition when you leave.

If you have a sleeping bag or air mattress, bring it with you.

If you are under 21, please have your parent or guardian sign a statement giving you permission to participate in the Arkansas Summer Project. Return this permission slip at once.

Write to us at 700 West Ninth Street, Little Rock, Arkansas if you have any further questions.

Source: Box 8, folder 7, Student Nonviolent Coordinating Committee—Arkansas Project Records, State Historical Society of Wisconsin, Madison

Orientation Schedule for Friday and Saturday, June 18, 19, 1965

Friday

11 to 12 noon	General orientation
1 to 2	What is Arkansas, SNCC history in Arkansas
2 to 4	History of each project
4 to 6	General Security and Conduct regulations and suggestions
7:30 to 9	Legal matters

Saturday

9 to 10:30 am	Political situation in Arkansas
10:45	Summer Programs

Each person will pose for an identification photograph during this session, preferably before noon of Friday.
Each person should fill out a medical form Friday morning.
Each person, who has not already done so, should get a drivers license at the State Capitol Friday morning.

31.

"82% Negro; 100% White" (1965)

The following document is an article written by Arkansas Project member Laura Foner for the October 26, 1965, issue of the Brandeis University student newspaper, The Justice. *Foner, a Brandeis graduate, spent nearly a year volunteering in Gould. In this article, Foner describes the state of the local civil rights movement and solicits donations for the financially strapped SNCC. Brandeis alumnae Nancy (Shaw) Stoller and Arlene (Wilgoren) Dunn also worked for the Arkansas Project.*

82% Negro; 100% White

By LAURA FONER, '65

Going South on Arkansas state highway 65 you will come to a cluster of three gas stations, and a sign:

GOULD, ARKANSAS
Population 1673

Gould is a town like 'most any other town in Southeast Arkansas. Look to your right and you are in typical small town America. The main street has two or three grocery stores, one general store, the post office, the bank, and the pool hall. City Hall, in the center of town, is one long room which serves as the police headquarters, the courtroom, the jail, and the "public library" (a few shelves of books along one wall). Except for the big cotton gin in the middle of town and the fields of white cotton which stretch every direction, you might imagine yourself to be somewhere in Massachusetts, just as much as in the middle of Mississippi delta country.

Source: *The Justice*, Brandeis University student newspaper, October 26, 1965, 4 and 7

Separate and Unequal

But look to your left—on the other side of Highway 65 and (literally) the other side of the railroad tracks. Is this still America? Are we not in the slums of some South American city?

Instead of the paved streets we find dirt roads. When it is dry, the dust covers you at every step; when it rains, the roads become impassable muddy streams. Houses are ramshackle two- or three-room wooden shacks where perhaps nine children share a bed (or the floor) and huddle together when the wind comes through the large cracks. The Negro high school, in the midst of a field of weeds and dust, consists of four old wooden buildings. Two of them are "Jap Houses"—or buildings that come from Japanese concentration camps during the war. "A rat's nest" is what the students call them, and indeed, many rats have found a home there. The description also applies to the general condition of the school—the large cracks and holes in the floors, ceilings and walls, the inadequate heating, and outdoor toilet facilities.

How can two worlds be so far apart and yet so close that only one two-lane highway lies between them?

That highway is easy to step across—and yet it forms "the line"— a line as impenetrable as a steel wall. By an unwritten law (unwritten on the statute books, yet branded into the flesh and hearts of millions of men), no Negro can step across that line *except* when he goes to cut the white man's yard or mop his floors, shop in the white man's store (where he can not get a job as a clerk), pay his bills at City Hall or the fine the white sheriff hands out whenever he wants some cash, or (before this summer) to eat at the side window of the white man's restaurant. Then he must quickly go back "where he belongs." We are in Gould to see what can be done to break down that wall.

Getting Things Done

What is needed is not tanks—but organization. What we are trying to do is to encourage the people in Gould to organize themselves to change their lives and the way this town is run. At present, Gould is run almost exclusively by a man named Howard Holtoff, one of the largest cotton planters in the state. Most of the people in the town who have jobs work for the Holtoff family—as tractor drivers, at the gin, or in the field. Gould is 82% Negro, yet there has never been a Negro mayor, city council member, sheriff, or school board member. Which is not to say that Negroes in Gould do not have the vote, as in Mississippi. Here, Negroes have always been voting (or been *voted*), but their vote and the whole political process is controlled by the same gang of white men.

And the few Negroes who have had the courage to run for office in the past have been defeated by all kinds of vote fraud and intimidation.

Our role as organizers is to urge people to get together to talk about whatever problems they feel are important and to search for ways of handling them. We are not here as missionaries, come to "save" anyone. We hope, rather, to encourage the people to help themselves—by helping them to realize their own abilities. Shortly after we began working in Gould, the people here set up their own organization—the Gould Citizens for Progress. They run their own meetings, and sponsor the various activities that have been going on since the summer, such things as voter registration drives, picketing the county courthouse when registration was taken out of Gould and removed to the county seat, testing two previously, segregated restaurants, picketing a gas station where a Negro was fired for work in the freedom movement, demonstrating in Gould and Little Rock to protest the conditions in the Negro school and the inadequacy of the desegregation plan (the case is now pending in federal court), and, for the first time, running a Negro candidate for the school board. Behind every action was much discussion, exchanging ideas, canvassing the town. And this takes time, because what you are fighting is a wall formed of the century-old attitudes of fear of the white man, of powerlessness in the face of a white world, of silent endurance of suffering and "waiting on the Lord." At each meeting, when people begin to share their hidden dreams, they begin to feel, perhaps for the first time, that they are something and that they have ideas worth listening to. When Negroes sit for the first time in an all-white restaurant, they begin to feel that things don't have to be as they have been. Things can change—and they are the ones with the power to change them.

A New Attitude

In this new beginning, the children are as much a part of the movement as the adults. The ones who have been coming to the freedom center know that it is not wrong to question. They are questioning their parents, their schools, their local government. They know it is not wrong to work for change—that to work for change is their right. (Some of the questions they have asked and we have tried to answer together are: "Why do policemen put you in jail when you are picketing for your rights?"; "Why did the guy beat up Tim for?" a (SNCC worker), "Why don't people who chop cotton get $1.25 an hour?"; "Why don't white parents let their children play with colored children?" to which the little girl who originally asked the question added—"If the parents would leave the children alone, they would all be friends.") They know it is their right to dream—

that they don't have to quietly bury those dreams under layers of indifference because of certain denial.

This is just the beginning. Any solution will demand change on a national level. But we must begin asking ourselves *today,* what can I do to contribute to the nationwide struggle for a new kind of life in a new kind of world?

*   *   *

Miss Foner is working for SNCC in Gould, Arkansas, a small town on the Mississippi border.

The SNCC operation is broke. They have six dollars in the bank and are $1300 in debt, with all of this month's utilities and rent bills to pay. They need money to keep from closing up the state office.

There will be collections in the dormitories on Thursday night to raise money. [Those interested in contributing] should contact Adele Smith '68.

32.

Letter to "Dear Friend" from Jim Jones (1965)

*Between June 1960 and December 1965, the national SNCC office pub-
lished a weekly newspaper, the* Student Voice *(later briefly renamed the*
Voice*). Although at times publication was irregular, the newspaper provided an avenue for SNCC volunteers in geographically distant places to
keep updated on the activities of their colleagues. The newspaper also
played an important role in fundraising. The historian Clayborne Carson
estimates that by 1964 more than 40,000 donors and supporters received
the publication. Inspired by the success of the national publication, the
Arkansas Project created a local counterpart, the* Arkansas Voice. *In the
letter below, then Arkansas Project director Jim Jones is soliciting funds
to keep the newspaper afloat.*

700 West 9th Street
Little Rock, Arkansas 72201
(501) Franklin 5-9081

July 20, 1965

Dear Friend,

We are including this note with the latest issue of the Arkansas Voice
because we need paper for printing the next issue.

Each issue is circulated free by SNCC workers to more than 8,000
people. In addition, a small mailing list of about 100 people who live in
Arkansas towns in which we don't work, are mailed the Voice. You and
about 350 other people, friends and relatives of current Arkansas SNCC
workers, are also mailed the Voice.

Source: Box 48, "Arkansas Correspondence," Student Nonviolent Coordinating Committee
Papers, 1959–1972, Martin Luther King, Jr. Center for Nonviolent Social Change, Inc.,
Atlanta

Formerly, Atlanta SNCC furnished the paper and covered the issue budget of about $50 (which included $18 worth of 4¢ stamps for the mailing list).

For the past 3 weeks SNCC has been broke and probably will be for the next month. We were able to mail you this issue thanks to donations by local newsmen. We would like to continue publication. We are sending you and the 350 others on the out-of-state mailing list this note. We ask you to send $1 to the Arkansas Voice for the next issue. Any money we receive over paper costs will go toward postage. (If you send a check or money order please make it out to Arkansas SNCC.) We are asking for donations of not more than $1 because we are only trying to get enough money to keep the Voice going.

Jim Jones
Arkansas Project Director

33.

"What We Shall Overcome Means to Me" (1965)

This document, a poem by an eleven-year-old Arkansas girl, demonstrates the role that the Arkansas Voice *hoped to play in providing a forum for local activists and citizens to document the activities and ideals of the civil rights movement.*

WHAT WE SHALL OVERCOME MEANS TO ME

It mean that Negro can do
what the White People do

We can own a Bank like White People
We can own a store like White People

And if we were in slave time we shall
overcome mean we shall be free one day.

And it mean that one day we shall have
color Negro salesmen

And we can go to the White Movie
We shall overcome mean that
White men can't kill color men anymore.

That we shall have best jobs as White
People.

Source: *Arkansas Voice*, July 16, 1965, page 3

And we shall overcome mean the color children
have good book in school like
White children

And the people who chop in the field
shall have more money

And it mean the policemen won't bother us anymore
And we shall overcome mean
the color police can arrest White People

It mean we shall have color teachers teaching
white children too
It mean that all children will go to
the same school
And we shall learn and play together.

White people have repaired street
and colored have dirt roads.
When we shall overcome our street
will be the same
And Negro have houses the same as White
People and we shall have bathroom on the
inside and color people have the right
to eat where White people do

Vote will be secret and fair for Negro.

The Negro of today want to have equal rights.
We shall overcome mean that we shall be treated the same way.

> Geraldine Smith, Age 11
> Forrest City Community Center

34.

Journal Entry by Mitchell Zimmerman (1965)

When he arrived in Arkansas in 1965, SNCC volunteer Mitchell Zimmerman was a graduate student in political science at Princeton University. While aiding the civil rights struggle, he hoped to conduct research about SNCC's unique style of community organizing. The following document is an excerpt from a journal he kept while living in Arkansas where he describes being arrested in West Memphis. As a white man who lived in the black part of town, local law enforcement officials regarded him with suspicion.

6 December 1965
Little Rock

For a lot of reasons, not worth going into here, I returned to our state project office here in Little Rock, where I'll be working on research. But my last days in West Memphis (shades of the last days of Pompeii!) gave me food for one last, long story from the field, for the time being.

I was North for a few days around Thanksgiving, and on my return to the state was greeted by a kind of official welcoming committee.

Following the breakdown of a car I was supposed to be driving South, in a desperate response to my lateness, I took a night flight to Memphis that I really couldn't afford. Via limousine and hitchhiking, I found myself on the outskirts of West Memphis at about three thirty a.m. with about a dollar and a half in my pocket. Loaded down with a suitcase, knapsack, and sleeping bag, I started walking to the place where we had been staying . . . On the way, a police car rolled past me, going the other way . . . I became somewhat more concerned when two minutes

Source: Box 8, folder 8, Student Nonviolent Coordinating Committee—Arkansas Project Records, State Historical Society of Wisconsin, Madison

later it went past me again. Luckily, I thought, I had reached the house where we had a room by the time it went past a third time . . . Safe at last, I thought, until I noticed that the door was locked. Crutch, my fellow SNCC worker, had the only key. I quickly surmised that he was in Forrest City, a project forty miles west of us. After a few minutes of standing and wondering what to do, I decided to wake some friends of ours a few blocks away, and sleep on their floor . . .

As I walked away from the house, the police car pulled up again, this time from behind me. As before, I ignored it, but this time they played a spotlight on me, and ordered me to stop. I could see that there were two white cops in the car. The cars that had passed me before at night in West Memphis had always had Negroes in them. That the cops were usually Negroes doesn't say they were any great shakes (these appointments don't exactly go by civil service exams, and Negro cops in the South are always Toms). But generally the Negro cops weren't allowed to arrest white people, and though a special dispensation might be allowed in the case of a white nigger, the fact that they hadn't bothered me before was encouraging. But these cops were white, and I knew they were going to pull me in. "What are you doing around here?" the driver asked me. When I told him that I lived in the house they had just seen me come out of, he grimaced. "You live with them? You live with them niggers?" Upon ascertaining that I did, indeed, live among the niggers, he ordered me into the patrol car.

"Am I under arrest?"

"You're damn right you're under arrest . . . under section 139, for investigation."

I rather exhaustedly piled my bags into the back seat, then slid in. They closed the door and we drove off.

"Who do you work for?"

"I work for the Student Nonviolent Coordinating Committee."

"What?"

"I work for the Student Nonviolent Coordinating Committee."

"How long have you been around here?"

"I've been around for a couple of weeks."

"What, do you hide during the daytime and work at night?"

"No, I work during the daytime."

"What do you do?"

"I just talk to people."

"Where you from?"

"New York."

"That figures. What do you want to come around here and cause trouble? Isn't there enough trouble in the world without you coming down here?"

"I'm not trying to cause trouble. I'm just trying to help people."

"What kind of people you trying to help?"

"Trying to help Negro people."

"You can't do nothing for them niggers."

We finally arrived at the police station. They waited for me to pick up all my bags, and carry them into a room in the front of the station. There they told me to put my bags down against the wall.

"You have any identification?" I gave them my Arkansas drivers license.

"Can I make a telephone call?" I asked.

"No you can't. Sit down over there."

They asked me a few more questions, and filled out a card on me. Then they brought me around to a room in the back. Along the way I wondered for a moment if they were going to beat me. But we were immediately at the cell block in the back of the police station. There my personal possessions were taken from me, and some more questions were asked, some by a few other cops who came in to look at me.

"If I'm being arrested, can't I make a telephone call?"

"Who you want to call?"

"My office." (This a blunder on my part—"my lawyer," I should have said.)

"You can't call them. You can only call your family to let them knew you're in jail."

I called my mother collect from a pay phone nearby, and asked her to call Bill Hansen, a SNCCer in Little Rock. When I was done with the call, there were a few more questions.

From a round one with a couple of gold teeth: "Ain't he the one that got the shit kicked out of him at the swimming pool?" (Alluding to the assault of one of our guys at an integration attempt early in the summer.)

Me: "No, that wasn't me."

Goldie: "Yeh, that was him."

Me: "That was somebody else."

Goldie: "It was him all right."

Me: Silence. I surrender to the realization that all white civil rights workers look alike to cracker cops.

By now it's about 5 a.m. They put me in a cell with one other white man. I'm not especially frightened because they let me call outside, and know that someone in the state is going to be contacted. I later find out that Bill called the FBI in both Little Rock and West Memphis, and also Mr. Yarbrough, the local NAACP President who's a friend of ours . . .

This whole thing is nothing particularly unusual for civil rights workers in the South, and is certainly not indicative of any particular heroism on my part. I go into detail because I know that, like all mass injustices, these incidents only become meaningful on the individual scale. I suppose the only way to try to comprehend what it means for this sort of thing to be going on hundreds of times every day across the country is just to imagine what each of those people, and their friends and relatives must be feeling, then to realize it's not just an individual thing, but part of a pattern, a policy . . .

Mitchell Zimmerman

35.

Letter from Rev. Benjamin S. Grinage to John A. Hannah (1966)

*In general, black Arkansans had more access to the polls than
African Americans in many other parts of the South. However,
due to the Arkansas poll tax and to the lack of appealing political candidates, many potential black voters were reluctant to
register until the 1960s. In 1964, the Twenty-fourth Amendment
to the U.S. Constitution, banning the use of the poll tax in federal elections, was passed, and in 1965, Arkansas introduced a
free, permanent voter registration system. These developments,
coupled with the voter education initiatives of SNCC and other
civil rights groups, persuaded even more African Americans to
register. However, even in areas with a significant black population, the goal of electing black officials initially proved elusive
due to voting irregularities. In the following letter, SNCC
Arkansas Project director Ben Grinage calls on the United States
Commission on Civil Rights to investigate evidence of voter
fraud in eastern Arkansas compiled by SNCC workers. The
commission responded by scheduling hearings in Forrest City on
April 23, 1966. The testimony of Grinage and others prompted
the commission to send two representatives to Arkansas to supervise elections and to monitor the use of absentee ballots.*

The Arkansas Project
Student Nonviolent Coordinating Committee
700 West 9th Street
Little Rock, Arkansas 72201
(501) FR 5-9081

Source: Box 149, folder 2, "Arkansas Project," Student Nonviolent Coordinating
Committee Papers, 1959–1972, Martin Luther King, Jr. Center for Nonviolent Social
Change, Inc., Atlanta

February 26, 1966

Mr. John A. Hannah, Chairman
U. S. Commission on Civil Rights
Washington, D. C.

Dear Mr. Hannah:

I am writing on behalf of the Arkansas Project of the Student
Nonviolent Coordinating Committee to file a formal complaint regarding
the denial of voting rights and to request that the U. S. Commission on
Civil Rights, pursuant to the mandate of the Civil Rights Act of 1957,
send a substantial number of observers to Eastern Arkansas polling
places to investigate the disfranchisement of Negro citizens through vote
fraud on election day. Members of the Coordinating Committee have earlier had conversations about this possibility with Mr. John W. Spence,
Assistant Director of the Memphis Field Office of the Commission. Mr.
Spence indicated to us that the Commission could conduct such an investigation by means of observers at the polling places.

But why should the Commission make a major investment of its
scarce resources to investigate Arkansas elections? The following four
points encompass the leading considerations.

1. In this summer's primaries and this fall's general election, Negro Arkansans will remain effectively disfranchised because of massive and systematic vote fraud.

Negroes have long been permitted to vote in Arkansas. But this does not
mean that whites here are prepared to allow Eastern Arkansas's Negro
majorities to use their votes to elect black mayors and sheriffs and county
assessors. In Phillips County, Arkansas, just as surely as in Neshoba
County, Mississippi, the racist way of life demands that politics stay the
instrument of whites. The difference lies only in the way the white minority stays in power.

The Arkansas way is vote fraud. This is not to suggest that violence
and intimidation are uncommon. But they are not the main bulwark of
"for-whites-only" politics.

The means by which vote fraud operates are set forth in a Special
Report of the Arkansas Project, "Fraud in the 1965 Arkansas School
Board Elections." (A copy is enclosed for your convenience.)

As the Special Report documents, in the most recent election to take
place in the state, illegal and unconstitutional practices predetermined the
outcome of the elections in Forrest City, Helena, Gould, and West

Memphis—and, it is likely, wherever Negroes ran in the state. These practices included the destruction of Negro ballots, the mistabulation of votes for Negro candidates, illegal voting of the ballots of illiterates by election officials, probable multiple white voting, segregation at the polling places (including ballot boxes), and denial of access to Negro poll-watchers. In practice there is, of course, no secret ballot in Arkansas. Voting is usually open and even if it were not, each ballot is marked with a number traceable to the voter who cast it.

The white men who control the political apparatus today are the same ones who controlled it during September's election. Now it will be their own offices which are at stake, not merely some school board positions. Can there be any doubt that this year they will be vigilant in protecting their own power from the votes of the Negro majority?

2. If the attempt to participate in politics through voting continues to be frustrated by fraud, the Negro community, will ultimately turn to violence.

We made this point in the Special Report:

> Until now, many Negro Arkansans have maintained their faith that the ballot box is the way to secure social justice. The continued denial of effective suffrage can be expected to erode that faith. And with disillusionment with the political process will come the heightened sense of alienation from American society that prevails in the ghettos of the North. There can be no assurance that, in such circumstances, the cities of Arkansas will be immune to eruptions of violence such as have stunned the cities of the North.

If the demand for political representation cannot find a legitimate channel, shall we be surprised when it finds its outlet on the streets?

3. The responsibility for correcting this situation lies with the Federal Government.

The practices outlined above represent more than a challenge to the principle of majority rule. They are violations of the U.S. Constitution and of Federal laws, some of which are long standing.

"The right of the citizens of the United States to vote," reads the Fifteenth Amendment, "shall not be denied or abridged by the United States or by any state on account of race, color, or previous condition of servitude." Refusal to count a man's vote after he casts his ballot must surely be considered a most effective means of abridging that right.

Only the latest of the laws in the intervening period to make this illegal is the Voting Rights Act of 1965. (See sections 11.(a), 12.(a) and (d), and 14.(c)(1). Yet none of these laws have been enforced against this way of denying a man the right to vote.

It would be naive to expect that state and local political leaders who are the beneficiaries of the system of disfranchisement will use their power to destroy that system. Only Federal power can do that. (If any further confirmation of this fact is needed, it was provided by the February 21, 1966 decision of the Arkansas Supreme Court, refusing to hold in contempt of court county officials who destroyed voting records to prevent the revelation of fraud.)

The laws exist to fulfill the oft-expressed intent. All that is lacking is determination to enforce the law. By drawing attention to the failures of the Executive Branch, particularly the Justice Department, the Commission could serve as an impetus toward that end.

4. The problem of vote fraud, which now looms large in the struggle of Arkansas Negroes for political representation, will soon be the problem all across the South.

In hundreds of counties in the South, Negroes are in the process of becoming the majority of registered voters, thanks to the Voting Rights Act of 1965. But it would be naive to expect that the mere registration of voters will mean an equal opportunity for Negroes to affect the political process through voting. The Arkansas experience proves that much. How can formal enfranchisement be transformed into operational enfranchisement? This is the unknown quantity in Southern politics for the next decade. A careful study of the problem in Arkansas, where it is of long standing, can point the way to solutions of significance for the whole South—and ultimately for the Nation. The Commission on Civil Rights is ideally suited to make that study.

What could Civil Rights Commission observers accomplish by being at the polling places in the coming elections? In the first place they would surely inhibit, by their mere presence, some of the practices. But we can be sure that the presence of these outsiders would not of itself be sufficient for the offending parties to end their illegal activities altogether—for the price would in most cases be their defeat.

A Commission study on vote fraud would, however, have a favorable effect on Federal enforcement policy. We believe that three related factors account for the failure of Federal policy. In the first place, there may be some misunderstanding in the Justice Department and elsewhere about the full nature of Federal responsibilities for elections. In the second place, the integrity of those making the charges of fraud is suspect in some quarters. And in the third place, the public at large is basically unaware of the scope of vote fraud in the South, and of how effective an instrument it is for the continued disfranchisement of the Southern Negro.

A careful report by the Commission can help alleviate all of these difficulties. The Commission can clarify some of the legal questions involved in Federal intervention in the election process; it can present a study whose integrity is unquestioned; and it can draw the attention of the public to the existence of this problem.

We are prepared to submit a somewhat more specific memorandum, at your request, for the deployment of Commission observers in implementation of this proposal.

We hope to hear from the Commission at the earliest possible date. Time is running out. We hope that the Commission will not hesitate to use its powers to help minimize the dangers that lie ahead. Thank you.

Yours truly,
Rev. Benjamin S. Grinage
Arkansas Project Director

36.

Press Statement: Rev. Ben Grinage (1966)

In 1966 the magnetic Stokely Carmichael was elected chairman of the national SNCC organization. At the time of his election, Carmichael was an experienced organizer who had helped regis-ter black voters in Lowndes County, Alabama. Local residents there even created their own political party, which used a black panther for a mascot. Increasingly, Carmichael and other like-minded activists began to focus their energies on empowering the black community, declaring, "Integration is irrelevant." This new change in emphasis inspired some civil rights activists and supporters and bewildered others. In the following press release, Ben Grinage, director of the Arkansas Project, disassociates himself from Carmichael's position and maintains a belief in the desirability of achieving integration.

29 May 1966

Press Statement: Rev. Ben Grinage, Ark. State Project Director, S.N.C.C.

I am making this statement at this time because of my basic and primary committment to the people of Arkansas with whom I have been working for the past 3 ½ years since I joined the staff of S.N.C.C.

I do not pretend to speak for all those who at present comprise the Snick Staff in Arkansas, but I do know that basically I speak for a major-ity of the Arkansas Staff and for many who are on the staff in other Southern Project areas.

It is our position that the announced new emphasis of Snick will not ultimately be in the best interests of the deprived Negro in Arkansas. Firstly, Negroes comprise only 22.2% of the total population of this state

Source: Arkansas Council on Human Relations Papers, 1954–1968, Box 33, folder 335, University of Arkansas Special Collections

and only in a very few counties are Negroes a majority. To attempt to organize a third party would not only be futile, but could not ever bring the poor, both Negro and white, into positions of power that could bring about the relief of oppression both politically and economically that our state suffers at this time.

We are committed to the dignity of all mankind, Black and non-Black alike. We have symbolized this not only in philosophy but by the very composition of our staff. We are and have always been very conscious of the fact that Negroes in this country have been the brunt of hatred, bigotry and injustice in this country and our efforts have been to organize people so that instead of being the victims of tokenism, de-humanization and pawns of political and economic conivers, every individual of all races and religions will be judged on the basis of their God Given Human Rights.

We do not feel that integration is irrelevant but is vital if this country is concerned with showing the rest of the world that peaceful co-existence is really what we are trying to achieve.

We abhor war and violence and take exception to this country's aggressive tactics as a means to realize peace. But we cannot make this statement and then suggest that civil war or violence, perpetuated by non-whites of this country will bring about a solution to the racial strife in this country.

We support the movements of independence of those countries throughout the world that refuse to be controlled or dominated by outside powers. And the right to hold Free Elections is one that we demand for all people of this country and do morally defend this right for all nations.

The struggle for Human Rights will continue in Arkansas regardless of internal opposition. Our work in Arkansas will expand and many varied types of programs will be initiated. People of both races are inviting our staff and our programs into their communities and are willing to give of themselves both time and resources. We will focus more on Urban Communities as well as Rural, in all of Eastern and Southern Arkansas. Politically, we will encourage and support both independent and party affiliated candidates, the pre-requisite being the individual candidate and his platform and committment to represent the disenfranchised population of his constituency. Economically, we will encourage programs that are designed to give relief to the here-to-fore neglected people of this state and will individually participate and or implement self-help programs for all people, whether they be Federal, State, Local Government or privately inspired. We will not decide for the communities, but they themselves will determine which community action programs are incorporated.

We as individuals may no longer be able to work under the Banners of S.N.C.C. , but as we suggested our committment is to the people of this state and this country not to any particular organization.

37.

"Black Power—Another Definition" (1966)

After his election as chairman of SNCC in 1966, Stokely Carmichael popularized the phrase "Black Power" to define the goals of the organization. Defenders of Black Power called for greater black political participation, for increased race pride, and for self-determination within the black community. For some, the ideology of Black Power also called for racial separatism. However, not all supporters of Black Power believed that the concept mandated separation. In the following letter to the editor of the Arkansas Gazette, *Mitchell Zimmerman, a white member of the Arkansas Project, defends the idea of Black Power.*

July 13, 1966

From the People

'Black Power'—Another Definition

To the Editor of the Gazette:

The charge of "black racism" is only another attack against the civil rights movement. But it is a very revealing attack because it indicates something that civil rights militants have long known: That when the struggle turned from attacking the symbols of oppression to dealing with the institutions which have profited from racism, there would be no "overwhelming national consensus."

Perhaps the fundamental error is the belief that (in the words of the Gazette) "the more important of the needed civil rights measures (have) been won in Congress. This ignores two things.

First, what has been "won" in Congress has always been lost in the White House. Laws have become only another symbol because no administration Democratic or Republican, has been willing to enforce the laws

Source: *Arkansas Gazette,* From the People, July 13, 1966

in a manner which makes them a reality for the great majority of American Negroes.

School desegregation under the 1964 Civil Rights Act is typical. The enforcement of this law has been so token, so gutless, so inadequate that 23 persons in the section of the Office of Education responsible for equal education have resigned in frustration in the last year. Orders from "on high" prevented them from doing their jobs—and from enforcing the law. And those orders came from the same one who sent his boy Hubert to attack SNCC and CORE as racists!

What does it mean to say this law has produced only tokenism? It means that the high goal of the Office of Education for this fall, 12 years after *Brown v. Board of Education*, three years after the Civil Rights Act, is that only 85 per cent of Negro schoolchildren should go to inferior, segregated schools. And the enforcement of the rights of black people to equal education has probably received more attention than any other matter.

The second thing that Gazette editors ignore in their assumption that the battle has been won, is that the laws which have been passed do not begin to face the problems of the black man who makes $3 a day.

The solution to the problem on this level is one which attacks the interests of many *within* the "great consensus." The whole pitch of the New South for industrialization rests on the low wage scales which could not be maintained if the government saw to it that the third of the South that is black earned a living wage. Perhaps this is part of the reason LBJ considered Senators Eastland, Byrd, and McClellan more important members of his coalition than Walther Reuther and Dr. King. Perhaps this is why the illegally elected racist congressmen from Mississippi were seated. If the President has given only token enforcement to laws granting *symbols,* can we expect him to be serious about changing the substance of life for black people in America?

As for the idea that we're all moving toward a great, integrated society (with the exception of a few rednecks, in other states), perhaps your readers might ponder some of the results of the 1963 Lou Harris polls on white attitudes toward Negroes (Cf. his "The Negro Revolution in America.") Thirty-nine percent of white Americans think Negroes have less native intelligence than whites. *Sixty-eight* per cent think Negroes laugh a lot. The world is not quite the way we would like it to be.

It is in recognition of this that SNCC has called for "black power." Black power does not mean hating white people—I am a white man and I feel no anomaly in working for black power. Nor does it mean the total exclusion of white persons from the struggle. Nor is it separatism.

The cry for black power is the cry of those who have always been powerless in our society—and subject to the power of others. They now make the outrageous suggestion that they should use power themselves, not only be the objects of power—and that they will use their power to better their own lot. Where poor black people are in the majority, they can use their ballots to elect their own. All along, Negroes have been asked why they don't make their own way, like all other ethnic groups. And now that they are doing it, they are racists. It is not racism, but realism to recognize that no white in a county 80 per cent Negro will work for poor black people. He is not excluded because of his color; he excludes himself.

The real racism, the real obsession with race is the belief that it is so important that there be white faces in government, that black people should allow racist plantation owners or their puppets to remain in government. The real racism is the belief that the government is bad just *because* it is black. The attempt to persuade Negroes that they can have pride in their color is seen as anti-white. This is a new, more sophisticated racism, for it does sophisticated Negro inferiority—it only insists that whites define the terms of black self-pride.

Where is the real racism—in those who, recognizing the effects of American racism, would create the preconditions of an egalitarian, integrated society, or those who, in the name of "integration," insist on maintaining white supremacy over Negroes? And the new racism is not less virulent for being sponsored by the Texas president of the United States.

For Freedom,
Mitchell Zimmerman
Student Nonviolent Coordinating
Committee
Little Rock

38.

"Arkansas Staff Meeting" (1966)

After Arkansas director Ben Grinage made a public statement revealing philosophical disagreements with SNCC chairman Stokely Carmichael over the desirability of achieving integration, Grinage resigned from the organization. The following document contains minutes from an Arkansas staff meeting, led by a visiting Stokely Carmichael. The staff elected Jim Jones as the new project director and discussed the immediate future of the Arkansas Project. Much of the discussion at the meeting touched on the role of whites in the organization. After Carmichael and others called for greater black empowerment and self-determination, a belief that was encapsulated in the phrase "Black Power," it was no longer clear what role whites would play in the new direction of the movement. Ultimately the national SNCC staff narrowly voted to expel white members at a meeting on December 1, 1966. By that time most white members of the Arkansas Project had already voluntarily resigned from SNCC.

ARKANSAS STAFF MEETING

9 June 1966

Decisions and some notes

Meeting attended by: Stokely Carmichael, Cleve Sellers, Jim Jones, Ben Grinage, Bob Cableton, Jerry Casey, Howard Himmelbaum, Myrtle Glascoe, Mitchell Zimmerman, Vincent O'Connor, Bill Hansen, Tex Lowe.

Source: Box 1, folder 7, Student Nonviolent Coordinating Committee—Arkansas Project Records, State Historical Society of Wisconsin, Madison

BEN'S STATEMENT

Stokely polled the staff at the beginning of the meeting (8:10 a.m.!) as to whether they agreed or disagreed with Ben's statement. Ben, Bill and Vince had not yet arrived, but practically everybody else expressed disagreement with Ben's statement and with the fact that he made a public statement. Stokely clarified the SNCC statements, and explained that he hadn't had any press conferences before the shit hit the fan, and that the only statements made were SNCC statements, not his. Stokely said that the staff outside of Arkansas was pissed off about Ben's statement and that it had hurt fund-raising. When Ben arrived he announced that because of financial pressures, he was unable to continue on staff, and was resigning effective the end of the week. In light of this, the discussion of Ben's statement was not resumed. Later in the meeting Jim Jones was elected Project Director. There was some discussion about how the press would interpret Ben's resignation. It was agreed that we would avoid for as long as possible letting the press know about it. Ben said that of course he would not issue any statement about his resignation, but that it was possible that he would be running a voter registration campaign for the Arkansas Council on Human Rights,[1] and that an announcement of that would be made.

PROGRAM AND GUIDELINES

Stokely read some guidelines for organizers that had been adopted by the Southwest Georgia staff. Generally, these involved things like—no more than three organizers in a county; no more than 2 consecutive meetings at the same place; no more than four consecutive meetings in the same part of the county; etc. Beyond that, the idea was to be more explicit about what your goals were, how you wanted to accomplish them and what the steps were in getting from here to there . . .

Stokely emphasized that these were the guidelines of the Southwest Georgia project and that he didn't think we should adopt them, but he felt we should draw up some of our own, and particularly some sort of timetable . . .

We talked a bit about the question of what it meant to talk about independent political organizing in this state. It was decided that a fuller discussion of guidelines for political program would wait until someone had a chance to go to Atlanta and talk to Jack Minnis. People thought Jack would be able to help us figure what was practical politically in light of the state's laws and population distribution.

RECRUITMENT

Next the question of recruitment came up. Stokely expressed the belief that if we could arrive at a program, recruiting staff would not be a problem. Many people agreed with this, but others were skeptical and felt that we should use the opportunity to go to Atlanta to get some new staff from among the students at an orientation session taking place there. Bill argued that we should stick to the principle that we weren't going to recruit any more staff from out of state, and after a discussion of this a vote was taken, and it was decided (7–3) that we would not bring back non-Arkansans from the orientation session to work on staff, and that as a general rule only Arkansans would be accepted on staff. Different people thought they could find people in the state interested in working for SNCC at least for the summer who would come to the orientation session beginning on the 11th in Atlanta. Jim said he had two people in mind, Myrtle said she knew one, and Howie said he knew of one. They will contact those people, and Jim will take whoever can go to Atlanta.

STAFF: WHO AND HOW LONG

Myrtle said she'd be gone for a month or two, then she'd be back to work indefinitely.

Jerry said he'd be here at least another month, but would be leaving to go back to school.

Vince said he would be here as long as he could be useful. Except he might be arrested at any time for non-cooperation with the draft. This might be a while because of his father's position in California.

Mitchell said he was here until at least September, and perhaps indefinitely.

Howie said he was here indefinitely.

Bill said he'd be in the state indefinitely, and how long he'd be with SNCC depended (on decisions at the meeting, and the like).

Jim said he was going back to school in September.

Tex said he anticipated going back to school in September, but he might stay longer depending on how things went.

Bob said he'd be here indefinitely.

(Crutch is now in the Soviet Union.)

This makes five or six blacks (depending on whether Jerry stays) and four whites.

WHITES ON STAFF

Vince is the only remaining white organizing in the black community in the state. The policy here was that a black should be placed in Pine Bluff as soon as possible, and that when he was able to operate on his own, Vince would either move out of Jefferson County, or would move into organizing poor whites there.

It was agreed that the office is too white. Howie and Mitchell said they thought they could recruit some Negroes to work in the office. Stokely suggested that they set a guideline for when this would be done. (They have subsequently done so: Two Negroes recruited for the office within a month; two more by the end of the summer.)

The approach that we felt should be adopted was that we'd decide what had to be done, then we'd see who could fill those jobs, rather than saying "What can this white person do?" Jim suggested that the sorts of things that called for work in the office included: research, fund-raising, newspaper. The possibility was mentioned that some Ozark organizing might take place. The question of who among the Little Rock staff could work with whom, at what and how, was postponed till the next meeting . . .

NEXT TIME

The following matters were left to be dealt with at the next staff meeting.

1. *A discussion of main tactics and goals.* Do we work within the Democratic Party? What is the balance between state-wide political goals and activity, and local goals and activity? Do we run people in areas where Negroes are in the minority? Should we establish some kind of political timetable—what we intend to try and what we think we can accomplish by when?
2. *Guidelines for organizers.* Some rules and timetables in our organizing activity, to measure progress by. Guidelines for recruitment.
3. *The organization of the Little Rock office* (or, How to Deal with the white peril, and other questions).
4. *A budget for the project.*
5. *Report on white community organizing* (to the extent that this doesn't come into other discussions).

M. Zimmerman (10 June 1966)

39.

"Ex-workers for SNCC Tell Why Group Faded in State" (1967)

The following article by Jack Baker appeared in the Arkansas
Gazette *on February 26, 1967. Baker is seeking to discover why
SNCC, which had been an active presence in the state since
1962, had all but vanished. Baker blames Stokely Carmichael's
call for "Black Power" and the 1966 expulsion of white members from the group for its disappearance in Arkansas. This
explanation is partially persuasive. Bill Hansen, a white man and
SNCC's most constant representative in the state, resigned from
SNCC in deference to African American calls for self-determination. However, SNCC faced other challenges as well as it charted
a new direction after passage of the Civil Rights Act of 1964 and
the Voting Rights Act of 1965. Having achieved desegregation
and federal protection of voting rights, two of the civil rights
movement's earliest and most tangible goals, SNCC was left with
the problem of charting a new more revolutionary agenda. The
organization had to do so from a precarious financial position as
donations had disappeared from former supporters who were
either leery of the new agenda or convinced that the goals of the
movement had already been achieved.*

Ex-workers for SNCC Tell Why Group Faded in State

By Jack Baker of the Gazette Staff

Robert Cableton has been convicted in the Mayor's Court of Gould on
charges of obstructing justice, assaulting an officer, disturbing the peace,
resisting arrest and public drunkenness.

Source: *Arkansas Gazette*, Sunday, February 26, 1967, 8A

All the charges stem from altercations with the police in 1965 and 1966 when Gould was the target of Civil Rights activism—or "aggravation," as a Gould school board member called it.

Hanging over Cableton, a Negro, are $671.50 in fines and costs and a nine-month jail term. Cableton, 25, has seen his latest appeal rejected in Lincoln County Circuit Court, but he plans to try once more to have his case heard by a federal court.

Robert Cableton is the last vestige in Arkansas of the Student Nonviolent Co-ordinating Committee.

SNCC is still in the Little Rock phone book but the number doesn't answer.

The office at West Ninth and Gaines was closed in the summer of 1966, in a manner which William W. (Bill) Hansen, now 27 and a pre-law student at Little Rock University describe like this: "We just moved everything out and tried to sneak out of sight as quietly as possible."

Carmichael Remarks Brought Troubles

Though SNCC, both in Arkansas and elsewhere, had always had financial troubles, its roof did not begin to cave in until SNCC's firebrand national chairman Stokely Carmichael joined the James Meredith March on Mississippi in June 1966.

He then began what was a new slogan: "Black Power."

Carmichael, who had defeated SNCC's perennial chairman, John Lewis, at an election in Nashville, Tenn., in May 1966, personified a new approach to race relations that alarmed the public, many SNCC members and the organization's primary financial backers, white liberals.

The Student Nonviolent Coordinating Committee was found in 1960 in Greensboro, N.C. by a group of Negro college students, who, with white sympathizers, had begun the first of the lunch counter "sit-ins." Although SNCC did not disdain legal maneuvers, it emphasized activism. Members organized demonstrations and boycotts, led marches, opened "Freedom Centers" in rural Negro neighborhoods and showed themselves willing to face clashes with the police, beatings from mobs, tear-gassings and imprisonment.

Four Big Projects Were Started

By 1964, there were four major SNCC projects: Southwest Georgia, Alabama, Mississippi, and Arkansas.

Operating in state headquarters first at Pine Bluff and later in Little Rock, SNCC organized Negroes in such places as Gould, Star City, Forrest City, Pine Bluff, Marvell, Helena, and West Helena.

Projects included school and store boycotts, voter registration and sit-ins.

After President Johnson began sending sizeable numbers of American troops to Vietnam early in 1965, SNCC leadership shifted to the left and added opposition to the Vietnam war to its list of projects. This caused the first tremor among the suppliers of SNCC money and contributions fell off.

Howard Himmelbaum, 26, was present when Stokely Carmichael was elected in Nashville on May 14, 1966 and was one of those who voted for Carmichael. Himmelbaum, who had been active in the "Arkansas Project" since 1965, returned to the state. Although a native of New York, Himmelbaum now is a permanent resident of Little Rock. "I like it here," he said.

But he no longer works for SNCC. He now is conducting research for the Southern Regional Council of Atlanta. Himmelbaum was the last of the whites.

Militant Workers are Dispersed

Where have they gone—those militant workers of the Arkansas Project?

Arlene Wilgoren. She came to the Arkansas Project in 1964 after two years with SNCC in New York. She was a graduate of Brandeis University at Waltham, Mass. It was she who announced in January 1965 that state headquarters would move from Pine Bluff to Little Rock. Miss Wilgoren is now a student at Brandeis again, working on a master's degree.

Mitchell Zimmerman. As a graduate student on leave from Princeton University, Zimmerman publically debated in Little Rock SNCC's controversial Vietnam position. He also publically defended Carmichael and Black Power. Zimmerman has returned to Princeton and is also working on a master's thesis.

Ben Grinage. The last state director of SNCC, Rev. Ben J. Grinage, 35, announced one month after the Carmichael victory in Nashville, his dissatisfaction with Carmichael's professed policy. In June 1966, Grinage resigned, pleading financial reasons, and joined the staff of the Arkansas Council of Human Relations in Little Rock, commuting daily from Pine Bluff for the sake of a voter education project.

Jim Jones. Originally of Williston, he was a student at AM and N College at Pine Bluff when he joined SNCC in 1963. For the next three years he was arrested, beaten, and denounced in several Arkansas counties during demonstrations. For a brief period, he was state director and was always a major voice in formulating SNCC policy in Arkansas. In the summer of 1966, he resigned and began attending classes at Little Rock University.

Hansen. For years, because of the amount of publicity he garnered, he was the very symbol of SNCC in Arkansas. Fresh from Cincinnati and Xavier University, he joined the 1961 "Freedom Rides" and the first sit-ins. He scouted the state for SNCC and founded the Arkansas Project in 1963, serving during the formative months as a one-man organizing staff. Hansen in 1963 married Ruthie Buffington of Pine Bluff, a Negro. It was Hansen who in 1965 led the SNCC sit-in against the last all-white lunch counter in Little Rock in the basement of the Capitol. Now Hansen, on a scholarship supplied by the Fund for Education and Legal Defense of New York, is at LRU.

Miss Wilgoren, Zimmerman, and Hansen are white. Jones and Grinage are Negroes. Their departures from SNCC—and those of scores of others—all date from about the same time: summer of 1966. Their announced reasons for leaving varied from "I just thought it was time to go back to school" to "Financial pressures got to be too much" to "I had a family and it was about time to settle down."

Notes

Preface

1. Howard Zinn, *SNCC: The New Abolitionists* (Boston, MA: Beacon Press, 1965); Clayborne Carson, *In Struggle: SNCC and the Black Awakening of the 1960s* (Cambridge, MA: Harvard University Press, 1981); Cheryl Greenberg, ed., *A Circle of Trust: Remembering SNCC* (New Brunswick, NJ: Rutgers University Press, 1998); Wesley C. Hogan, *Many Minds, One Heart: SNCC's Dream of a New America* (Chapel Hill: University of North Carolina Press, 2007). Zinn mentions SNCC in Arkansas seven times (11, 167, 185, 186, 214, 262, 268); Carson twice (150, 232); Greenberg, ed., once (182); and Hogan once (in the footnotes, 316). This highlights not only the collective amnesia about Arkansas SNCC in the historiography but also the fact that that amnesia has increased rather than decreased over time.

2. See, for example, William H. Chafe, *Civilities and Civil Rights: Greensboro, North Carolina, and the Black Struggle for Freedom* (New York: Oxford University Press, 1980); Raymond Arsenault, *Freedom Riders: 1961 and the Struggle for Racial Justice* (New York: Oxford University Press, 2006); Patrick Henry Bass, *Like a Mighty Stream: The March on Washington, August 28, 1963* (Philadelphia: Running Press, 2002); John Dittmer, *Local People: The Struggle for Civil Rights in Mississippi* (Urbana: University of Illinois Press, 1994); Charles Payne, *I've Got the Light of Freedom: The Organizing Tradition and the Mississippi Freedom Struggle* (Berkeley and Los Angeles: University of California Press, 1995); David J. Garrow, *Protest at Selma: Martin Luther King, Jr., and the Voting Rights Act of 1965* (New Haven, CT: Yale University Press, 1978); J. Mills Thornton, *Dividing Lines: Municipal Politics and the Struggle for Civil Rights in Montgomery, Birmingham, and Selma* (Tuscaloosa: University of Alabama Press, 2002); Peniel E. Joseph, *Waiting Till the Midnight Hour: A Narrative History of Black Power in America* (New York: Holt, 2007).

3. See, for example, Emilye Crosby, *A Little Taste of Freedom: The Black Freedom Struggle in Claiborne County, Mississippi* (Chapel Hill: University of North Carolina Press, 2005); Adam Fairclough, *Race and Democracy: The Civil Rights Struggle in Louisiana, 1915–1972* (Athens: University of Georgia Press, 1995); Cynthia Griggs Fleming, *In the Shadow of Selma: The Continuing Struggle for Civil Rights in the Rural South* (Lanham, MD: Rowman and Littlefield, 2004); John A. Kirk, *Redefining the Color Line: Black Activism in Little Rock, Arkansas, 1940–1970* (Gainesville: University of Florida Press, 2002); Stephen G. N. Tuck, *Beyond Atlanta: The Struggle for Racial Equality in Georgia, 1940–1980* (Athens: University of Georgia Press, 2001).

4. The civil rights struggle in Mississippi is one of the most covered events in the historiography of the civil rights movement. In addition to Dittmer and Payne in note 2, see, for example, Kenneth T. Andrews, *Freedom Is a Constant Struggle: The Mississippi Civil Rights Movement and Its Legacy* (Chicago: University of Chicago Press, 2004); Len Holt, *The Summer That Didn't End: The Story of the Mississippi Civil Rights Project of 1964* (New York: Da Capo, 1992); Charles Marsh, *God's Long Summer: Stories of Faith and Civil Rights* (Princeton, NJ: Princeton University Press, 1997); Doug McAdam, *Freedom Summer* (New York:

Oxford University Press, 1988); Nicolaus Mills, *Like a Holy Crusade: Mississippi 1964—The Turning Point of the Civil Rights Movement in America* (Chicago: I. R. Dee, 1992).

1.

1. For accounts of the Greensboro sit-ins, see William H. Chafe, *Civilities and Civil Rights: Greensboro, North Carolina, and the Black Struggle for Freedom* (New York: Oxford University Press, 1980); William Chafe, "The Greensboro Sit-ins," *Southern Exposure* 6 (Fall 1978): 78–87; Deidre B. Flowers, "The Launching of the Sit-in Movement: The Role of Black Women at Bennett College," *Journal of African American History* 90 (Winter 2005): 52–63; Eugene Pfaff, "Greensboro Sit-ins," *Southern Exposure* 9, no. 1 (1981): 23–28; Howell Raines, ed., *My Soul Is Rested: The Story of the Civil Rights Movement in the Deep South* (New York: Putnam, 1977); Fredric Soloman and Jacob R. Fishman, "Youth and Social Action II: Action Identity Formation in the First Student Sit-in Demonstration," *Journal of Social Issues* 29 (April 1964): 36–47; Miles Wolff, *Lunch at the Five and Ten, The Greensboro Sit-Ins: A Contemporary History* (New York: Stein and Day, 1970).

2. Overviews of the sit-ins include Clayborne Carson, *In Struggle: SNCC and the Black Awakening of the 1960s* (Cambridge, MA: Harvard University Press, 1981), 9–18; Wesley C. Hogan, *Many Minds, One Heart: SNCC's Dream of a New America* (Chapel Hill: University of North Carolina Press, 2007), 13–14; James H. Laue, *Direct Action and Desegregation, 1960–1962: Toward a Theory of the Rationalization of Protest* (Brooklyn, NY: Carlson Publishing, 1989), 75–95; Aldon D. Morris, *The Origins of the Civil Rights Movement: Black Communities Organizing for Change* (New York: Free Press, 1984), 195–228; Aldon D. Morris, "Black Southern Student Sit-in Movement: An Analysis of Internal Organization," *American Sociological Review* 46, no. 6 (1981): 744–67; Martin Oppenheimer, "The Southern Student Movement: Year I," *Journal of Negro Education* 33 (1964): 396–403; Martin Oppenheimer, *The Sit-in Movement of 1960* (Brooklyn, NY: Carlson Publishing, 1989); Howard Zinn, *SNCC: The New Abolitionists* (Boston, MA: Beacon Press, 1965), 16–39. The sit-ins generally met with much less success in the Deep South. See, for example, James W. Ely Jr., "Negro Demonstrations and the Law: Danville as a Test Case," *Vanderbilt Law Review* 27 (1974): 927–68.

3. On the Greensboro sit-ins, see note 1. On Nashville, see David Halberstam, *The Children* (New York: Random House, 1998); Diane Nash, "Inside the Sit-ins and the Freedom Rides: Testimony of a Southern Student," in Matthew Ahmann, ed., *The New Negro* (Notre Dame, IN: Fides Publishers, 1961), 43–60; republished in David G. Garrow, ed., *We Shall Overcome: The Civil Rights Movement in the United States in the 1950s and 1960s,* vol. 3 (Brooklyn, NY: Carlson Publishing, 1989), 955–74; Linda T. Wynn, "The Dawning of a New Day: The Nashville Sit-ins, February 13–May 10, 1960," *Tennessee Historical Quarterly* 50, no. 1 (1991): 42–54. On Atlanta, see the essays in David J. Garrow, ed., *Atlanta, Georgia, 1960–1961: Sit-Ins and Student Activism* (Brooklyn, NY: Carlson Publishing, 1989), and Clifford M. Kuhn, "'There's a Footnote to History!' Memory and the History of Martin Luther King's October 1960 Arrest and Its Aftermath," *Journal of American History* 84 (September 1997): 583–95.

4. Cynthia Griggs Fleming, "White Lunch Counters and the Black Consciousness: The Story of the Knoxville Sit-Ins," *Tennessee Historical Quarterly* 49 (Spring 1990): 40.

5. Gretchen Cassell Eick, *Dissent in Wichita: The Civil Rights Movement in the Midwest, 1954–72* (Urbana: University of Illinois Press, 2001); Fleming, "White Lunch Counters"; Garrow, ed., *Atlanta, Georgia, 1960–1961;* Carl R. Graves, "The Right to be Served: Oklahoma City's Lunch Counter Sit-Ins, 1958–1964," *Chronicles of Oklahoma* 59 (Summer 1981): 361–73; August Meier, "The Successful Sit-Ins in a Border City: A Study in Social Causation," *Journal of Intergroup Relations* 2 (Summer 1961): 230–37; Donald Seals Jr., "The Wiley-Bishop Student Movement: A Case Study in the 1960 Civil Rights Sit-Ins," *Southwestern Historical Quarterly* 106, no. 3 (2003): 418–40; Peter Wallenstein, "To Sit or Not to Sit: The Supreme Court of the United States and the Civil Rights Movement in the Upper South," *Journal of Supreme Court History* 29, no. 2 (2004): 145–62; Ronald Walters, "The Great Plains Sit-In Movement, 1958–1960," *Great Plains Quarterly* 16, no. 2 (1996): 85–94; Wynn, "The Dawning of a New Day."

6. Sociological studies include Kenneth T. Andrews and Michael Biggs, "The Dynamics of Protest Diffusion: Movement Organizations, Social Networks, and News Media in the 1960 Sit-ins," *American Sociological Review* 71, no. 5 (2006): 752–77; Lewis M. Killian, "Organization, Rationality and Spontaneity in the Civil Rights Movement," *American Sociological Review* 49 (December 1984): 770–83; Morris, *Origins of the Civil Rights Movement;* Morris, "Black Southern Student Sit-in Movement"; Anthony Oberschall, *Social Conflict and Social Movements* (Englewood Cliffs, NJ: Prentice-Hall, 1973); Martin Oppenheimer, "The Southern Student Sit-ins: Intra-Group Relations and Community Conflict," *Phylon* 27, no. 1 (1966): 20–26; Oppenheimer, *The Sit-in Movement of 1960;* Anhtony M. Orum and Amy W. Orum, "Class and Status Bases of Negro Student Protest," *Social Science Quarterly* 49, no. 3 (1968): 521–33; Frances F. Piven and Richard A. Cloward, *Poor People's Movements: How They Succeed, Why Some Fail* (New York: Vintage Books, 1979); Ruth Searles and J. Allen Williams Jr., "Negro College Students: Participations in Sit-ins," *Social Forces* 40 (March 1962): 215–20; Charles U. Smith, "The Sit-ins and the New Negro Student," *Journal of Intergroup Relations* 2 (1961): 223–29; Donald Von Eschen, Jerome Kirk, and Maurice Pinard, "The Organizational Substructure of Disorderly Politics," *Social Forces* 49 (1971): 529–43.

Legal studies include Brad Ervin, "Notes: Result or Reason: The Supreme Court and the Sit-in Cases," *Virginia Law Review* 93 (March 2007): 181–233; Jole B. Grossman, "A Model for Judicial Policy Analysis: The Supreme Court and the Sit-In Cases," in *Frontiers of Judicial Research*, ed. Joel B. Grossman and Joseph Tanenhaus (New York: John Wiley and Sons, 1969), 405–60; Peter Irons, *The Courage of Their Convictions: Sixteen Americans Who Fought Their Way to the Supreme Court* (New York: Free Press, 1988); Thomas P. Lewis, "The Sit-in Cases: Great Expectations," *Supreme Court Review* (1963): 101–51; "Note: Constitutional Law: Supreme Court Avoids Constitutional Question of State Action in Sit-in Cases by Extending the Doctrine of Abatement," *Duke Law Journal* 3 (1965): 640–48; Monrad G. Paulsen, "The Sit-in Cases of 1964: 'But Answer Came There None,'" *Supreme Court Review* (1964): 137–70; Daniel H. Pollitt, "Dime Store Demonstrations: Events and Legal Problems of the First Sixty

Days," *Duke Law Journal* 10 (Summer 1960): 315–65; Wallenstein, "To Sit or Not to Sit"; McKenzie Webster, "The Warren Court's Struggle with the Sit-in Cases and the Constitutionality of Segregation in Places of Public Accommodations," *Journal of Law and Politics* 17, no. 2 (2001): 373–407.

7. For overviews of the historiography of the Little Rock crisis, see John A. Kirk, *Beyond Little Rock: The Origins and Legacies of the Central High Crisis* (Fayetteville: University of Arkansas Press, 2007), 1–14, and John A. Kirk, "Bigger than Little Rock? New Histories of the 1957 Central High Crisis," *Reviews in American History* 36, no. 4 (December 2008): 624–38.

8. Elizabeth Jacoway, *Turn Away Thy Son: Little Rock, the Crisis That Shocked a Nation* (New York: Free Press, 2007), 353.

9. Frank James, "'Up Against the Obstacles,' Little Rock, Arkansas," item 17, reel 4, frame 0980, Student Nonviolent Coordinating Committee Papers, Microfilm, Roosevelt Study Center, Middleburg, the Netherlands (hereafter SNCC Papers [RSC Microfilm]); Daisy Bates to Roy Wilkins, February 23, 1960, group III, series A, container 20, folder "Bates, Daisy, 1957–1960," National Association for the Advancement of Colored People Papers, Manuscript Division, Library of Congress, Washington, D.C. (hereafter NAACP Papers [Washington, D.C.]); "Arkansas Council on Human Relations, Narrative Quarterly Report, January–March, 1960," series 1, box 27, folder 228, Arkansas Council on Human Relations Papers, 1954–1968, Special Collections Division, University of Arkansas Libraries, Fayetteville (hereafter ACHR Papers); *Arkansas Democrat* (Little Rock), March 10, 1960, and March 17, 1960; *Arkansas Gazette* (Little Rock), March 11, 1960.

10. *Arkansas Gazette,* March 11, 1960.

11. Act 17 of the 1958 Session of the Arkansas General Assembly.

12. Act 226 of the 1959 Special Session of the Arkansas General Assembly.

13. "An Appeal to the Negroes of Little Rock," series 1, box 33, folder 335, ACHR Papers; *Arkansas Democrat,* March 13, 1960.

14. For a discussion of these issues, see Hurley Doddy, "Editorial Comment: 'The Sit-In' Demonstrations and the Dilemma of the Negro College President," *Journal of Negro Education* 30 (Winter 1961): 1–3.

15. *Arkansas Democrat,* March 15 and 16, 1960.

16. Memorandum from C. D. Coleman to M. T. Puryear, October 5, 1959, group II, series D, container 26, folder "Affiliates File, Little Rock, Arkansas," National Urban League Papers, Manuscript Division, Library of Congress, Washington, D.C.

17. John Walker to Paul Rilling, November 17, 1959, reel 141, frame 0234–0235, Southern Regional Council Papers, Microfilm, Manuscript Division, Library of Congress, Washington, D.C.

18. *Arkansas Democrat,* March 11, 1960.

19. "Arkansas Council on Human Relations, Narrative Quarterly Report, January–March, 1960," series 1, box 27, folder 228, ACHR Papers; "Monthly Report of Clarence A. Laws, Field Secretary, SWR, February 26–March 31, 1960," box 4, folder 10, Daisy Bates Papers, State Historical Society of Wisconsin, Madison (hereafter Bates Papers [Madison]); *Arkansas Democrat,* March 17, 1960; *Arkansas Gazette,* March 18, 1960.

20. *Arkansas Democrat,* March 17, 1960; *Arkansas Gazette,* March 17, 1960.

21. Memorandum from Rev. J. C. Crenchaw to all religious groups, fraternal organizations, fraternities, sororities, civic and political groups, March 30, 1960, series 1, box 31, folder 322, ACHR Papers; "Monthly Report of Clarence Laws, Field Secretary, SWR, February 26–March 31, 1960"; "1960 Annual Report of L. C. Bates, Field Secretary, Arkansas, December 3, 1960," both in box 4, folder 10, Bates Papers (Madison); *Arkansas Democrat,* April 1, 1960; *Arkansas Gazette,* April 1, 1960; Gilbert Jonas, *Freedom's Sword: The NAACP and the Struggle Against Racism in America, 1909–1969* (New York: Routledge, 2005), 174–77.

22. Jack Greenberg, *Crusaders in the Courts: How a Dedicated Band of Lawyers Fought for the Civil Rights Revolution* (New York: Basic Books, 1994), 275–76. For discussion of the equal protection clause, see Michael Klarman, "An Interpretive History of Modern Equal Protection," *Michigan Law Review* 90 (November 1991): 213–318.

23. *Civil Rights Cases,* 109 U.S. 3 (1883).

24. *Shelley v. Kraemer,* 334 U.S. 1 (1948).

25. For a discussion of housing, race, and the law, see Stephen Grant Meyer, *As Long As They Don't Move Next Door: Segregation and Racial Conflict in American Neighborhoods* (Lanham, MD: Rowman and Littlefield, 2000).

26. Greenberg, *Crusaders in the Courts,* 276.

27. *Arkansas Democrat,* April 11, 1960.

28. *Arkansas Democrat,* April 12, 1960.

29. Act 14 of the 1959 Special Session of the Arkansas General Assembly.

30. *Arkansas Gazette,* April 16, 1960.

31. "1960 Annual Report of L. C. Bates, Field Secretary, Arkansas, December 3, 1960," box 4, folder 10, Bates Papers (Madison); *Arkansas Democrat,* April 13, 21, 1960.

32. *Arkansas Democrat,* April 27, 1960; *Arkansas Gazette,* April 28, 1960.

33. *Arkansas Gazette,* May 31, 1960; June 1, 1960.

34. "1960 Annual Report of L. C. Bates, Field Secretary, Arkansas, December 3, 1960," box 4, folder 10, Bates Papers (Madison); *Arkansas Democrat,* April 27; June 17, 18, August 17, 1960; *Arkansas Gazette,* April 27, 1960; June 1, 1960. On Branton, see Judith Kilpatrick, *There When We Needed Him: Wiley Austin Branton, Civil Rights Warrior* (Fayetteville: University of Arkansas Press, 2007).

35. *Arkansas Democrat,* May 11, 1960, June 29, 1960, August 17, 1960.

36. *Arkansas Democrat,* June 4, 1960, October 4, 1960.

37. "Arkansas Council on Human Relations, Narrative Quarterly Report, October–November, 1960," series 1, box 27, folder 228, ACHR Papers; *Arkansas Democrat,* September 6, 1960, November 29, 1960.

38. Worth Long Jr. to Edward B. King Jr., n.d., item 88, reel 19, frame 0189, SNCC Papers (RSC Microfilm).

39. *Arkansas Democrat,* November 29, 1960.

40. *Arkansas Democrat,* November 30, 1960; *Arkansas Gazette,* December 1, 1960.

41. *Arkansas Democrat,* December 1, 1960. In the case of Charles Parker, who had already been arrested and sentenced for his role in the March 1960 sit-in, Glover handed down a $500 fine and a six-month prison sentence.

42. *Arkansas Gazette,* January 1, 1961, January 17, 1961.

43. *Arkansas Gazette,* January 17, 1961.

44. *Arkansas Democrat,* December 1, 1960; January 16, 1961; *Arkansas Gazette,* April 20, 28, 1961; March 18, 1962; July 11, 1962, October 17, 1962; November 1, 1962, May 14, 1963.

45. *Congressional Record,* 84th Congress Second Session, Vol. 102, part 4, March 12, 1956 (Washington, D.C.: Government Printing Office, 1956), 4459–60.

46. On massive resistance to Brown, see Numan V. Bartley, *The Rise of Massive Resistance: Race and Politics in the South during the 1950s* (Baton Rouge: Louisiana State University Press, 1969); George Lewis, *The White South and the Red Menace: Segregationists, Anticommunism and Massive Resistance* (Gainesville: University of Florida Press, 2004); George Lewis, *Massive Resistance: The White Response to the Civil Rights Movement* (London: Hodder and Arnold, 2006); Neil R. McMillen, *The Citizens' Council: Organized Resistance to the Second Reconstruction, 1955–1964* (Urbana: University of Illinois Press, 1971); Clive Webb, ed., *Massive Resistance: Southern Opposition to the Second Reconstruction* (New York: Oxford University Press, 2005); Jeff Woods, *Black Struggle, Red Scare: Segregation and Anti-Communism in the South, 1948–1968* (Baton Rouge: Louisiana State University Press, 2004).

47. *Boynton v. Virginia,* 364 U.S. 454 (1960); *Garner v. Louisiana,* 368 U.S. 157 (1961). On the Supreme Court's 1960 and 1961 terms and the sit-ins, see Derek Bell, *Race, Racism and American Law,* 5th ed. (New York: Aspen Publishers, 2004), 544–47; Ervin, "Notes: Result or Reason," 188–200; Greenberg, *Crusaders in the Courts,* 306–8; Lewis, "The Sit-in Cases," 101–51; Schwartz, *Super Chief,* 402–4; Webster, "Note: The Warren Court's Struggle," 376–79.

48. Memo from Little Rock ACHR to SRC, December 6, 1960, reel 141, frame 0218, Southern Regional Council Papers, Microfilm, Manuscript Division, Library of Congress, Washington, D.C.

49. *Morgan v. Virginia,* 328 U.S. 373 (1946). On the Freedom Rides, see Arsenault, *Freedom Riders.*

50. ACHR Minutes of the Executive Committee, July 13, 1961, box 22, folder 219, ACHR Papers.

51. On the Freedom Rides in Little Rock, see John A. Kirk, *Redefining the Color Line: Black Activism in Little Rock, Arkansas, 1940–1970* (Gainesville: University of Florida Press, 2002), 146–50. On Little Rock's white business elite, see Elizabeth Jacoway, "Taken By Surprise: Little Rock Business Leaders and Desegregation," in *Southern Businessmen and Desegregation,* ed. Elizabeth Jacoway and David R. Colburn (Baton Rouge: Louisiana State University Press, 1982), 12–41.

52. *Arkansas Gazette,* August 14, 1961.

53. *Arkansas Gazette,* September 7, 1961; March 14, 1962.

54. Ozell Sutton, August 7, 1993; Dr. Maurice A. Jackson, February 10, 1993; Dr. W. H. Townsend, April 25, 1993, all interviews with author and

deposited in the Pryor Center for Arkansas Oral and Visual History, Special Collections Division, University of Arkansas Libraries, Fayetteville (hereafter Pryor Center); *Arkansas Gazette*, November 15, 1962.

55. *Arkansas Gazette*, March 9, 1962.

56. *Arkansas Gazette*, March 10, 1962.

57. Telegram from Dorothy Miller to Nat Griswold, n.d, series 1, box 33, folder 335, ACHR Papers.

58. "Report, May 30, 1962," box 8, folder 5, "Field Reports—Maryland, Georgia and Arkansas: Hansen, William W.," Student Nonviolent Coordinating Committee Arkansas Project Records, State Historical Society of Wisconsin, Madison (hereafter SNCC Papers [Madison]).

59. Worth Long, August 8, 1993, interview with author, Pryor Center.

60. "Field Report, Thursday October 23, 1962–Thursday November 1, 1962," box 8, folder 5, "Field Reports—Maryland, Georgia and Arkansas: Hansen, William W," SNCC Papers (Madison).

61. Ibid.; *Arkansas Gazette*, November 8, 1962; *Arkansas Democrat*, November 8, 1962.

62. "Field Report, Friday November 2, 1962–Wednesday November 7, 1962," box 8, folder 5, "Field Reports–Maryland, Georgia and Arkansas: Hansen, William W.," SNCC Papers (Madison); *Arkansas Gazette*, November 8, 1962; *Arkansas Democrat*, November 8, 1962.

63. "Arkansas Council on Human Relations, Quarterly Narrative Report, October–December 15, 1962," series 1, box 28, folder 289, ACHR Papers; Hugh Patterson, May 6, 1993, Ozell Sutton, August 7, 1993, B. Finely Vinson, February 25, 1993; and E. Grainger Williams, April 30, 1993, all interviewed by author and deposited in the Pryor Center; Irving J. Spitzberg, *Racial Politics in Little Rock 1954–1964* (New York: Garland Publishing, 1987), 143–47.

64. "Field Report, Monday November 26, 1962–Monday December 3, 1962"; "Field Reports—Maryland, Georgia and Arkansas: Hansen, William W.," both in box 8, folder 5, SNCC Papers (Madison); "Arkansas Council on Human Relations, Quarterly Narrative Report, October–December 15, 1962," series 1, box 28, folder 289, ACHR Papers; *Arkansas Gazette*, November 29, 1963; Townsend interview, Pryor Center.

65. "First Little Rock Sit-Ins in Two Years," item 88, reel 19, frame 0174, SNCC Papers (RSC Microfilm), *Arkansas Gazette*, December 8, 1962.

66. "Dates and Procedures for Making Changes," series 1, box 19, folder 190, ACHR Papers; Vinson and Williams interviews, Pryor Center; Spitzberg, *Racial Politics*, 144–45.

67. Sutton and Vinson interviews, Pryor Center; Spitzberg, *Racial Politics*, 144–45.

68. "Dates and Procedures for Making Changes," series 1, box 19, folder 190, ACHR Papers; Spitzberg, *Racial Politics*, 145.

69. "Public Facilities Integrated in Little Rock, Jan. 24, 1963, Jan. 24, 1963," item 88, reel 19, frame 0176, SNCC Papers (RSC Microfilm).

70. *Freeman, et al. v. City of Little Rock* ED Ark., W. Div., #LR-62-C-40; *Arkansas Gazette*, February 14, 16, 1963.

71. "Public Accommodations and Downtown Employment, May, 1964," series 1, box 19, folder 190, ACHR Papers.

72. *Peterson v. Greenville*, 373 U.S. 244; *Lombard v. Louisiana*, 373 U.S. 267; *Griffin v. Maryland*, 378 U.S. 130. On the Supreme Court's 1962 term and the sit-ins, see Bell, *Race, Racism and American Law*, 547–48; Ervin, "Notes: Result or Reason," 200–212; Greenberg, *Crusaders in the Courts*, 306–8; Schwartz, *Super Chief*, 479–86.

73. *Briggs v. State*, 236 Ark. 596, 367 S.W. 2d 750. On Johnson's career see Elizabeth Jacoway, "Jim Johnson of Arkansas: Segregationist Protoype," in *The Role of Ideas in the Civil Rights Movement*, ed. Ted Ownby, (Jackson: University Press of Mississippi), 137–55.

74. *Briggs v. State*, 236 Ark. 596, 367 S.W. 2d 750.

75. *Arkansas Gazette*, May 15, 1963; June 4, 1963.

76. *Arkansas Gazette*, June 14, 1963; June 16, 1963.

77. *Arkansas Gazette*, June 26, 1963.

78. *Bell v. Maryland*, 378 U.S. 226; *Barr v. City of Columbia*, 378 U.S. 146; *Bouie v. City of Columbia*, 378 U.S. 347. On the Supreme Court's 1963 and 1964 terms and the sit-ins, see Bell, *Race, Racism and American Law*, 548; Ervin, "Notes: Result or Reason," 212–21; Greenberg, *Crusaders in the Courts*, 311–15; Paulsen, "The Sit-in Cases of 1964"; Lucas A. Powe, *The Warren Court and American Politics* (Cambridge, MA: The Belknap Press of Harvard University Press, 2000); Schwartz, *Super Chief*, 508–25; Webster, "The Warren Court's Struggle," 379–83, 388–405.

79. Civil Rights Act of 1964 (*Pub.L.* 88–352, 78 *Stat.* 241, July 2, 1964). On the act, see Hugh D. Graham, *The Civil Rights Era: Origins and Development of National Policy, 1960–1972* (New York: Oxford University Press, 1990); Robert D. Loevy, *To End All Segregation: The Politics of the Passage of the Civil Rights Act of 1964* (Lanham, MD: University Press of America, 1990); Robert D. Loevy, ed., *The Civil Rights Act of 1964: The Passage of the Law That Ended Racial Segregation* (Albany: State University of New York Press, 1997); Clifford M. Lytle, "The History of the Civil Rights Bill of 1964," *Journal of Negro History* 51 (October 1966): 275–96; Robert Mann, *When Freedom Would Triumph: The Civil Rights Struggle in Congress, 1954–1968* (Baton Rouge: Louisiana State University Press, 2007); Denton L. Watson, *Lion in the Lobby: Clarence Mitchell, Jr.'s Struggle for the Passage of Civil Rights Laws* (New York: William Morrow and Co., 1990); Charles W. Whalen and Barbara Whalen. *The Longest Debate: A Legislative History of the 1964 Civil Rights Act* (Cabin John, MD: Seven Locks Press, 1985); Rebecca Zietlow, *Enforcing Equality: Congress, the Constitution, and the Protection of Individual Rights* (New York: New York University Press, 2006), 97–127.

80. *Hamm v. Rock Hill*, 379 U.S. 306 (1964); *Lupper v. Arkansas*, 379 U.S. 306 (1964). *Arkansas Gazette*, October 11, 13, 1964; "Note: Constitutional Law"; Schwartz, *Super Chief*, 552–55. According to one source, the sit-ins had a 93.4 percent success rate before the Supreme Court, Grossman, "A Model for Judicial Policy Analysis," 438.

81. *Heart of Atlanta Motel Inc. v. United States*, 379 U.S. 241 (1964); *Katzenbach v. McClung*, 379 U.S. 294 (1964). On the two cases, see Richard C. Cortner, *Civil Rights and Public Accommodations: The Heart of Atlanta and McClung Cases* (2001).

82. *United States v. Lopez,* 514 U.S. 549 (1995); *United States v. Morrison,* 529 U.S. 598 (2000). On Morrison, the Rehnquist Court, and Equal Protection, see Robert C. Post and Reva B. Siegal, "Equal Protection by Law: Federal Anti-Discrimination Legislation after Morrison and Kimmel," *Yale Law Journal* 110 (December 2000): 441–526.

83. Martin Luther King, Jr., "Letter from Birmingham Jail," April 16, 1963, accessed online June 5, 2010 at http://mlk-kpp01.stanford.edu/index.php/encyclopedia/documentsentry/annotated_letter_from_birmingham/

84. Martin Luther King Jr., "Statement to the Press at the Beginning of the Youth Leadership Conference Raleigh, N.C.," April 15, 1960, in Clayborne Carson, Tenisha Armstrong, Susan A. Carson, Adrienne Clay, and Kieran Taylor, eds., *The Papers of Martin Luther King, Jr. Vol. V: Threshold of a New Decade, January 1959-December 1960 (*Berkeley and Los Angeles: University of California Press, 2005), 427.

2.

1. Quoted in Howard Zinn, "Kennedy: The Reluctant Emancipator," in *The Zinn Reader* (New York: Seven Stories Press, 1997), 72.

2. *New York Times,* July 28, 1962, 1.

3. William Hansen, e-mail correspondence with author, April 10, August 2, 2004.

4. Ibid., August 2, 2004.

5. William Hansen, correspondence with author, April 21, 2004.

6. Ibid.

7. Clayborne Carson, *In Struggle: SNCC and the Black Awakening of the 1960s* (Cambridge, MA: Harvard University Press, 1981), 2.

8. William Hansen, e-mail correspondence with author, March 4, 2002.

9. See Carson's seminal *In Struggle,* as well as Howard Zinn's participatory memoir, *SNCC: The New Abolitionists* (Boston: Beacon Press, 1964).

10. Hansen, e-mail correspondence, August 2, 2004. See also telegram to SNCC communications director Julian Bond, October [?], 1962, series 1, box 33, folder 335, Arkansas Council on Human Relations Papers, Special Collections Division, University of Arkansas Libraries, Fayetteville.

11. Hansen, e-mail correspondence, August 2, 2004.

12. Emily Stoper, "The Student Nonviolent Coordinating Committee: Rise and Fall of a Redemptive Organization," *Journal of Black Studies* 8 (September 1977): 15.

13. "Will the Circle Be Unbroken" (transcript of a documentary produced by the Southern Regional Council, 2000), 5.

14. Hansen, e-mail correspondence, August 2, 2004.

15. John A. Kirk, *Redefining the Color Line: Black Activism in Little Rock, Arkansas, 1940–1970* (Gainesville: University Press of Florida, 2002), 154–58; Ben F. Johnson III, *Arkansas in Modern America, 1930–1999* (Fayetteville: University of Arkansas Press, 2000), 151.

16. Hansen, e-mail correspondence, August 2, 2004.

17. "Will the Circle Be Unbroken," 7.

18. Ibid., 8.

19. Ibid., 10.

20. Ibid., 12.

21. Stokely Carmichael headed SNCC's national office during the organization's final years.

22. John A. Kirk, "The Other Freedom Summers: SNCC in the Arkansas Delta 19621967" (unpublished paper, Royal Holloway Archives, University of London, 1998), 1–8.

23. Hansen, e-mail correspondence, August 2, 2004.

24. Ibid., e-mail correspondence with author, March 22, 2002.

25. William Hansen, Field Report to National SNCC National Office, Atlanta, January 1964, box 8, folder 5, Student Nonviolent Coordinating Committee Arkansas Project Records [hereafter SNCC Arkansas Project Records], Wisconsin Historical Society, Madison.

26. Ibid.

27. Hansen, Field Report, February 1965, box 8, folder 5, SNCC Arkansas Project Records.

28. Mitchell Zimmerman to United States Justice Department, Civil Rights Division, February 1966, box 8, folder 5, SNCC Arkansas Project Records.

29. Hansen, Field Report, February 1965.

30. Ibid.

31. Ibid.

32. Ibid.

33. *Arkansas Gazette* (Little Rock), November 4, 1964, B1.

34. Hansen, e-mail correspondence, March 22, 2002.

35. *Student Voice,* August 5, 1964, quoted in The *Student Voice 1960–1965: Periodical of the Student Nonviolent Coordinating Committee,* compiled by the staff of the Martin Luther King Jr., Papers Project, Clayborne Carson, senior editor and director (London: Meckler, 1990), 179.

36. Hansen, Field Report, February 1965.

37. Hansen, e-mail correspondence, March 22, 2002.

38. "Will the Circle Be Unbroken," 9.

39. Ibid., 5.

40. Hansen, e-mail correspondence, March 22, 2002.

41. "Will the Circle Be Unbroken," 13. See also Kirk, *Redefining the Color Line,* 181–82.

42. *Arkansas Gazette,* August 26, 1964, A10.

43. Carson, *In Struggle,* 232.

44. Hansen, e-mail correspondence, March 22, 2002.

45. Ibid.

46. Ibid.

47. *Arkansas Gazette,* May 25, 1966, 1B.

48. Ibid., July 1, 1966, 12A. See also Pine Bluff Commercial, July 1, 1966, in clippings file, series 1, box 33, folder 335, Arkansas Council on Human Relations Papers.

49. Hansen, e-mail correspondence, March 22, 2002. Hansen pointed out that he did not consider Stokely Carmichael to be part of this "looney ultra-nationalist fringe." While Hansen never endorsed Carmichael's most radical beliefs, they remained friends.

50. Hansen, e-mail correspondence, March 22, 2002.

51. See Ward Churchill and Jim Vander Wall, *The COINTELPRO Papers: Documents from the FBI's Secret Wars against Dissent in the United States* (Cambridge, MA: South End Press, 2002); Nelson Blackstock, *COINTELPRO: The FBI's Secret War on Political Freedom* (New York: Pathfinder Press, 1988).

52. Hansen, correspondence with author, July 1, 2004.

53. Ibid.

54. Hansen, e-mail correspondence, August 2, 2004.

55. Ibid.

3.

1. The downtown Walgreen had been initially chosen as the site for the protest, but at the last moment the PBSM changed its focus to the lunch counter at Woolworth; *Pine Bluff Commercial*, February 2, 1963.

2. Recent scholarship has shown the importance of expanding attention beyond well-known sites of civil rights struggle, such as Little Rock or Birmingham; John Dittmer, *Local People: The Struggle for Civil Rights in Mississippi* (Urbana: University of Illinois Press, 1994).

3. Bureau of the Census, *Census of Population and Demographics*, 1960 (Ann Arbor: Inter-university Consortium for Political and Social Research, 2002), http:// www.icpsr.umisc.edu/ (accessed October 2002). Flowers had opened a private practice in Pine Bluff in 1938. Largely responsible for bringing Arkansas in general and Pine Bluff in particular to the attention of the National Association for the Advancement of Colored People, Flowers corresponded with both Walter White and Thurgood Marshall to solicit aid in organizing blacks in the state. In 1940, after months of being ignored by the NAACP, Flowers founded the Committee on Negro Organizations, which sought to consolidate the power of numerous black groups and individuals. From canvassing for greater participation in the political process to lawsuits demanding equitable pay for black teachers, Flowers remained for decades a well-known figure for the cause of civil rights in Arkansas; John A. Kirk, *Redefining the Color Line: Black Activism in Little Rock, Arkansas, 1940–1970* (Gainesville: University Press of Florida, 2002), 25–33; Judith Kilpatrick, "(Extra)Ordinary Men: African-American Lawyers and Civil Rights in Arkansas before 1950," *Arkansas Law Review* 53 (2000): 299.

4. *Arkansas Voice*, May 27, 1965.

5. William Hansen, Field Report: Pine Bluff, October 23–November 2, 1962, reel 9 in *Student Nonviolent Coordinating Committee Papers, 1959–1972* (Sanford, NC: Microfilm Corporation of America, 1982).

6. *Pine Bluff Commercial*, January 1, 1963.

7. Joanna Edwards of Pine Bluff, telephone interview with author, November 2002.

8. Clearly, Sheriff Norton recognized that a window *had* been broken on Howard's vehicle, but refused to recognize the damage actually occurred in the manner William Howard and both children claimed it had. Denying the damage to Howard's car was an act of violence and emphasizing that "neither of the students [*sic*] was harmed in any way during the whole incident" prevented Howard from claiming his own act of violence was actually self-defense.

9. *Pine Bluff Commercial,* January 24, 1963; Kirk, *Redefining the Color Line,* 160.

10. William "Bill" Hansen and Ruthie Buffington, interview with Bob Gabriner, August 7, 1966, SNCC Arkansas Project, Social Action Collection, State Historical Society of Wisconsin, Madison. For a more in-depth look at Hansen, see Brent Riffel, "In the Storm: William Hansen and the Student Nonviolent Coordinating Committee in Arkansas, 1962–1967," *Arkansas Historical Quarterly* 63 (Winter 2004): 404–19.

11. *Pine Bluff Commercial,* January 26, 1963.

12. Edwards interview.

13. *Pine Bluff Commercial,* February 4, 5, 6, 8, 1963.

14. Ibid., February 5, 6, 1963; *Arkansas Democrat* (Little Rock), February 9, 1963.

15. *Pine Bluff Commercial,* February 21, 1963.

16. Ibid., February 14, 15, 24, 1963; *Arkansas Democrat,* February 21, 1963.

17. *Pine Bluff Commercial,* February 17, 1963.

18. *Arkansas Democrat,* February 28, March 1, 1963.

19. *Pine Bluff Commercial,* January 26, 1963.

20. William H. Chafe, *Civilities and Civil Rights: Greensboro, North Carolina, and the Black Struggle for Freedom* (New York: Oxford University Press, 1980), 21–22.

21. "General Information about UAPB," http://www.uapb.edu/admissions/about_uapb.htm (accessed January 29, 2007); "USAD Liaison Office," http://www.uapb.edu/academics/safhs/safhs_usda_liason_office.htm (accessed January 29, 2007).

22. Hansen-Buffington interview.

23. Chancellor Lawrence A. Davis Sr. to students of AM&N College, February 11, 1963, University Museum Collections and Archive, University of Arkansas at Pine Bluff.

24. Edwards interview; Hansen-Buffington interview.

25. Edwards interview.

26. *Pine Bluff Commercial,* February 13, 1963.

27. Ibid., February 12, March 1, 1963; *Arkansas Gazette* (Little Rock), February 12, 1963; *Arkansas Democrat,* February 13, 1963.

28. Lawrence A. Davis Jr. interview with author, April 2003.

29. Ibid. During the same week, King journeyed to Little Rock where he

attended graduation ceremonies at Central High as the guest of the family of Ernest Green, one of the nine students who integrated the school; Ben F. Johnson, *Arkansas in Modern America: 1930–1999* (Fayetteville: University of Arkansas Press, 2000), 113.

30. Davis interview.

31. *Pine Bluff Commercial*, May 27, 1958; *Arkansas Gazette*, May 28, 1958.

32. Chancellor Davis Jr. could not recall the name of the Faulkner County statesman, only that the individual hailed from the city of Conway.

33. "Historical Census Browser," University of Virginia Libraries,http:// fisher.lib.virginia.edu/collections/stats/histcensus/ (accessed January 29, 2007).

34. Davis interview.

35. AM&N had not always had such a contentious relationship with elected officials. In 1949, Gov. Sidney McMath doubled the appropriations of AM&N, allowing the college to receive North Central Association academic accreditation. McMath proved to be one of only a small number of officials who believed in racial moderation in the state, although he believed it "could be pursued only indirectly"; Johnson, *Arkansas in Modern America*, 103.

36. Charles Payne, *I've Got the Light of Freedom: The Organizing Tradition and the Mississippi Freedom Struggle* (Berkeley and Los Angeles: University of California Press, 1995), 79.

37. Edwards interview.

38. Hansen-Buffington interview.

39. Ibid.

40. Ibid.

41. Though often derided in both Pine Bluff's black and white communities, the relationship that slowly developed between Hansen and Buffington led to marriage on October 12, 1963. Humorously, Hansen reported the marriage to the legal counsel for the Pine Bluff Movement almost as an afterthought in a letter discussing the tardy title to a Plymouth used by SNCC; William Hansen to Leo Branton Jr., no date, folder 2, box 8, Correspondence and Related Materials, SNCC Arkansas Project. During the first few years of marriage, the couple worked for SNCC throughout Arkansas, raised a family, and sought to pass along their desire for racial equality to their children. In February 1966, while still working for SNCC, William Hansen took his eleven-month-old son, William Walter Hansen III, to a protest march against the Vietnam War in Little Rock. A placard taped to the baby's carriage read, "Stop the War. I Want a World to Grow Up In"; *Arkansas Democrat*, February 13, 1966.

42. Edwards interview; *Arkansas Voice*, May 27, 1965; Hansen to Ruby Doris Smith, February 23, 1963, reel 9 in SNCC Papers. James O. Jones, a victim of the first wave of student expulsions, continued his work with SNCC as the Arkansas state project director in Little Rock. As late as 1965, Jones was organizing voter registration drives, establishing community centers, and working to end discrimination in both the public and private sectors; *Arkansas Voice*, June 25, 1965; Randy Finley, "Crossing the White Line: SNCC in Three Delta Towns, 1963–1967," *Arkansas Historical Quarterly* 65 (Summer 2006): 122–23, 125, 127.

43. *Pine Bluff Commercial,* March 1, 1963; Edwards interview.

44. *Arkansas Voice,* May 27, 1965.

45. *Pine Bluff Commercial,* February 11, 13, 15, 1963.

46. Ibid., February 25, 1963.

47. Ibid., March 4, 1963; Bill Hansen, Field Report: Pine Bluff, March 23–April 5, 1963, reel 9, *SNCC Papers.*

48. *Pine Bluff Commercial,* March 6, 1963; Ruthie Buffington to Jim [Forman], March 5, 1963, reel 9, *SNCC Papers.*

49. *Pine Bluff Commercial,* March 15, 16, 1963.

50. Ibid., March 3, 15, 16, 18, 1963; Buffington to Forman, March 5, 1963.

51. *Pine Bluff Commercial,* March 19, 1963.

52. Ibid., March 26, 1963; Edwards interview; Hansen, Field Report: Pine Bluff, March 23–April 5, 1963.

53. *Pine Bluff Commercial,* March 20, 28, 29, 1963; Hansen, Field Report: Pine Bluff, March 23–April 5, 1963.

54. Helen Hughes Jackson of Pine Bluff, telephone interview with author, April 2003.

55. Ibid.

56. Ibid.

57. Hansen, Field Report: Pine Bluff, March 23–April 5, 1963; Benjamin Grinage, Field Report: Pine Bluff, May 10–May 28, 1963, reel 9, *SNCC Papers;* SNCC press releases, May 8, July 29, 1963, ibid., reel 19; *Arkansas Democrat,* June 1, 1965; *Arkansas Voice,* May 27, June 9, 25, July 16, 1965.

58. The "master narrative" of the Arkansas civil rights movement that I was taught in public school goes something like this: Nine black children wanted to attend an all-white school; violent white mobs prevented the black students from entering the school for a number of days; a benevolent federal government stepped in to ensure the civil liberties of the black children were no longer trod upon; and, today in Arkansas, blacks and whites hold hands singing "Kum ba yah."

59. Randy Finley, in briefly discussing integration efforts in Pine Bluff, notes that activists faced "stiffer white resistance than in Little Rock," but credits local blacks with a readiness for change that resulted in "city officials [drawing] up timetables for integration of public parks, restaurants, swimming pools, and schools." No mention is made of the student suspensions or arrests of activists, creating the misleading impression of quick success in Pine Bluff that allowed SNCC to turn its attention to other parts of the state; Finley, "Crossing the White Line," 119.

60. Payne, *I've Got the Light of Freedom,* 395, 364.

4.

1. SNCC Field Report: Arkansas, November 18, 1965, reel 16 in *Student Nonviolent Coordinating Committee Papers, 1959–1972* (Sanford, NC: Microfilm Corporation of America, 1982) [hereinafter, SNCC Papers]; SNCC Field Report: Phillips County, AR, October 21, 1963, reel 5, ibid.; Johnny E. Williams, *African American Religion and the Civil Rights Movement in Arkansas* (Jackson: University Press of Mississippi, 2003), 147.

2. *Helena World,* January 23, October 26, 1964; SNCC Field Report: Arkansas, April 1, 1965, reel 16, SNCC Papers; *Arkansas Gazette* (Little Rock), January 16, 1964; Williams, *African American Religion,* 145.

3. Claybome Carson, *In Struggle: SNCC and the Black Awakening of the 1960s* (Cambridge, MA: Harvard University Press, 1981), 19; David Halberstam, *The Children* (New York: Random House, 1998), 215–19; Joanne Grant, *Ella Baker: Freedom Bound* (New York: John Wiley & Sons, 1998), 102–6; Aprele Elliott, "Ella Baker: Free Agent in the Civil Rights Movement," *Journal of Black Studies* 26 (May 1996): 600; Taylor Branch, *Parting the Waters: America in the King Years, 1954–1963* (New York: Simon & Schuster, 1988), 291–92; John Lewis, *Walking with the Wind: A Memoir of the Movement* (New York: Harcourt Brace and Company, 1998), 107–8; John A. Kirk, *Redefining the Color Line: Black Activism in Little Rock, Arkansas, 1940–1970* (Gainesville: University Press of Florida, 2002), 11, 142–45; Frank James Report, March 12, 1960, reel 1, SNCC Papers.

4. Ruth Arnold to Margaret Long, September 19, 1962, reel 6, SNCC Papers; SNCC Field Report: Arkansas, August 4, 1962, reel 19, ibid.; SNCC Field Report: Arkansas, February 21, 1963, reel 15, ibid.; Brent Riffel, "In the Storm: William Hansen and the Student Nonviolent Coordinating Committee in Arkansas, 1962–1967," *Arkansas Historical Quarterly* 63 (Winter 2004): 407; Ben F. Johnson III, *Arkansas in Modern America, 1930–1999* (Fayetteville: University of Arkansas Press, 2000), 151; Kirk, *Redefining the Color Line,* 154.

5. Kirk, *Redefining the Color Line,* 155–57; *Arkansas Gazette,* November 8, 29, 1962; Johnson, *Arkansas in Modern America,* 151; SNCC Field Report: Arkansas, November 8, 1962, reel 13, SNCC Papers; *Student Voice* (Arkansas), December 1962, reel 37, ibid.; SNCC Field Report: Arkansas, January 24, 1963, reel 13, ibid.; SNCC Field Report: Arkansas, Spring 1963, reel 10, ibid.

6. Hansen Field Report: Arkansas, March 23, 1963, reel 8, SNCC Papers; SNCC Field Report: Arkansas, July 29, 1963, reel 13, ibid.; *Arkansas Gazette,* June 13, 1963.

7. Cheryl Lee Greenberg, *A Circle of Trust: Remembering SNCC* (New Brunswick, NJ: Rutgers University Press, 1998), 182; 1960 Census, http://fisher.lib.va.edu/egi-local/censusbin/census/cen.pl (accessed October 31, 2003); SNCC Field Report: Phillips County, AR, October 27, 1963, reel 5, SNCC Papers.

8. SNCC Field Report: Phillips County, AR, October 27, 1963, reel 5, SNCC Papers.

9. SNCC Field Report: Phillips County, AR, October 27, 1963, April 6, July 13, 1964, reel 5, SNCC Papers; SNCC Field Report: Helena, AR, July 26, 1964, reel 15, ibid.

10. SNCC Field Report: Helena, AR, October 27, 1963, reel 8, SNCC Papers; SNCC Field Report: Helena, AR, December 13, 1963, reel 15, ibid.; *Arkansas Gazette,* November 19, 1963. For an excellent analysis of the Elaine riot, see Grif Stockley, *Blood in Their Eyes: The Elaine Race Massacres of 1919* (Fayetteville: University of Arkansas Press, 2001).

11. *Arkansas Gazette,* January 26, 1964; SNCC Field Report: Phillips County, AR, July 13, 1964, reel 5, SNCC Papers.

12. *Student Voice* (Arkansas), December 11, 1963, reel 37, SNCC Papers;

SNCC Field Report: Helena, AR, December 11, 1963, reel 13, ibid.; SNCC Field Report: Helena, AR, December 16, 17, 1963, reel 15, ibid.; *Arkansas Gazette,* November 18, 1963; Riffel, "In the Storm," 411.

13. SNCC Field Report: Arkansas, June 6, 1964, reel 15, SNCC Papers.

14. *Helena World,* June 21, 1964; SNCC Field Report: Helena, AR, July 25, 1964, reel 15, SNCC Papers; *Arkansas Gazette,* July 8, 1964.

15. SNCC Field Report: Phillips County, AR, March 22, 1965, reel 7, SNCC Papers.

16. *Arkansas Voice,* June 9, 1965, reel 19, SNCC Papers.

17. SNCC Field Report: Arkansas, March 22, 1965, reel 7, SNCC Papers; SNCC Field Report: Arkansas, July 3, August 5, 1965, reel 16, ibid.

18. *Arkansas Voice,* July 16, 1965, reel 19, SNCC Papers.

19. SNCC Field Report: Phillips County, AR, April 1964, reel 5, SNCC Papers; *Helena World,* February 25, August 12, 1964.

20. *Arkansas Gazette,* August 4, 8, 9, 19, 1964; SNCC Field Report: Helena, AR, August 1, 1964, reel 15, SNCC Papers; SNCC Field Report: Arkansas, August 5, 1964, reel 15, ibid.; *Helena World,* August 9, 1964.

21. SNCC Field Report: Forrest City, AR, January 29, 1964, reel 7, SNCC Papers; SNCC Field Report: Forrest City, AR, November 1, 1963, reel 17, ibid.; *Arkansas Gazette,* May 23, 1964; *Helena World,* May 24, 1964; Hansen to Bond, June 3, 1964, reel 15, SNCC Papers.

22. Johnson, *Arkansas in Modern America,* 161; SNCC Field Report: Helena, AR, July 23, 1964, reel 5, SNCC Papers; *Voice of Freedom,* April 18, 1964, reel 10, ibid.; SNCC Field Report: Arkansas, January 1965, reel 1, ibid.; SNCC Field Report: Arkansas, November 1964, reel 14, ibid.; *Arkansas Gazette,* November 4, 1964; Riffel, "In the Storm," 411–12.

23. Prospectus for Arkansas Project, May 8, 1964, reel 5, SNCC Papers; SNCC Field Report: Pine Bluff, AR, October 14, 1964, reel 14, ibid.; SNCC Field Report: Arkansas, January 1965, reel 1, ibid.; SNCC Field Report: Arkansas, July 6, 1965, reel 16, ibid.; *Arkansas Gazette,* November 4, 1964; *Helena World,* July 29, September 13, 1964.

24. Robert Dallek, *Flawed Giant: Lyndon Johnson and His Times, 1961–1973* (New York: Oxford University Press, 1998), 219–21; *Arkansas Gazette,* February 23, 27, April 21, 24, July 1, 1966.

25. SNCC Field Report: Little Rock, AR, July 22, 1966, reel 10, SNCC Papers; SNCC Field Report: Arkansas, September 12, 24, November 29, 1966, reel 16, ibid.; Michael Dougan, *Arkansas Odyssey: The Saga of Arkansas From Prehistoric Times to Present* (Little Rock: Rose Publishing Company, 1993), 08–9.

26. *Helena World,* April 9, May 24, 1964.

27. SNCC Field Report: Arkansas, November 12, 1965, reel 16, SNCC Papers; SNCC Field Report: Arkansas, October 25, 1965, reel 19, ibid.; SNCC Field Report: Arkansas, November 1965, reel 1, ibid.

28. SNCC Field Report: Arkansas, September 17, 21, 22, 23, 1965, reel 16, SNCC Papers; SNCC Field Report: Arkansas, October 25, 1965, reel 19, ibid.

29. SNCC Field Report: Forrest City, AR, September 18, 19, October 4, 15, November 12, 15, 1965, reel 16, SNCC Papers.

30. *Arkansas Gazette,* September 21, 23, 1965.

31. Johnson, *Arkansas in Modern America,* 168.

32. 1965 Special Report on Education, reel 20, SNCC Papers; SNCC Field Report: Arkansas, June 10, November 15, 1965, reel 16, ibid.

33. SNCC Field Report; Helena, AR, March 7, 1965, reel 19, SNCC Papers; 1965 School Board Report, 1965, reel 19, ibid.; SNCC Field Report: Little Rock, AR, September 28, 1965, reel 16, ibid.; SNCC Field Report: Arkansas, October 25, 1965, reel 19, ibid.

34. 1965 School Board Report, reel 19, SNCC Papers. The only black candidate to win was Arthur Miller, who survived a bitter race for a seat on the Pine Bluff School Board.

35. Executive Committee Report, October 18, 1964, reel 3, SNCC Papers; *Arkansas Voice,* June 9, 1965, reel 19, ibid.; SNCC Field Report: Arkansas, August 3, 1965, reel 16, ibid.; SNCC Field Report: Arkansas, May 6, 1965, reel 11, ibid.; SNCC Field Report: Arkansas, November 1965, reel 1, ibid.; SNCC Field Report: Arkansas, February 18, 1966, reel 16, ibid.; *Arkansas Gazette,* February 27, 1966.

36. SNCC Field Report: Helena, AR, July 23, 26, 1964, reel 5, SNCC Papers; SNCC Field Report: Phillips County, AR, July 13, 1964, reel 5, ibid.

37. SNCC Field Report: Arkansas, June 21, 29, 1965, reel 16, SNCC Papers; SNCC Field Report: Forrest City, AR, June 23, July 2, 1965, reel 16, ibid.; SNCC Field Report: Arkansas, July 1966, reel 15, ibid.; SNCC Field Report: Arkansas, September 25, 1966, reel 16, ibid.; *Arkansas Voice,* June 12, 1965, reel 19, ibid.

38. SNCC Field Report: Arkansas, January 9, 1965, reel 14, SNCC Papers; SNCC Field Report: Arkansas, July 3, 20, November 12, 1965, reel 16, ibid.; SNCC Field Report: Arkansas, January 26, 1965, reel 15, ibid.

39. SNCC Field Report: Arkansas, September 6, 1965, reel 16, SNCC Papers; FBI Files, September 7, 1965, Part 1C: http://libproxy.library.unt.edu:2617/sncc.htm (accessed October 14, 2002).

40. SNCC Field Report: Arkansas, November 1, 1963, reel 17, SNCC Papers; Voter Registration Project Report: Arkansas, September 5, 1963, reel 6, ibid.; *Student Voice* (Arkansas), November 18, 1963, reel 37, ibid.; SNCC Field Report: Pine Bluff, AR, November 19, 1963, reel 15, ibid.; *Arkansas Gazette,* November 19, 1963.

41. SNCC Field Report: Phillips County, AR, April 6, 1964, reel 5, SNCC Papers; SNCC Field Report, 16th Senatorial District, April 20, 1964, reel 5, ibid.; SNCC Field Report: Helena, AR, July 26, 1964, reel 15, ibid.

42. Lewis to Grinage, October 26, 1965, reel 1, SNCC Papers; Riffel, "In the Storm," 415–16.

43. SNCC Field Report: Arkansas, February 17, 1966, reel 16, SNCC Papers; SNCC Field Report: Arkansas, March 23, 1966, reel 17, ibid.; Himmelbaum to Liz, February 5, 1966, reel 19, ibid.; Grinage to Jordan, March 18, 1966, reel 19, ibid.

44. Lewis, *Walking With the Wind,* 380–84.

45. *Arkansas Gazette,* May 25, 1966; Arkansas Staff meeting notes, June 6, 1966, reel 3, SNCC Papers; Riffel, "In the Storm," 416–17.

46. SNCC Field Report: Arkansas, April 1966, reel 3, SNCC Papers.

47. SNCC Field Report: Gould, AR, January 9, 1967, reel 10, SNCC Papers.

5.

1. Stokely Carmichael and Ekwueme Michael Thelwell, *Ready for Revolution: The Life and Struggles of Stokely Carmichael (Kwame Ture)* (New York: Scribner, 2003), 306.

2. Brian Ward, "Forgotten Walls and Master Narratives: Media, Culture, and Memories of the Modern African American Freedom Struggle," in *Media, Culture, and the Modern African American Freedom Struggle,* ed. Brian Ward (Gainesville: University Press of Florida, 2001), 8–9. For an analysis of the media's role as interpreters of the movement, see Julian Bond, "The Media and the Movement: Looking Back from the Southern Front," ibid., 16–40, and Jenny Walker, "A Media-Made Movement?: Black Violence and Nonviolence in the Historiography of the Civil Rights Movement," ibid., 41–66.

3. Many movement scholars have critiqued this tendency toward stark periodization. See, for example, Jacquelyn Dowd Hall, "The Long Civil Rights Movement and the Political Uses of the Past," *Journal of American History* 91 (March 2005): 1233–63. For a rejoinder to Hall, see Sundiata Keith Cha-Jua and Clarence Lang, "The 'Long Movement' as Vampire: Temporal and Spatial Fallacies in Recent Black Freedom Studies," *Journal of African American History* 92 (Spring 2007): 265–88. Others have tried to rescue the Black Power movement from oversimplification and demonization. See, for example, Peniel Joseph, ed., *The Black Power Movement: Rethinking the Civil Rights-Black Power Era* (New York: Routledge, 2006), and Jeffrey O. G. Ogbar, *Black Power: Radical Politics and African American Identity* (Baltimore: Johns Hopkins University Press, 2004).

4. C. Vann Woodward, "What Happened to the Civil Rights Movement?" *Harper's Magazine,* January 1967, 37. For a critique of several scholarly works that embrace a "turning point" thesis, see Winifred Breines, "Whose New Left?" *Journal of American History* 75 (September 1988): 528–45. In a more subtle fashion, the structure of Clayborne Carson's groundbreaking *In Struggle: SNCC and the Black Awakening of the 1960s* (Cambridge, MA: Harvard University Press, 1981) also supports a Black Power declension narrative. Chapter 13, entitled "Racial Separatism," is followed by Part 3, entitled "Falling Apart." Carson both explicitly and implicitly makes a linkage between the rise of black nationalism and the demise of SNCC.

5. *The Jewish Americans,* DVD, directed by David Grubin (Sherman Oaks, CA: JTN Productions, 2008).

6. Quoted in Jonah Raskin, *For the Hell of It: The Life and Times of Abbie Hoffman* (Berkeley and Los Angeles: University of California Press, 1997), 76.

7. Casey Hayden, preface to Mary King, *Freedom Song: A Personal Story of the 1960s Civil Rights Movement* (New York: William & Morrow, 1987), 7.

8. Quoted in Carson, *In Struggle,* 241.

9. Emily Stoper, "The Student Nonviolent Coordinating Committee: Rise

and Fall of a Redemptive Organization," *Journal of Black Studies* 8 (September 1977): 22.

10. For more information on the Mississippi Project, see Sally Belfrage, *Freedom Summer* (New York: Viking, 1965); Doug McAdam, *Freedom Summer* (New York: Oxford University Press, 1988); and James Forman, *The Making of Black Revolutionaries* (Washington, D.C.: Open Hand, 1985), 422.

11. Stoper, "Student Nonviolent Coordinating Committee," 23, 24.

12. Both Clayborne Carson's landmark *In Struggle* and the latest SNCC monograph, Wesley Hogan, *Many Minds, One Heart: SNCC's Dream for a New America* (Chapel Hill: University of North Carolina Press, 2007), highlight the Mississippi experience. Neither had much to say about the activities of the much smaller Arkansas Project.

13. In his important article, "In the Storm: William Hansen and the Student Nonviolent Coordinating Committee in Arkansas, 1962–1967," *Arkansas Historical Quarterly* 63 (Winter 2004): 404–19, Brent Riffel claims that "A number of white northern activists, including Mitchell Zimmerman, joined SNCC in 1963–64, yet by 1966 Hansen was one of only a handful of whites still involved in the project" (415). This is misleading. For one thing, Zimmerman did not join the staff until 1965, the same year as white staffer Howard Himmelbaum. Both Zimmerman and Himmelbaum outlasted Hansen's involvement with SNCC, and by late 1966 only a handful of blacks or whites belonged to the Arkansas Project. See Personal Information Form, Mitchell Zimmerman, January 13, 1965, and Personal Information Form, Howard Himmelbaum, January 18, 1966, William Hansen Papers, Martin Luther King, Jr., Center for Nonviolent Social Change, Atlanta, GA; Jack Baker, "Ex-workers for SNCC Tell Why Group Faded in State," *Arkansas Gazette* (Little Rock), February 26, 1967, sec. A8.

14. Memo to Friends of SNCC Offices from Arlene Wilgoren, April 3, 1965, Arkansas SNCC Project, May 7, 1965–March 21, 1976, box 149, folder 2, Student Nonviolent Coordinating Committee Papers, 1959–1972, King Center [hereinafter, SNCC Papers—King Center].

15. William Hansen, telephone interview with author, July 22, 1997.

16. For one hint at a small conflict, see Mitchell Zimmerman to Hardy, November 18, 1965, box 8, folder 8, Student Nonviolent Coordinating Committee—Arkansas Project Records, State Historical Society of Wisconsin, Madison [hereinafter, APR]. In this letter, Zimmerman admits to "growing to detest" an unnamed SNCC coworker.

17. Riffel, "In the Storm," 404–19; John A. Kirk, "The Other Freedom Summers: SNCC in the Arkansas Delta, 1962–1967" (Paper presented at the British Association of American Studies Conference, Glasgow, April 1999).

18. Randy Finley, "Crossing the White Line: SNCC in Three Delta Towns, 1963–1967," *Arkansas Historical Quarterly* 65 (Summer 2006): 135.

19. Robert Cableton, interview by Robert Wright, September 24, 1968, Ralph J. Bunche Collection, Moorland-Spingarn Research Center, Howard University, Washington, D.C.

20. See Finley, "Crossing the White Line," 117–38, for a summary of SNCC activities in the state.

21. Roy Reed, *Faubus: The Life and Times of an American Prodigal*

(Fayetteville: University of Arkansas Press, 1997), 303; John A. Kirk, *Redefining the Color Line: Black Activism in Little Rock, 1940–1970* (Gainesville: University Press of Florida, 2002), 156, 169–71. In helpful comments on this essay, John A. Kirk points out that although the desegregation of Little Rock did occur peacefully, it also occurred relatively late.

22. Mitchell Zimmerman, Student Nonviolent Coordinating Committee Application, April 23, 1965, box 8, folder 8, APR.

23. Kwame Shaw, telephone interview with author, September 26, 2006. During the 1960s, Shaw went by the name Don Shaw.

24. Kirk, *Redefining the Color Line*, 168; Adam Fairclough, *To Redeem the Soul of America: The Southern Christian Leadership Conference and Martin Luther King, Jr.* (Athens: University of Georgia Press, 1987), 253.

25. For an early attempt to define the term, see Stokely Carmichael and Charles V. Hamilton, *Black Power: The Politics of Liberation* (1967; reprint, New York: Vintage, 1992).

26. Carson, *In Struggle*, 240.

27. Central Committee Meeting transcript, March 6, 1967, reel 3 in Student Nonviolent Coordinating Papers, 1959–1972 (Sanford, NC: Microfilm Corporation of America, 1982) [hereinafter, SNCC Papers-Microfilm]; Decisions of the Central Committee, May 1967, ibid.; Gloria House, "Black Power," in *A Circle of Trust: Remembering SNCC*, ed. Cheryl Lynn Greenberg (New Brunswick, NJ: Rutgers University Press, 1998), 161; Carson, *In Struggle*, 241–42.

28. The responses of white members of the SNCC Arkansas Project to Black Power are better documented than black reactions. This is likely due, in part, to the fact that Black Power did not threaten black membership in the organization. Thus, black members did not have to make the same kind of difficult decisions about leaving the group or attempting to stay in it that whites did. Furthermore, in Arkansas, many of the record keepers were white, including Bill Hansen, Arlene Dunn, Nancy Stoller, and Mitchell Zimmerman. Whites were often given office jobs so that blacks could be freed up to work in the field. In addition, white members Howard Himmelbaum, Collin Minert, and Vincent O'Connor seem to have been responsible for donating the Arkansas Project records to the State Historical Society of Wisconsin where they remain; Howard Himmelbaum, telephone interview with author, July 24, 1997; Christopher Hexter and Alicia Kaplow to Collin Minert, August 18, 1966, box 8, folder 7, APR; Vicki Gabriner to Vincent O'Connor, January 6, 1967, box 6, folder 1, APR.

29. See, for example, "White Integration Leader in Pine Bluff Is Married in Cincinnati to Negro," *Arkansas Gazette*, November 11, 1963, sec. A2.

30. Doug Smith, "Mood Is Changing Among Snick Youths," *Arkansas Gazette*, June 7, 1964, sec. A11.

31. Anne Reeves, "Hansen Resigns SNCC Post; Says Negroes Should Lead but He'll Stay as Advisor," *Arkansas Gazette*, August 26, 1964, sec. A10.

32. Hansen interview.

33. Ibid.

34. Reeves, "Hansen Resigns SNCC Post."

35. Hansen interview.

36. Ibid.

37. Ibid.

38. Howard Zinn, "Kennedy: The Reluctant Emancipator," *Nation,* December 1, 1962, 375.

39. Hansen interview; Arlene Wilgoren Dunn, telephone interview with author, August 15, 2006; Himmelbaum interview; Mitchell Zimmerman, correspondence with author, September 3, 2006; Nancy Stoller, correspondence with author, July 14, 2006.

40. Quoted in Riffel, "In the Storm," 416.

41. Riffel, "In the Storm," 415.

42. "SNCC Hurting for Funds; Arkansas Employees Unpaid and Outlook Appears Dim," *Arkansas Gazette,* March 25, 1964, sec. A5.

43. Hansen interview.

44. Carmichael, *Ready for Revolution,* 565.

45. Hansen interview.

46. Wilgoren Dunn interview; Stoller correspondence.

47. Himmelbaum interview; Zimmerman correspondence.

48. Howard Himmelbaum, correspondence with author, March 31, 1997.

49. Arlene Wilgoren Dunn, "My SNCC Story," unpublished manuscript in author's possession.

50. Ibid.

51. Wilgoren Dunn interview.

52. Central Committee of SNCC, Baltimore, MD, October 28–30, 1968, reel 3, SNCC Papers-Microfilm.

53. Arlene Wilgoren to Howard Himmelbaum, July 10, 1966, box 1, folder 2, APR.

54. Stoller correspondence.

55. Arlo Tatum to Vincent O'Connor, March 16, 1966, box 6, folder 10, APR; Arlo Tatum to Vincent O'Connor, October 23, 1965, ibid.; Mary Carey, "O'Connor on the case: Activist keeps eye on town affairs," *Amherst Bulletin,* March 24, 2006, http://www.amherstbulletin. com/story/id/32400372006/ (accessed May 13, 2008).

56. Vincent O'Connor to Peter Beemer, August 5, 1966, box 6, folder 10, APR.

57. Vincent O'Connor to SWAP, March 15, 1967, box 6, folder 7, ibid.

58. Vincent O'Connor to Carl and Ann Braden, October 24, 1966, box 6, folder 6, ibid.

59. Mitchell Zimmerman to Bill Hansen, August 17, 1965, box 8, folder 8, ibid.; Mitchell Zimmerman, correspondence with author, May 31 and June 1, 2006.

60. Mitchell Zimmerman to Professor Lockhard, September 25, 1965, box 8, folder 8, APR; Mitchell Zimmerman research notes, December 6, 1965, ibid.

61. Mitchell Zimmerman, "'Black Power'—Another Definition," Arkansas Gazette, July 13, 1966, sec. A6.

62. Little Rock Field Report by Howard Himmelbaum and Mitchell Zimmerman, July 2, 1966, reel 3, SNCC Papers-Microfilm.

63. Mitchell Zimmerman research notes, September 20, 1965, box 8, folder 8, APR.

64. Zimmerman correspondence.

65. Michael Thelwell, "Black Power," in *Circle of Trust: Remembering SNCC*, 153.

66. Himmelbaum correspondence.

67. Himmelbaum interview.

68. "SNCC in Arkansas," undated memo, folder 335, Arkansas Council on Human Relations Papers [hereinafter ACHR Papers], Special Collections, University of Arkansas Libraries, Fayetteville.

69. Baker, "Ex-workers for SNCC Tell Why Group Faded in State"; Himmelbaum interview.

70. Central Committee Meeting transcript, March 6, 1967, reel 3, SNCC Papers- Microfilm.

71. Himmelbaum interview.

72. Shaw interview; Toni Morrison, "The Talk of the Town," *New Yorker,* October 5, 1998. Available at http://www.newyorker.com/archive/1998/10/05/1998–10–05–031-TNYLIBRY- 000016504 (accessed July 20, 2008).

73. Carmichael, *Ready for Revolution,* 308.

74. Zimmerman correspondence.

75. May 29, 1966, Press Statement: Rev. Ben Grinage, Ark. State Project Director, S.N.C.C., folder 335, ACHR Papers; Chris Kazan, "State SNCC Chief Attacks New Policy and Threatens to Resign," *Arkansas Gazette,* May 25, 1966, sec. B1.

76. Hansen interview.

77. Ibid; Kazan, "State SNCC Chief Attacks New Policy, Threatens to Resign."

78. "Director of SNCC Resigns and Joins Relations Council," *Arkansas Gazette,* July 1, 1966, 12A.

79. Michael Simmons, "In Search of a Left Agenda: A Personal Journey," unpublished manuscript in author's possession.

80. Michael Simmons, telephone interview with author, June 2, 2006.

81. Michael Simmons, interview with author, September 1, 2006, Atlanta.

82. Jim Jones, interview by Robert Wright, October 15, 1970, Bunche Collection.

83. Millard Lowe, correspondence with author, July 1997.

84. Cableton interview.

85. "SNCC in Arkansas,"ACHR Papers. Although undated, this report was likely written in autumn 1966 or later.

86. Finley, "Crossing the White Line," 135.

87. Ibid.

88. Howard Himmelbaum to Liz, February 5, 1966, box 48, SNCC Papers—King Center.

6.

1. My seventieth birthday came and went as I was writing this article. The events about which I am writing occurred nearly half a century ago. I have fond memories of those days, but I must also confess that some of them are, inevitably one supposes, a bit frayed around the edges. I am an academic and have been for the nearly four decades. I am familiar with the nature and style of academic research. This "memoir-essay" is not a "researched" article. I am writing it from memory with all the pitfalls such an effort entails. My memory is certainly as selective as anyone's. Furthermore, this is my first attempt to write for publication anything about my years with the Student Nonviolent Coordinating Committee. Why? I'm not certain but I think it was a fear that I could not be objective about a six- or seven-year period that was the most compelling and important of my life. For these possible shortcomings I beg the reader's indulgence.

I would also like to thank Jennifer Wallach and John Kirk for giving me this opportunity.

2. *Time* magazine used the phrase "windowless cubicle" to describe the SNCC office in 1962.

3. I could be mistaken about Bert's surname.

4. Ruthe Jena Buffington—September 17, 1943–July 12, 2009—passed away at her home in Punta Gorda, Florida, as I was writing the first part of this memoir at the home of a friend in Blagoevgrad, Bulgaria. After twelve years of marriage we separated in 1976. We had two sons, Bill and Malcolm. A retired specialist in drug and alcohol rehabilitation, she is survived by her husband of twenty-eight years, Dick Datson, our second son, Malcolm, and two grandsons, Ramsey and Wren. Although we haven't been together in more than three decades, I was shaken by the news. I would like to dedicate this memoir to her memory and that of our first son, Bill, who died in a plane crash in 1985 at the age of twenty. *Requiescant in pace.*

5. In the summer of 1998, just a month or so before I moved to Central Asia to take up a teaching job, I went from my then home in Hartford, Connecticut, to New York City accompanied by my eighteen-year-old youngest son. We spent the day with a dying, bedridden Stokely Carmichael. Stokely and I had kept in touch, albeit irregularly, over the years. So near death, Stokely was hardly the commanding physical presence that he'd been in his younger days, but he still was able to flash that magnetic Carmichael grin regularly and he still answered the phone (it rang many times while we were there) "Ready for the revolution." We knew this was the last time we'd ever see each other. Doug, a high school graduate a month earlier, was transfixed by this (in)famous character about whom he'd learned so much from his father and from his high school courses. (He went to a very progressive high school.) After about ten hours together Doug and I went back to Hartford. In August 1998 I left for Kyrgyzstan. Stokely died that fall.

6. Forrest City was named after Nathan Bedford Forrest, the founder of the Ku Klux Klan.

7.

1. Jones was born in Willisville, Arkansas.—Eds.

2. He is likely referring to Bob Whitfield.—Eds.

3. "Ben Grenish" likely refers to Ben Grinage.—Eds.

4. This is actually the date of the famous sit-ins in Greensboro, North Carolina, which inspired sit-ins all over the South, including in Arkansas.—Eds.

5. He may be referring to SNCC executive director James Forman.—Eds.

8.

1. My brother John Ali became the national secretary for the Nation of Islam. My other brother, Nathaniel Simmons, was the chief caretaker of Muhammad Ali's training camp in Pennsylvania.

10.

1. He is referring to the Mississippi Freedom Democratic Party.—Eds.

2. He is likely referring to Benjamin Grinage.—Eds.

3. Again, he is likely referring to Ben Grinage.—Eds.

4. He is likely referring to John Walker.—Eds.

14.

1. Foner's father is the labor historian Philip S. Foner.—Eds.

2. In *Arthur Lee Raney v. the Board of Education of the Gould School District* (1968) the Supreme Court ruled that the "freedom of choice" plan was inadequate for achieving a "unitary, nonracial" school system.—Eds.

15.

1. In a series of rulings in 1968, 1969, 1970 (*Jackson v. the Marvell School System*) the 8th Circuit U.S. Court of Appeals ordered the Marvell school district to quickly adopt an effective desegregation plan.—Eds.

19.

1. Stokely Carmichael was elected chairman of SNCC in 1966. Griswold did not approve of Carmichael's philosophy of "Black Power," which he interpreted as an unwise rejection of white, liberal allies of the civil rights movement.—Eds.

22.

1. Although the letter is dated 1963, it likely was written in 1964 as the couple was not yet married in February of 1963.—Eds.

2. Aaron Henry was a pharmacist and civil rights activist based in Clarksdale, Mississippi. Among other positions he was president of the Mississippi branch of the NAACP and was instrumental in founding the Council of Federated Organizations (COFO), an umbrella civil rights group, and the Mississippi Freedom Democratic Party (MFDP), which coordinated a challenge of the all-white Democratic Party in Mississippi.—Eds.

3. Hansen is referring to visiting the African American comedian Dick Gregory. Hansen and Gregory were arrested and imprisoned in February 1964 for attempting to integrate a local restaurant, the Truckers' Inn.—Eds.

23.

1. The Civil Rights Act of 1964 outlawed discrimination in public accommodations.—Eds.

26.

1. The Princeton Plan originated in Princeton, New Jersey, in 1948 when a black elementary school and a white elementary school were paired. In order to achieve substantial, rather than token, desegregation, both black and white children attended each school. All children in grades K–5 went to one school; all children grades 6–8 attended the other.—Eds.

2. Fourteen activists traveled from Forrest City to Washington, D.C., to present their complaints to John Doar, assistant attorney general, Civil Rights Division of the Department of Justice.—Eds.

38.

1. He is referring to the Arkansas Council on Human Relations.—Eds.

Contributors

Randy Finley is professor of history at Georgia Perimeter College in Dunwoody, Georgia, and the author of *From Slavery to Uncertain Freedom: The Freedmen's Bureau in Arkansas, 1865–1869* (1996). This article originally appeared in the summer 2006 issue of the *Arkansas Historical Quarterly.*

John A. Kirk is chair and Donaghey Professor of History at the University of Arkansas at Little Rock. He is the author of numerous books, articles, and essays on the civil rights movement, including *Redefining the Color Line: Black Activism in Little Rock, Arkansas, 1940–1970* (2002), *Martin Luther King, Jr.* (2005), and *Beyond Little Rock: The Origins and Legacies of the Central High Crisis* (2007).

Holly Y. McGee is a graduate student at the University of Wisconsin-Madison and is at work on a dissertation entitled *When the Window Closed: Gender, Race, and (Inter)Nationalism in the United States and South Africa, 1920s–1960s.* She was the 2010–2011 recipient of the Erskine A. Peters Dissertation Year Fellowship. This article originally appeared in the spring 2007 issue of the *Arkansas Historical Quarterly.*

Brent Riffel holds a doctorate in modern American history from the University of Arkansas-Fayetteville and has written on topics related to Arkansas history for a number of publications. He currently teaches American history at College of the Canyons in Valencia, California. This article originally appeared in the winter 2004 issue of the *Arkansas Historical Quarterly.*

Jennifer Jensen Wallach is the author of *Closer to the Truth Than Any Fact: Memoir, Memory, and Jim Crow* (2008) and *Richard Wright: From Black Boy to World Citizen* (2010). She teaches African American history at the University of North Texas. This article originally appeared in the autumn 2008 issue of the *Arkansas Historical Quarterly.*

Index